Knowledge
STRUCTURES

Knowledge
STRUCTURES

James A. Galambos
Robert P. Abelson
John B. Black

Editors

LAWRENCE ERLBAUM ASSOCIATES, PUBLISHERS
1986   Hillsdale, New Jersey   London

Lawrence Erlbaum Associates, Inc., Publishers
365 Broadway
Hillsdale, New Jersey 07642

Cover design by Brian Regal

Library of Congress Cataloging in Publication Data

Galambos James A. (James Andrew), 1951-
    Knowledge structures.

    Bibliography: p.
    Includes index.
    1. Cognition. 2. Artificial intelligence.
I. Abelson, Robert P. II. Black, John B. (John
Benjamin), 1947-   . III. Title.
BF311.G26 1986   153.4   86-16738
ISBN 0-89859-816-8

Printed in the United States of America
10 9 8 7 6 5 4 3 2 1

Contents

Preface

The story of this book goes back to the mid-1970s, when a collaboration began at Yale between the computer science and psychology departments, anchored by the joint work of Roger Schank and Robert Abelson. In 1977, these collaborators produced the book, *Scripts, Plans, Goals, and Understanding,* and initiated the Yale Cognitive Science Program. The book hypothesized a conceptual framework for a set of "knowledge structures" used by both people and certain computer programs to comprehend social behavior, as presented in simple stories. The Cognitive Science Program, financed first by the Sloan Foundation and later by the System Development Foundation, brought together students, faculty, and postdocs in artificial intelligence and in cognitive (and social) psychology, with occasional input from linguists and philosophers as well. Joint lectures, seminars, training courses, and bull sessions helped create an environment with a novel perspective on how humans understand their social world.

The artificial intelligence people, under the guidance of Roger Schank, devised computer programs which demonstrated some aspect of "understanding" of pieces of text from human interest stories, news clippings, conversations, etc. The intent of these programs was expressly psychological; the attempt was to model the way human understanding processes might work. Among the many outstanding individuals participating were Wendy Lehnert, Chris Riesbeck, Robert Wilensky, Jaime Carbonell, Mike Lebowitz, Gerard DeJong, Janet Kolodner, Michael Dyer, Lawrence Birnbaum, Mark Burstein, Gregg Collins, and Natalie Dehn. Many of these names will be encountered later in this volume.

Meanwhile, the psychologists in the group were busy arguing with the computer scientists whether the artificial intelligence models *really* captured the essence of human cognitive process. We labored to devise experiments testing aspects of the models, and also phenomena not captured by the programming efforts. The faculty members of "the psychos," as we called ourselves, were Robert Abelson and John Black. Postdoctorates or research associates for one or more years included James Galambos, Noel Sharkey, Steve Shwartz, Gail McKoon, Ray Gibbs, Rolf Pfeifer, Rand Spiro, and Stephen Read. Visitors too numerous to list were on the scene for shorter time periods. Graduate students participated in a highly structured way. On Cognitive Science Fellowships, they pursued Ph.D.'s in psychology, with a curriculum combining cognitive psychology and artificial intelligence courses and requirements. The first two Ph.D.'s from this program were Brian Reiser and Scott Robertson. Others still matriculating as we write this include Colleen Seifert, Dana Kay, Stuart McGuigan, and Robert Rist.

Publications from the artificial intelligence side by Roger Schank and his associates and students have been many and varied, mainly concentrated in the journal *Cognitive Science.* A book by Schank (1982) sets forth a whole set of new ideas going beyond Schank and Abelson (1977). The psychological side has been slower to publish, as it took some years to shape apt experiments. Our recent publications have been scattered among several journals, technical reports, and conference papers. This book collects in one place the research work on which we have concentrated, covering topics in the representation, processing, and recall of meaningful verbal materials. Several of the chapters are first reports of research; others are specially prepared reviews and elaborations of research reported previously. Here it is all together: Studies of scripts, plans, and higher-level knowledge structures; analyses of knowledge structure activation, of autobiographical memory, of the phenomenon of reminding, of the summarization of text, of explanations for events, and more.

Preparation of this book was enabled by the support of the System Development Foundation. Running of the experiments was aided by several research assistants, including Valerie Abbott, Amanda Sharkey, Maren Jones, and Peter Kalamarides. For typing the chapters in various incarnations, we thank Linda Rodman, Julie Williams, and especially Marilyn Cassella, who also helped with editorial tasks.

This book marks a watershed in cognitive science activity at Yale. Over the past decade, the cognitive science orientation has become more and more integrated into the mainstream of cognitive psychology, and artificial intelligence workers now feel comfortable thinking about psychological experimentation. Meanwhile, heavy external financial support for cognitive science programs has run its course. We no longer have a formally structured Cognitive Science Program at Yale. We don't need one, however, because its activities have become embedded in the normal flow of activity in psychology and computer science. This volume, which closes a chapter on an exciting period of cognitive science history, also represents a new beginning. The topics we cover here have now been opened up for exploration with a new and broader interdisciplinary outlook in cognitive psychology.

James Galambos
Robert Abelson
John Black

1 Introduction

Robert P. Abelson
John B. Black

This book reports a large number of experiments carried out in the Yale Cognitive Science Program, concerned with how people organize their knowledge of the world so as to understand and retain new information. A fundamental supposition throughout our work is that knowledge is *schematized,* that is, organized in chunks or packages so that, given a little bit of appropriate situational context, the individual has available many likely inferences on what might happen next in a given situation.

To say that knowledge is schematized is not to say much, without a great deal of further elaboration. In this volume, we organize many details concerning schemas, or as we tend to call them, "knowledge structures." We see this book as the continuation of a new tradition in cognitive science and cognitive psychology, as represented earlier by the Schank and Abelson (1977) volume, *Scripts, plans, goals, and understanding.* Perhaps it is presumptuous to speak of a tradition and paradoxical to label it "new." Yet the work that has been in progress at Yale for the past eight or 10 years on "knowledge structures" is different enough from previous approaches to alter sharply our ways of thinking about how people comprehend information, and store, remember, and apply knowledge.

The influence of this new tradition can be seen in many parts of cognitive psychology (including cognitive social psychology), artificial intelligence (AI), and to a limited extent, linguistics. While the concept of schema has been available in modern psychological literature for some time (Bartlett, 1932; Piaget, 1926), the number of references to schemas of various kinds has escalated astronomically in the last ten years (see Alba &

1

Hasher, 1983; Brewer & Nakamura, 1984; Taylor & Crocker, 1981; and Thorndyke & Yekovich, 1980, for reviews).

The use of schemas in remembering textual information has been well documented. In early work, Bransford and Johnson (1972, 1973) and Dooling and Lachman (1971; also Dooling & Mullet, 1973) demonstrated that ambiguous stories were easy to understand and recall if they were given a title that referred to appropriate background knowledge, but very difficult without the title. Goodman (1980) demonstrated similar effects with memory for pictures, and Nelson and Gruendel (1981) discussed the role of generalized representations in children's cognitive development. Similarly, experts, who can provide extensive background knowledge for themselves, do better at recalling information in their area than nonexperts (Chiesi, Spilich, & Voss, 1979). Schemas have been shown to determine not only how much of a text will be recalled but which parts of a text will be recalled. If a schema is mentioned at the time a text is read, information relevant to the schema is more likely to be recalled (Pichert & Anderson, 1977) and more likely to be recognized (Graesser, Woll, Kowalski, & Smith, 1980; Schallert, 1976). Schema-relevant information that has not actually appeared in the text is also more likely to intrude gratuitously into recall protocols than schema-irrelevant information (Bower, Black, & Turner, 1979). Finally, facts that can be organized by well-known schemas seem to be more tightly connected in memory than facts that cannot be so organized (McKoon & Ratcliff, 1980a).

It is a tempting vision, albeit clearly untrue, for us to suppose that a revolution in cognitive psychology was brought about by heroic, single-handed Yale initiatives against the dead weight of older paradigms. In truth, the revolution includes contributions by many individuals and research groups, reflecting the broad emergence of many parallel ideas whose times had come. The role of schemas in memory representation has been emphasized by Fillmore (1975), Minsky (1975), Rumelhart and Ortony (1977), Rumelhart (1980), Bobrow and Winograd (1977), Anderson, Kline, and Beasley (1979), Bobrow and Norman (1975), and in social cognition, Cantor and Mischel (1977, 1979), Hamilton (1979), and Fiske and Taylor (1984). Related research developments are in the areas of categorization (Rosch, 1978; Smith, & Medin, 1981; Landauer & Meyer, 1972); mental models (Johnson-Laird, 1980, 1983; Gentner & Stevens, 1983; Brown & van Lehn, 1980); planning (Brewer & Dupree, 1983; Lichtenstein & Brewer, 1980); memory organization (Anderson & Bower, 1973; Anderson, 1983; Collins & Quillian, 1970; Hayes-Roth & Hayes-Roth, 1977; Newell, 1982); metaphor (Lakoff & Johnson, 1980; Norman & Rumelhart, 1975; Gick & Holyoak, 1983); and text understanding (Thorndyke, 1977; Thorndyke & Hayes-Roth, 1979; Kintsch & van Dijk, 1978; van Dijk, 1980; Graesser, 1981; Mandler & Johnson, 1977; Stein & Glenn, 1979). We can claim, however, that the Yale approach was early, and that it is an important and prototypical representative of the new tradition. Whether it is also the most detailed, and best backed by available empirical evidence, the reader will have to judge after reading this volume.

Judgment of the empirical evidence is a delicate matter. As Schank and Abelson (1977) noted: "the usual style of experimentation [in cognitive psychology] is both too unnatural and too slow" (p. 6). The scope of even a very limited theory of knowledge structures is ambitious and full of ambiguities. The data of experimental psychology come in bits and pieces. As the evidence builds up, it may suggest clarifications of some of these ambiguities, but this process is very gradual.

We at Yale have had a good deal of interaction over several years between artificial intelligence programmers and experimental psychologists. In the early days there was some mistrust, even incredulity, about the nature of the Other's enterprise. The experimentalists have come to understand programming, however, and the programmers, experiments. But the development of trust and understanding has not automatically engendered some amazing method for making joint progress. The ways of AI and of experimental psychology are indeed quite different, and it is very hard work to make them complement each other effectively. For the present discussion, the main point is that empirical progress will inevitably come at a modest pace. We are, after all, asking big questions about the nature of human memory and knowledge representation, and it would be presumptuous to expect instant success.

That's the bad news. The good news is that in this volume we present some two dozen studies carried out over the past four years, illuminating a wide set of aspects of knowledge structure application. We deal with memory distortions, with autobiographical memory, with how one idea reminds a person of another, with the process of summarization of prose, with the ways people produce explanations for events, and many other topics. Types of knowledge structures we explore are scripts, goals, and plans, building on Schank and Abelson (1977), and several higher-level knowledge structures developed more recently, such as *MOP*s (Schank, 1982), plot units (Lehnert, 1981), and *TAU*s (Dyer, 1983).

The emphasis throughout is on what the experimental data are trying to tell us. To that extent this volume is quite different from Schank and Abelson (1977) and Schank (1982), which, while based on the same essential point of view, largely consisted of assertions about how knowledge structures seemed to function, without coming to grips seriously with the kind of empirical tests familiar to psychologists. Here, we will sometimes discover that in certain of their details, knowledge structures behave in practice a little differently than we originally supposed, and we are led to useful modifications of our views. In other cases, we find pretty much what we expected, but we are able to fill in more detail and establish empirical norms, and open up new empirical approaches to old issues.

The most useful way to set the context for what follows is to outline the basic premises of schema theories of knowledge representation, and then make explicit the Yale versions of the details. In the process we will sketch alternative viewpoints still very much active despite the popularity of the new tradition. A lot of what we say will cover familiar territory, but new issues will be raised in the process of recapitulation.

MAJOR PRESUPPOSITIONS

As we see it, there are three major presuppositions on which schema theories are based. These are: (1) the importance of *"top-down" processing* of input information; (2) the *content specificity* of schemas; and (3) the *flexibility of function* of schemas. We discuss each of these in turn.

Top-down Processing

"Top-down" processing is a term used in artificial intelligence (e.g., by Barr & Feigenbaum, 1981), where it is opposed to "bottom-up" processing. This basic distinction has to do with the competition between previous context and present input for dominance in the control of present cognitive processing. If the previous context has created strong implications about what else might follow, then control of processing is mainly determined by that context. If, on the other hand, the context is weak and/or the present input is rich with its own implications, then processing is governed by that input. The metaphoric sense of "bottom-up" is that meaning lies in the text, and its implications spread "upward" to higher abstractions; "top-down" implies that the meaning lies "above" the text, and implication moves down to assimilate the text.

For example, suppose one is presented with the context: "The pirates blindfolded the victim, and started him on his walk." While the reference to "his walk" is elliptical without context, the reader has no difficulty imagining that a plank is being walked. Later references to the "water below" and the "cheers of the pirates" would be easily understood because of the strength of the available context. One might be tempted to say that the reader *expects* references to "water," "cheers," etc., although we should be careful not to interpret the concept of expectation as implying inexorability.

Certainly there is no ironclad guarantee that the text will follow precisely as the context suggests. Suppose, in fact, that the continuation were as follows: "The pirates blindfolded the victim, and started him on his walk to the penthouse, where the masquerade party was in full sway." Here, when "penthouse" appears, top-down processing founders because the prior context offers little useful interpretation. The best the reader can do is to wait and see what comes next. When "masquerade party" arrives, bottom-up processing can take over. The entailments of masquerades are computed to provide a new context. Then (top-down again), the previous details ("pirates," "walk," "penthouse") are reinterpreted to fit the new schema.

One might say here that the "pirate cruelty schema" was replaced by the "masquerade party schema," or, in an alternative terminology, that there was a change in the "framing" (Goffman, 1959; Minsky, 1975) of the action. What these terminologies mean to suggest with their metaphors is that larger structures are used in the comprehension process to interpret new pieces of information.

Presumably, the interplay between top-down and bottom-up processing is continual, with new or revised schemas or frames being activated, then their details filled in, then further schemas activated, and so on. This type of yin and yang has been articulated in the greatest detail at the most concrete level of text understanding, namely, the parsing of sentences—the fitting of the constituents of a sentence into a coherent grammatical or conceptual structure. In "semantic parsing" by computer (Riesbeck & Schank, 1979), certain words or phrases create "requests," which scan the remainder of the sentence for words or phrases filling those requests. In the process, new requests may be activated, and so on.

At a very much higher level of abstraction, a somewhat similar cyclical interplay obtains between theories and data, either of a scientific or of an everyday variety. A theory proscribes what kind of data will be sought, and the actual data may, if sharply enough different from what was expected, serve to modify the theory or provoke a new one. Nisbett and Ross (1980) speak of "theory-driven" versus "data-driven" processing of information. Piaget long ago suggested that individuals not only modify structures in reaction to external events, they also use their own structures to incorporate elements of the external world (Piaget, 1960). Thus, Piaget contrasted the "assimilation" of new information into old schemas with the "accommodation" of old schemas to new information, both processes being crucial to formal reasoning.

So we have a variety of levels of abstraction at which "schemas"—the structures that constrain top-down or theory-driven processing—can operate. The apparent universality of the general idea of schemas, however, raises two perplexing intellectual issues: First, is there any alternative to the general notion that "top-down" structures—schemas—are necessary to knowledge processing? Second, if schemas exist on levels of abstraction as disparate as noun phrases and the Theory of Relativity, can any coherent principles be established for them which would apply to all levels? These two issues together can be rephrased by asking: "If everything is a schema, and they are always necessary, what leverage do we have for a schema theory? Of what use is such a bland, universal concept?"

The question of whether there is an alternative to the necessity for a "top-down" component of processing has a surprising answer: yes. Or, at least the answer is yes, if one takes the traditions of certain disciplines seriously. The discipline of linguistics is the most obvious example. Linguists seek structure within the text itself, typically within the sentence, without reference to nontextual or mentalistic entities which lie "above" the text and interpret it. This point of view is, in effect, totally "bottom-up." There are some linguists who are exceptions, notably Lakoff (1972) and Fillmore (1975), but most linguists adopt the bottom-up conception of the theoretical task (Katz & Fodor, 1964). This does not mean that linguists do not postulate structure within sentences. Chomsky (1968), of course, has practically made "deep structure" a household word. But the deep structure of a sentence is embodied within it, to be revealed by close analysis, not somehow used as an active hypothesis aiding sentence processing. Indeed, the very notion of "processing," in the sense a psychologist or an AI worker might use it, is not usually regarded by linguists as within their province. Thus there is at least one tradition where "top-down" processing is not taken for granted (Marcus, 1980). Another discipline that emphasizes bottom-up processes is, to some extent, classical experimental cognitive psychology. But of this, more later.

Content Specificity

Our other rhetorical question, whether the schema concept is of any use if there are so many varieties of schemas, raises sharp issues of scientific procedure. The Yale approach has been to focus on particular classes of schemas, such as scripts, goals, and plans, and to attempt to show how they in particular are (or might be) used in processing. Schank and Abelson (1977) assert: "A knowledge structure theory must make a commitment to particular content schemas" (p. 10). We have not tried to formulate abstract principles applying to all types of schemas. We have even avoided the use of the general term "schema," believing that its generality can be illusory. The schema concept is too easy to overextend. In accounting for how people can understand the pirate episode above, one could appeal to the "pirate schema." In explaining that people know how to hammer nails, one could invoke the "hammer-and-nail schema." That schoolchildren sing patriotic songs no doubt could be mediated by the "My country 'tis of thee" schema, among others. And so on and on, every use of knowledge about X being attributed to the "X schema." While in some sense there may be a certain truth to this position, it is much too weak to help much with further assumptions. But if formal assumptions were made with intended application to *all* schemas, the resulting propositions would probably be too strong, because schemas at different levels may act very differently. This is why we have chosen to emphasize particular schematic forms such as scripts, with particular contents, yes, restaurants, for example. If we can understand the particular principles for knowledge structure application in these cases, we will be in a stronger position to make more abstract assertions later.

A knowledge structure theory must make a commitment to particular content schemas. Recent research has pointed out that some processes depend upon the content of the knowledge (Keil, 1981). When presented with problems in abstracted settings, subjects perform poorly compared with when the problems are presented in a familiar context. In one experiment (Wason & Johnson-Laird, 1972), subjects were given four exemplars with particular features: four cards were displayed, one with the letter "E" showing, one with the letter "K" showing, one with the number "4" up, and one with the number "7" showing. The task was to turn over only those cards which had to be turned over to determine the correctness of the rule, "if the card has a vowel on one side, then it has an even number on the other side." Only 4 percent of subjects elected to turn over E and 7, the correct answer. It appeared that most subjects looked for only confirming (turn over the E and 4) rather than disconfirming (turn over the 7) evidence to evaluate the truth of the rule. When the problem set was instantiated in a domain very familiar to subjects, they did much better in recognizing and applying the strategy of looking for disconfirming evidence. In this experiment (Johnson-Laird, Legrenzi, & Legrenzi, 1972), subjects were given four pictures of envelopes—one unsealed, one sealed, one face up with a 50-lira stamp, one face up with a 40-lira stamp. When given the rule, "if a letter is sealed, then it has a 50-lira stamp on it," 21 out of 24 subjects were correctly able to choose the sealed letter and the letter with the 40-lira stamp. Thus, in a context that is familiar, where subjects have had experience with strategies for "catching cheaters," subjects can apply general principles ("look for disconfirming evidence"). In unfamiliar domains, they can not.

The research strategy of specifying the particular schemas involved in a domain is lamented by some as being too ad hoc, too unscientific, too much like engineering (Dresher & Hornstein, 1976; Thorndyke & Yekovich, 1980; Feldman, 1975; Dreyfus, 1979). There is pressure toward more abstract statements in the formulation of cognitive science theories of knowledge structure. This comes not merely from an obsession with the need for formalisms—though that is part of the story (Abelson, 1981b)—but more legitimately, from a puzzlement over the basis for selection of such entities as scripts, plans, goals, etc., as schematic objects to study. Why these? What is there about them that makes them special? If we could articulate some principle(s) giving rise to a privileged status for these particular knowledge structures, we would undercut the charge of being ad hoc, and be on the way toward abstract generality. Thus these are questions to be taken seriously, and we will address them in what follows.

Functional Flexibility

Besides "top-down" processing and commitment to particularity, a third feature of our point of view is that knowledge structures have *functional flexibility*. Both words are operative. The "functional" part says that knowledge structures *do* something. They aid comprehension, they organize memory, they guide learning and abstraction, and so on. The "flexibility" says that knowledge structures and the processes that use them can be combined efficiently to serve multiple purposes. While each of these ideas may seem obvious enough, it is all too easy for the theorist to slide into knowledge structure analyses which simply outline static forms, categories, or networks of knowledge. When functions are given to knowledge structures, sometimes they are so specific that it would seem that whole new knowledge representations would have to be invented to handle a slightly different function.

One interesting example of functional flexibility will come up later in this volume (Chapter 7). It concerns the overlap between how people understand questions and how they understand assertions. Presumably many of the mechanisms involved in sentence parsing are used in both cases. A few years ago, it was realized by Yale AI programmers (e.g., Lehnert, 1978) that the parsing programs being written to understand questions were rather different from those available for understanding stories. This seemed odd, and it was decided to try to reduce the differences. This approach of "integrated parsing" (Schank, Lebowitz, & Birnbaum, 1980) not only was successful in producing more efficient programs, it also provoked consideration of psychological possibilities. When integrated parsing is used, it has as a possible side-effect the confusion of premises stated as facts with premises slipped into questions, in other words, that people can be tricked by misleading questions. "Misleading questions effects" are a well-known curiosity in cognitive psychology (Loftus, 1975), but there has not been much of a theory behind why they occur. Integrated parsing provides part of such a theory (Lehnert, Robertson, & Black, 1984).

We do not mean to imply that functional flexibility leads to errors of performance. There are other examples where the consequences are increased cognitive economy without unfortunate side-effect. An important class of cases comes from differing manifestations of the basic process of understanding. Schank (1982) has suggested that the phenomenon of reminding, in which one experience spontaneously calls to mind a related experience, has a great deal in common with the process of understanding. Apt reminding is a by-product of apt understanding. We deal in Chapter 8 with some experiments attempting to capture the flavor of Schank's ideas on reminding.

Another transfer of the understanding process is to the process of providing explanations for events. Social psychologists have in the past 10 or 15 years been much devoted to "attribution theory" (Kelley, 1967; Jones & Davis, 1965), which is a system of concepts purported to explain explanations—that is, to account for how people attribute causes to events. The conceptual systems of attribution theory are special-purpose systems, evoked only when there is an explanatory problem—they lack the functional flexibility to perform other cognitive tasks besides explaining events. And they are not very specific in their content details. Both of these features seem undesirable to us. Lalljee and Abelson (1983) have suggested that a knowledge structure theory of attribution might be superior to available theories. (See also Druian & Omessi, 1982.) The basic idea of this approach would simply be that "explanation" is part and parcel of what goes on in general during understanding. To understand the actions of others, individuals construct representations of their goals and plans, among other things. These representations then provide the stuff of attribution, should explanations be requested. In Chapter 5, we present some preliminary experiments addressed to the ways in which explanations tend to reflect goal and plan representations.

The three features—top-down processing, commitment to particularity, and functional flexibility—thus provide the core of our general approach to knowledge structures. To these three might be added a fourth feature, partly because it has historically been a part of our environment, and partly because it fits well with the other three.

Compatibility With Artificial Intelligence Concepts

The historical place of AI in our enterprise has been clearly established by many joint publications. The connection of our three features with AI might bear spelling out, however. The basic message that an AI orientation carries for the psychologist is that whatever mechanisms are postulated to perform certain functions, they must "run"—they must be capable of being simulated in detail on a computer (although actual simulations may not in fact be carried out). The reasons for this have often been stated, chief among them being the discipline that programming imposes. Vague theoretical arm-waving doesn't make programs run, but exact specification of process detail does.

Once one thinks in terms of a running system, other features follow. The knowledge in the system is best organized in some kind of efficient chunks, thus, top-down processing. The system has to be designed with potential inputs in mind, thus commitment to particularity. If the system is to be efficient, it should be capable of many task performances with few mechanisms, thus functional flexibility. Hence, our three major principles could be viewed as corollaries of an AI commitment. This view is fair enough, perhaps, but we should stress that our three features could in principle be advocated quite independently of AI considerations, on the ground of better psychological modeling *per se.*

This book will not in fact deal in close detail with AI models. Our job here is to focus on the results of psychological experiments, and to puzzle out what these results imply. Where there is interesting interplay between psychological data and related AI models we will, of course, discuss the issues raised.

COMPARISON TO OTHER APPROACHES

In this section, we clarify our approach (which we call the *function content* approach) by contrasting it to two other popular approaches and discuss what seems to us to be the best level of description for theories of cognition. The two other approaches that we compare with ours are the *propositional network* approach and the *structured schema* approach.

Three Contrasting Approaches

The propositional-network approach (e.g., Anderson & Bower, 1973; Norman & Rumelhart, 1975; Kintsch, 1974; Anderson, 1976) forms propositional meaning units and links together those that share common concepts. This approach differs from ours in all three presuppositions: i.e., it is bottom-up rather than top-down, it is structural rather than content-oriented, and it is descriptive instead of functional. The structured-schema approach (e.g., Meyer, 1975; Rumelhart, 1975a; Thorndyke, 1977; Mandler & Johnson, 1977), on the other hand, shares a top-down orientation with the function-content approach, but conflicts with it by being structural rather than content-oriented and descriptive instead of functional. The structured-schema approach concentrates on representing the structure of some entity (e.g., a story has a setting, goal, attempts, and resolution) rather than the content of the entity (e.g., the kind of goal and type of resolution) and the way in which the content will be used in other tasks (e.g., to answer questions, to recall related experiences, to learn new generalizations).

These contrasting approaches are best clarified with an example, so we will consider how all three approaches would represent the following example story:

The Stanford University Psychology Department advertised an assistant professor position and seven students from Yale University applied. The students all wanted this prestigious job, so they each wrote letters criticizing the others. Later they heard that the Stanford department had decided not to hire anybody this year.

Fig. 1.1 gives a typical propositional-network representation of this example story, while Fig. 1.2 gives a typical structured-schema representation, and Fig. 1.3 gives an illustrative function-content representation. For simplicity, the representations in these figures are not from any specific theories, but are simplifications that still contain the typical features of the theory-categories they exemplify (e.g., Miller & Kintsch, 1981; Rumelhart, 1977).

The Fig. 1.1 propositional-network representation starts with the proposition (*Advertise, Stanford, Position*) at the top of the hierarchy (at the far left of Fig. 1.1) because that is the first major proposition contained in the text. The next proposition is that the Yale students applied for the position; that repeats the concept *Position* from the first proposition, so this proposition is connected by a referential link to the first and is one level down (to the right) in the hierarchy. The next two propositions are that the Yale students applied for the position; that they wrote the critical letters. These two propositions are subordinate and connected by referential links to (*Apply, Yale Students, Position*) because they repeat the concept *Yale Students* that was introduced in that proposition. Finally,

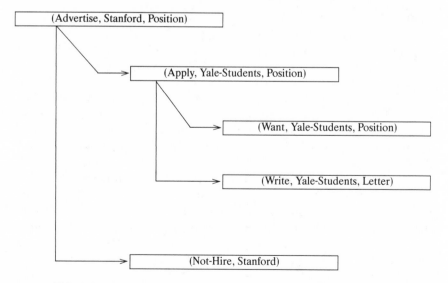

FIG. 1.1. Example of propositional-network representation.

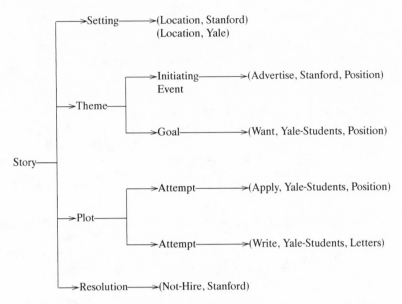

FIG. 1.2.   Example of structured-schema representation.

the last paragraph is that Stanford decided not to hire anyone and that proposition appears at the second level in the hierarchy linked to the first proposition because it repeats the concept *Stanford* that was introduced in that proposition.

The Fig. 1.2 structured-schema representation contains the same propositions, but connects them with structural links rather than referential links. In particular, the structured schema has preconceived notions about what kinds of information should be present, which guides the search for propositions that fulfill these preconceptions. When these propositions are found, they are put at the appropriate place in the structural schema representation. At the top level, the schema in Fig. 1.2 says there should be *Setting, Theme, Plot,* and *Resolution* information. It then finds the propositions (*Location, Stanford*) and (*Location, Yale*), which are *Setting* information, so it connects them to the *Setting* part of the structural schema. It then further specifies the *Theme* into *Initiating Event* and *Goal,* and finds propositions that fit these two labels—namely, (*Advertise, Stanford, Position*) is the *Initiating Event* and (*Want, Yale Students, Position*) is the *Goal. Plot* also gets further specified into *Attempts,* and the propositions (*Apply, Yale Students, Position*) and (*Write, Yale Students, Letters*) are connected to the representation there because they constitute *Attempts* to attain the *Goal.* Finally, proposition (*Not Hire, Stanford*) is connected to the *Resolution* part of the representation because it gives the outcomes of the *Attempts* to attain the *Goal.*

The function-content representation in Fig. 1.3 links propositions into a network at the lowest level and has two other levels of more abstract content patterns that serve to organize and index the propositional information. At the lowest level, this representation states that Stanford's advertising a position motivated (m link) the students to want the position. The students then executed two plans (p links) to try to attain this goal—namely, applying for the position and writing letters about the other students. However, the outcome (o link) of this was Stanford's not hiring anyone. The next level of abstraction corresponds to the network of plot units embodied in the text (Lehnert, 1981). This level starts by noticing that the story involves competition, so it links this plot unit with the proposition that specifies it (s link)—namely, the students' wanting the position. Further, the representation notes that writing the malicious letters is a specific version (s link) of malicious acts and then notes that these malicious acts result (r link) in a failure for everybody (o link to competition) since

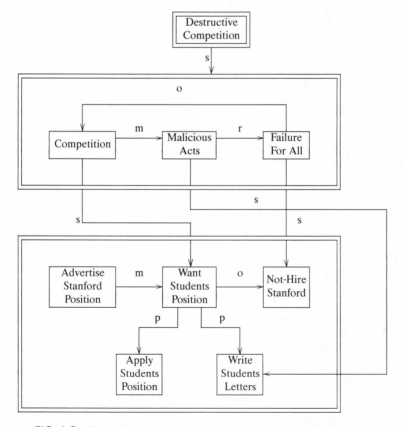

FIG. 1.3.   Example of function-content representation.

Stanford decided not to hire anyone (s link from failure). Finally, at the top level, the representation notes that this pattern of plot units corresponds (s link) to the Thematic Abstraction Unit (Dyer, 1983) of Destructive Competition in which everybody loses.

All three of these kinds of representations have received some empirical support. However, the support has usually involved showing that they predict the results in specific tasks such as recalling the entire contents of a text or recognizing statements as having occurred in the text. For example, Kintsch, Kozminsky, Streby, McKoon, and Keenan (1975) showed that the level of a proposition in a hierarchy such as the one in Fig. 1.1 predicts the probability that the proposition will be recalled when the full text is being recalled. Anderson and Bower (1973) showed that statements corresponding to inferences used to link propositions such as those in Fig. 1.1 are recognized even when they are only implied rather than explicit in the text. Similarly, Thorndyke (1977) showed that the level in a structured-schema hierarchy like the one in Fig. 1.2 predicts the probability that a proposition will be recalled, and Seifert, Robertson, and Black (1985) found that readers falsely recognized statements corresponding to the implicit linkages (goals and plans) in function-content representations like the one shown in Fig. 1.3.

While these results demonstrate some support for the models, tasks such as full recall and detail recognition are not typically encountered in everyday life, and are not representative of the cognitive processes needed to deal with normal situations. What do people do with information they have understood and stored in memory? In fact, a variety of tasks involve the memory representation of information, from learning new generalizations to recalling particular experiences. For example, the memory representation has to be suited to answering questions posed by people to themselves (e.g., What did I do last time the video recorder stuck?) or to other people (e.g., Why did the Marines invade Grenada?). Therefore, memory representations should be adapted for tasks such as question answering and learning, as well as the experimental tasks of full recall and recognition verification. One way to evaluate representational schemes, then, is to compare how they are suited to performing particular tasks. We will evaluate what kinds of questions a given kind of representation makes easy to answer and those it makes hard, and whether this division into easy and hard questions corresponds to the same division in people.

Because the links between propositions in propositional-network representations connect propositions involving common referents (Fig. 1.1), there is a built-in ability to answer questions such as "What was said (or do you know) about Yale students?" Also, answering questions about concepts that were mentioned earlier in the text would be easier than those mentioned later (e.g., answering questions about Stanford would be easier than questions about Yale students) because the earlier concepts are generally close to the top (or in Fig. 1.1, closer to the left) of the hierarchy. Thus propositional-network representations provide direct support for questions concerning the retrieval of propositions involving particular referent concepts, but any other kind of question would require additional processing to supplement search of the representation.

In contrast, structured-schema representations like the one shown in Fig. 1.2 do not necessarily provide direct links between propositions, so retrieving all the propositions involving a given concept would not necessarily be easy. Instead, questions are easy to answer when the question specifies the route through the structured schema to the propositions that provide the answer. For example, "How did the Yale students attempt to get what they wanted?" would be easy to answer from the representation in Fig. 1.2 because "attempt" specifies the path story–plot–attempt–apply (and write). Similarly, questions such as "Where did the story happen?" and "What did the Yale students want?" would be easy to answer because they specify the setting retrieval path and the theme–goal path respectively. Retrieving propositions with a concept in common would only be easy when the relevant propositions are part of the same constituent of the structured schema (and hence retrievable by the same or very similar paths). For example, in Fig. 1.2, if asked for the propositions involving Yale students, it would be comparatively easy to retrieve the proposition (*Write, Yale Students, Letters*) once the proposition (*Apply, Yale Students, Position*) had been retrieved because they are in the same constituent (namely, plot). However, it would be harder to remember also that the proposition (*Want, Yale Students, Position*) involved Yale students because the proposition is in a different constituent (namely, theme) from the others.

Function-content representations like the one in Fig. 1.3 make yet another set of predictions about what kinds of questions are relatively easy to answer. In particular, the easiest questions to answer here are ones such as "What is the main point of the story?" (or more colloquially, "What happened?") since the answer to that question is given by the top levels of the representation. For example, in Figure 1.3 the point is "A group of people destroyed each others' chances for something they all wanted." As with the structured-schema representation, questions about details can be answered easily only if the question explicitly or implicitly provides the information needed to find a path through the representation to the needed information, but the kinds of paths in the function-content representation are different from those in the structured-schema representation. In particular, while the path-specification in the structured-schema representation required the question to provide structural information (e.g., is the sought information in the setting, theme, plot or resolution), the function-content representation requires the question to provide information about the content information related to the sought information. For example, in Fig. 1.3 these are questions such as "What was the competition between the students?" (Answer: "They all wanted a position at Stanford."), "What did the competition lead to?" (Answer: "The students wrote malicious letters about each other."), "What was the result of the malicious acts?" (Answer: "The students failed to get what they wanted when Stanford decided not to hire anyone.") and "What did the students do about wanting the position?" (Answer: "They applied for the position and wrote letters criticizing their competitors.")

We claim that the questions that the function-content representation makes easy are the very ones that people find easy to answer, while the questions the propositional-network and structured-schema predict to be easy are comparatively hard for people to answer. After reading stories like our example, people are most likely to answer something like "A bunch of students screwed each other" when asked "What happened?" This is the kind of answer that the function-content representation in Fig. 1.3 makes easy, but the other representations make hard.

What is it about the function-content approach that allows it to construct better (more functional) memory representations than the propositional-network and structured-schema approaches? One reason for the superiority of the function-content approach is that it constructs schemas that are better for memory retrieval because the schemas allow top-down processing of new information and top-down memory search for old information. Further, the schemas are better constructed so as to organize and index the information content in order to facilitate information retrieval when needed to perform tasks, that is, the schemas are functionally oriented. Thus, the characteristics that make the function-content approach better are the features we have been emphasizing throughout this chapter—namely, top-down, content-oriented, and functionally based.

Level of Description

We believe that a complete theory of cognition must contain not only a description of representations and processes, but also of representation and process interactions. Most memory models have had very general description of representations and a description of processes in terms of a small number of very general principles (e.g., spread of activation, intersection search, etc.). We claim that these general principles of representations and processes need to be supplemented with more detailed models of "higher level" representations and rules about representation-specific processes. Theories of cognition must contain theories of content. Newell (1982) has also argued that a theory of cognition in a particular domain first demands a theory of the domain itself, which he calls the "knowledge level." One component of a complete model is a description of the more complex structures in memory and their characteristic properties. Although differences between such structures may be reducible in part to more general representational principles, such as number of associations or level of abstraction, these properties are not sufficient to capture the observed differences.

There is a body of experimental data comparing the memorability of different types of representational links. Black and Bern (1981) found that when pairs of statements were linked with a causal inference, they were remembered better than when there was no causal inference linking them. Similarly, Abbott and Black (1982) found that sentence triples linked by motivational inferences were remembered better than those not so connected. We claim that the best level of description and explanation for such phenomena is the function-content level. Thus our explanation is that function-content representations like the one given in Fig. 1.3 are constructed during comprehension, and such representations use causal and motivational links between propositions. When such links are not explicitly or implicitly present, the propositions are not connected in the representation and therefore they are not remembered as well as when they are connected.

However, we could also try to explain this phenomenon of better memory for related propositions using a propositional-network level of description.

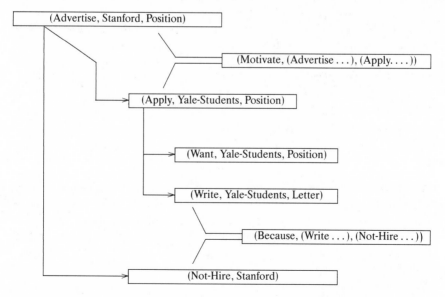

FIG. 1.4.   Example of propositional-network representation with inferences.

This would involve a representation such as the one shown in Fig. 1.4. This representation supplements the one in Fig. 1.1 by adding second-order propositions denoting motivational inferences that provide extra linkages between pairs of propositions. For example, the second-order proposition (*Motivate*, [*Advertise, Stanford, Position*], [*Apply, Yale Students, Position*]) adds two more referential links which together form a new path (ignoring the original direction of the links) connecting the simple propositions embedded in the second-order one—namely, connecting (*Advertise, Stanford, Position*) and (*Want, Yale Students, Position*). Similarly, (*Because*, [*Write, Yale Students, Letters*], [*Not Hire, Stanford*]) provides a new path linking its component propositions. These new paths in the memory representation would increase the linkage between the component propositions and thus increase the memorability of the propositions, so such a supplemented propositional-network representation explains the results of superior memory for causally and motivationally linked statements. Further, propositional networks can explain why adding a causal link increases memory more than adding a referential link (Black & McGuigan, 1983) by assuming that the links between propositions have various strength values associated with them (Anderson, 1976) and that linkages formed from causal and motivational inferences have higher strength values than other linkages.

Now we have considered explanations at the function-content level and at the propositional network level: Which do we use? We claim that the function-content level provides the more natural and parsimonious explanation because the propositional-network explanation has an ad hoc character that assumes the function-content mechanisms as part of its more complicated explanation. For example, the only way we know when a second-order proposition should be inferred to add another stronger link between the propositions is that a causal inference should be made. Thus, a more parsimonious explanation is merely saying that the causal inference provides the link (a function-content level explanation), omitting the cumbersome propositional-network level.

SECTIONS TO FOLLOW

We will detail our views on knowledge structures for different levels of such structures: the simplest and most concrete, *scripts;* the somewhat more complex and flexible level of *goals* and *plans;* and finally, the thematic or *higher level structures.* The book is divided into sections corresponding to these three levels, with two to four chapters and an explanatory introduction in each.

SCRIPTS

Scripts are probably the most experimentally tractable of the knowledge structures that we will examine in this book. This is not to say that script experiments are easily designed and performed compared with experiments on the more traditional objects of a psychologist's attention. Quite the contrary; examination of these knowledge structures requires considerable attention to a wide variety of extraneous variables whose effects must be controlled in order to observe the phenomena of interest. Part of the point made by the next three chapters is, indeed, methodological in that the authors show by example the care involved in studying scripts in human memory.

Scripts are mental representations of the causally connected actions, props, and participants that are involved in common activities. The most overused example is the restaurant script with its stereotypical cast of players, their goals, and the sequence of actions in which they interact. Other activities, such as grocery shopping, bus riding, and throwing a birthday party, are similarly represented in memory by this sort of knowledge structure.

Scripts have three general functions in the realm of cognitive processing. These functions are roughly characterized as repository, comprehension, and recollection. Each of the next three chapters concentrates on one of these functions.

In chapter 2, James Galambos uses methods adapted from the study of semantic memory to explore the main representational features of scripts. He examines the relationships among component actions of scripted activities as well as those between the actions and the general activity concepts (script headers). Some of these relationships are examined further in later chapters.

In chapter 3, Noel Sharkey provides us with a number of temporal snapshots of scripts involved in comprehension. He describes some of the important details of how scripts are activated, and, perhaps more importantly, deactivated during the immediate course of story comprehension. Sharkey also examines how activated scripts aid processing by providing top-down expectations as well as interpretation of information presented in a story.

In chapter 4, Brian Reiser examines how script knowledge structures are involved in the retrieval from memory of personal experiences. Reiser argues that the script context that was active at the time of encoding the experience must be reactivated in order to begin searching memory of the specific experience. Using both protocol analysis and retrieval latency experiments, Reiser goes on to describe a number of search strategies which involve using various content features of the general script to recover the details of experienced instances of the script activity.

What emerges from these three chapters is the view of script knowledge structures as extremely flexible and multifunctional cognitive constructs.

2 Knowledge Structures for Common Activities

James A. Galambos

INTRODUCTION

Clearly there are important differences among various types of knowledge structures, but I consider knowledge of common activities to be the paradigmatic case. Representations of common activities are particularly amenable to observation and provide important insight into the functional design of knowledge structures in general. We seek to identify those features of knowledge of common activities that are useful to the efficient functioning of the comprehensive system.

Knowledge structures for common activities represent information about the component parts of an activity and the relations connecting the component actions to each other and to the superordinate concept of the activity. Here, the term *activity* refers to a self-contained series of actions performed to attain a goal in a particular situation. It is synonymous with *script,* but since I have used the word "activity" in instructions to subjects, I will stick with that terminology here. The term *action* refers to the component actions of the activity.

In the following series of studies, norms were obtained for 30 common activities on four dimensions that may play a role in the cognitive function of these knowledge structures. Some examples of the activities examined are "Changing a Flat," "Shopping for Groceries," "Washing your Hair," "Taking the Subway," and "Making the Bed." Each of the four dimensions has been examined in reaction time studies in a fashion similar to those involving natural categories in semantic memory. Some of these results are reported in Galambos and Rips (1982) and Galambos and Black (1982).

The Membership Decision Task

There is a type of experimental task in which representational features of knowledge structures are observed as they exist independent of any particular stimulus story. The most frequent such method is called the *membership decision task*. In this task, subjects are timed as they decide whether an action is involved in performing a given activity. Subjects are presented with two phrases, the *action* phrase and the *activity* phrase, and are instructed to press one of two buttons ("yes" or "no"), indicating their decision whether the action is a component of the activity.

The stimulus actions are chosen using the norms described in Galambos (1983). The norms reported there allow an experimenter to design studies of common activities that either *manipulate* levels of these dimensions or *control* for their effects. For example, Galambos and Rips (1982) examined the centrality dimension (see definition of centrality later in this chapter) in the membership decision paradigm. We selected two sets of actions, one set containing actions highly central to their activities, and the other, actions not central to their activities. We then compared membership decision latencies for central and noncentral actions. We found the latencies significantly shorter in "yes" responses to highly central actions than to less central actions. Thus, retrieval of the action is facilitated by the centrality of that action to the activity.

The Activities and the Actions

As stimulus materials, I used 30 common activities and 12 component actions of each. The activities cover a fairly wide range of situations varying in length, complexity, and number of participants. These activities were originally chosen to be *scripts* according to the definition and examples in Schank and Abelson (1977).

A three-word name beginning with a nominalized verb was selected to refer to each activity. Examples are: "Starting a Car," and "Going to Restaurants." For each activity, 12 component actions were chosen, each represented by a three-word description. Typically they had the linguistic form of subjectless imperatives. For example, in the "Changing a Flat" activity, some of the actions were "Position the Jack," "Take off Hubcap," and "Raise the Car."

The criteria for the selection of the action phrases were that they referred to actions at approximately the same level of generality, and that the actions were unambiguous and nonoverlapping. The resultant action sets may be thought of as composite representations of their activities and not necessarily precise characterizations of any one individual's memory. These sets are intended to be free to some extent from idiosyncrasies in the way in which people perform these activities and yet to constitute a representation of the activities which would not differ markedly from person to person.

Features of Action Components of Activities

In a number of memory retrieval experiments (Galambos, 1983; Galambos & Black, 1982; Galambos & Rips, 1982; and Reiser, Galambos, & Black, 1982), four features of the representations of actions have been shown to influence the time to answer questions about activities. *Centrality* was introduced earlier. Three other features examined were *distinctiveness* and *standardness* of actions, and the *sequence* in which they occur.

Distinctiveness

The distinctiveness of an action is a measure of whether the action occurs in one or many different activities. Thus, the action *See Head Waiter* is distinctive to the "Going to Restaurants" activity because it appears in few if any other activities. *Eat the Meal* or *Stand in Line* are low in distinctiveness because they occur in a large number of activities.

Centrality

The centrality of an action is a measure of how important an action is to its activity. Thus, *Eat the Meal* is central to the "Restaurant" activity because it is one of the main reasons for doing the activity. In contrast, *See Head Waiter* is low in centrality because it is not as important to that activity.

Standardness

The standardness of an action is a measure of the frequency with which an action is performed in an activity. For example, when "Starting a Car," the action *Turn the Key* is always done, while the action *Fasten Seat Belts* is done less frequently. The former action is high in standardness and the latter low.

Sequence

Finally, the sequential position of the actions in the course of performing the activities can be rated (e.g., the action *Put on Apron* occurs early in the sequence of actions involved in the activity "Doing the Dishes," while the action *Wash the Pans* occurs later).

EXPERIMENTS ON CENTRALITY AND SEQUENCE

Centrality of Actions

In most schema theories, information varies in terms of its prominence in the representation. For example, in Schank and Abelson (1977), the action of *Eating the Meal* is the *Main Conceptualization* of the Restaurant script: It realizes the primary goal of the restaurant activity. Similarly, in models by Graesser (1981), Mandler and Johnson (1977), Thorndyke (1977), and Trabasso, Secco, and van den Broek (1984), the story schemas are hierarchical, and the superordinate nodes have higher prominence in the representation. Thus, one general feature that may be shared by knowledge structures is the tendency to represent differences in importance or centrality among the components. The centrality of an action may influence its retrievability when the activity context is present. It may be that central actions are more readily available to serve as expectations to guide a top-down comprehension process.

Quantifying the Centrality Dimension

Fifteen subjects were asked to rank the 12 actions in each of the 30 scripts in terms of "the importance of doing the action when performing the activity." Each subject was given a computer-printed packet of 30 randomized pages. Each page had one of the activity names at the top of the page followed by the 12 actions in that activity. The subjects were asked to rank the action within the activity using number one to indicate least central, 12 to indicate most central. Mean rank order across subjects for each action is taken to be the centrality value of the action.

For example, in the activity "Going to Restaurants" some representative centrality values are:

Action	Centrality
See Head Waiter	2.87
Tip the Waiter	5.27
Ask for Menu	7.20
Eat the Meal	10.60

The Sequence of Actions in Common Activities

One of the most striking claims made by script theory is that the *temporal sequence* in which the actions occur in an activity provides the basis for the representation. Thus, an action is connected by causal links with preceding and succeeding actions. This temporal information may be relevant to predictions and inferences made by a comprehension system. If one knows that John ate a meal at a restaurant, it can be inferred that at some earlier time, he ordered said meal. Clearly causal and plan relationships may be involved in this inference. Thus, one may rely on the knowledge that ordering a meal is causally related to getting and eating it. This causal relationship may be more relevant to the inference than mere temporal precedence. To make this distinction it is necessary to have a metric for sequential order to be able to contrast with a causal interpretation.

Quantifying the Sequence Dimension

To examine these issues we asked subjects to order the actions in each activity "according to the temporal sequence in which the actions are normally performed." This feature was quantified in the same fashion as the centrality feature. The lower the number, the earlier the action in the activity. Again, the mean rank across subjects of the action is taken to be the sequence value of the action. For example, in the activity "Starting a Car," subjects gave the following actions these mean sequence rankings:

Action	Sequence
Open the Door	1.94
Adjust the Seat	5.00
Check the Mirrors	7.19
Shift into Drive	11.00

Centrality and Sequence in Retrieval

High agreement among subjects in their ranking of actions was obtained, and is evidence that they possess knowledge of the centrality and sequence of actions in common activities. However, in order to support a claim that these dimensions are structural characteristics of the schematic organization of the actions, it is necessary to examine their effects on retrieval from memory. Specifically, if the schema organizes actions in a temporal chain, then it might be expected that earlier actions would be easier to retrieve than later actions. Alternatively, if actions are represented in a hierarchical fashion, where the more central actions are superordinate nodes, then it should be easier to retrieve high centrality actions than low centrality actions.

Experiment 1

To test these questions the membership decision task was employed. This experiment is described in greater detail in Galambos and Rips (1982). Subjects were presented with stimuli that consisted of an activity paired with an action that might or might not be a part of the activity. For example, subjects might see the following stimulus:

CHANGING A FLAT

RAISE THE CAR

Subjects were asked to verify whether the action is a component of the activity, and their button-press responses were timed. In this case, of course, the answer is yes, the action *Raise the Car* is part of the activity "Changing a Flat."

Four actions from each of 16 activities were used as stimuli. Two of these actions were from early in the activity sequence and two were from late in the sequence. Within these groups, one action was high in centrality and one action was low in centrality. The mean decision times (in milliseconds) for the main experimental conditions were as follows:

| | Centrality | |
Sequence	High	Low
Early	1304	1361
Late	1305	1381

There is a significant effect of centrality but none of sequence. That is, central actions are more rapidly retrieved than noncentral actions. However, earlier actions are not retrieved significantly faster than later actions. It seems therefore that the temporal sequence of actions in an activity is not likely to be the only, or even primary, organizer of the knowledge structure. It is also possible that there may be sequential relations among actions that were not tapped in this study.

Experiment 2

In this experiment, we examined the possibility that sequence relations are present in the knowledge structure but are not necessarily used in the retrieval process for the task in Experiment 1. To test this, we designed a new version of the membership decision task called the *paired membership decision task.* In this paradigm (described in detail in Galambos and Rips, 1982), we presented pairs of actions as in the following stimulus:

CHANGING A FLAT

RAISE THE CAR   TAKE OFF HUBCAP

Subjects were asked to indicate whether or not *both* actions are part of the activity. It was hoped that subjects might use sequence relations between the actions to facilitate the membership decision. To examine this, we compared two types of stimuli. In the first, the two actions were close together in the sequence ratings. In the second type, the actions were at a larger distance from each other. If there are sequence links between actions then the *close* stimuli should, generally, be more rapidly verified as belonging to the same activity than the *far* stimuli. For the close pairs, the activation of one of the actions should prime the second action along the sequence links.

In addition, centrality of the action pairs was also varied. Thus, a given pair was either composed of both high, or both low, centrality actions. In this experiment, mean reaction times for "yes" answers were:

| | Centrality | |
Distance	High	Low
Close	1417	1464
Far	1424	1488

It is easier to decide that pairs of central actions are both in the activity, than to decide about pairs of less central actions. However, there is still no significant support for priming on sequence links for the close stimuli. Perhaps subjects did not use sequence links and merely turned the task into a "double membership decision task."

Experiment 3

In a final attempt to find strong effects of sequential organization of actions in these knowledge structures, Galambos and Rips designed an experiment that explicitly required subjects to use temporal information to determine their response. In Experiments 1 and 2, the task was merely to report whether the actions were part of the script. In Experiment 3, subjects were asked which of two actions occurred earlier (or in another condition, later) in the activity. As in Experiment 2, the stimulus items were pairs of actions with their activity. For example:

CHANGING A FLAT

POSITION THE JACK   RAISE THE CAR

The distance in temporal sequence rankings between the two actions was varied. Pairs of actions (either high or low in centrality) were separated by three different distances: *close, intermediate,* and *far.* The prediction was that if the sequence information were structural, it would be easier to report the temporal relationship between actions that are close together in the activity than to report the relationship between more distant actions.

This task is a version of the mental comparison task used by Banks (1977), Moyer and Dumais (1978), and others. The prediction above, however, is in direct opposition to the results of these other mental comparison experiments. In other domains (e.g., size, amount), results show that the farther apart the stimuli, the easier the comparison.

Our data demonstrate this same pattern, and, therefore, do not show the results predicted by the notion that subjects trace sequential links along the knowledge structure. The mean reaction times were:

Distance	*Centrality*	
	High	*Low*
Close	1626	1664
Intermediate	1588	1610
Far	1490	1475

In this experiment, the centrality of the action pairs did not significantly influence response latency. However, separation by varying sequential distance did have a strong effect on latency. As in other types of mental comparison, the closer the items, the more difficult the comparison. These results show that decisions based on activity sequence information can be reliably used by subjects, but are inconsistent with a model where sequential *links* between actions are represented explicitly in the knowledge structure. Nottenburg and Shoben (1980) report similar results.

A Revised View of Action Sequence

The implication of this series of experiments is that sequence information is *not* stored in terms of a serial chain linking the first to the last actions via single relations to adjacent actions. Insofar as the notion of a "script" representation involves the explicit presence of this sort of relationship, that notion needs revision. In retrospect, an explicit serial chain model is implausible on functional grounds, because rigid representation of actions in a particular order would tend to have less utility than a more flexible representation. A rigid representation does not take into account a number of important features of these common activities. One of these features is that component actions are performed more than once in an activity. Indeed, in many of the activities a set of actions may be iterated. For example, in the "Washing the Dishes" activity, the subsequence of actions:

> Get the Dirty Dish
>
> Put it into the Soapy Water
>
> Scrub it until Clean
>
> Rinse the Dish
>
> Put it into the Drying Rack

is repeated a number of times in the successful performance of the activity. Thus the link between the final instance of the action of putting a rinsed dish into the drying rack and the next new action (say, getting a dish towel to dry the dishes) is likely to be quite different than the link between the actions of scrubbing the dish clean and rinsing it off. It would complicate matters to account for these problems in a purely serial, sequence-based representation.

Furthermore, there is a good deal of optionality in the choice of which actions to perform in which order. There are at least three different varieties of optionality. One sense of optionality is that an action may or may not be needed to accomplish the goal of the activity. An action is optional in this sense if it can be left out of the activity or replaced with another action. For example, some people may always dry their dishes with a dish towel while others leave them to dry in a drying rack. Another sort of optionality involves the possibility that the temporal order of certain actions is completely arbitrary. This is true for most actions which are preparatory in nature. It does not much matter whether one runs the hot water before collecting the dirty dishes from the table or after. Indeed, efficiency dictates that these two actions might occur to some extent in parallel.

There is also the optionality associated with variations in the units within the activity knowledge structure. These may vary in size and content. For example, the list of actions given above is a unit that may vary depending on the individual and the situation. On one occasion of the dishwashing activity, one might put all of the dirty dishes into soapy water first and then iterate on the last three actions. On another occasion, one might iterate the first three actions in the list but save the rinsing and drying until all the dishes were scrubbed clean.

This flexibility is necessary, both for the ability to adapt to changing environments within which the activity takes place, and for the ability to recognize and understand the inherent similarity across many and perhaps quite different variants of the same activity. If knowledge structures were representations of strict serial order, their functionality would be severely limited. They would neither serve effectively as guides to prepare the system to behave appropriately in varying circumstances, nor would they facilitate comprehension of experiences which diverged from the standard sequence.

Moreover, structures which required a serial search through their components might well be representationally inefficient because such a search would slow the activation of components occurring late in the sequence. A different inefficiency might be introduced if components that were not particularly well ordered temporally (as described above) were forced into a sequential representation. For example, let us say that action A is not well ordered with respect to action B. However, the constraints of a sequential system force a representation of B as following A. Finally, assume that the comprehension system encounters an instance of action B at some point in the processing of the relevant activity. Since A precedes B in the knowledge structure, A will not be generated as an expectation to facilitate comprehension. In fact, the A concept may be relatively difficult to activate at all. If so this would be representational inefficiency at its worst—having information present in a knowledge structure and yet not having it activated when needed.

Clearly sequential orderings might be present on a much more local level where the temporal order is unvarying. Where sequence can be relied on, it would be very predictive and serve the expectation generation function of knowledge structures quite well. However, invariant temporal orderings are typically epiphenomenal with other features of the actions, for example, their causal structure. Where B always follows A, it may be because A causes B. It is possible that causality is a strong candidate as the basis for the representation of sequence information.

The Representation of Centrality Information

The experiments described above indicate that the centrality of actions in an activity has an influence on response latency. The question arises, what is the functional advantage of representing this centrality information in the knowledge structure? To answer this we need to unpack the notion of centrality. What does it mean to say that one action is more central than another?

One way to think of centrality is in terms of the notion of typicality in natural categories (Rips, Shoben, & Smith, 1973; Rosch, 1973; see Smith &

Medin, 1981 for a review of this extensive literature). For example, a robin is a very typical member of the category, "bird," and, therefore, it is readily classified as a bird. A chicken is not a typical bird and thus is more difficult (or takes longer) to classify as a bird. On the view that centrality is a form of typicality, responses in the membership decision task were facilitated because the more central actions were more typical than were the less central actions. This view seems not entirely appropriate, however. While there is certainly some similarity between centrality effects in probes of knowledge structures on one hand, and typicality effects in retrieval of information from semantic memory on the other, there are also considerable differences. Prototype theories are based on similarities of attributes across instances of the category. The component actions of an activity rarely share much in the way of attribute similarity. The decomposition of prototypes into features does not appear to have any analogue in the concepts representing actions in activities. Thus centrality does not seem effectively explained as simply a variant of typicality.

A second view holds that central actions are the major goals or subgoals of the activity. Less central actions are those that are part of the lower-level plans to serve these goals. This view is akin to that discussed by Graesser (1978) and Lichtenstein and Brewer (1980). From this perspective, the centrality effects result from the intentional structure of the activities. Thus, it is easier to recognize that the intention of performing a main goal action is to accomplish the activity than it is to recognize the same intention for less central actions. This implies a hierarchical representation where less central actions (steps in the plan) are subordinated to the more central goal actions.

This general view is consistent with models developed by Abelson (1981a) and Bower, Black, and Turner (1979), where the notion of a *scene* is discussed. Scenes are substructures within larger knowledge structures. An activity might have a number of scenes. Each scene has a major goal and a series of plan actions that serve to attain that goal. A plausible explanation of the centrality effect is that more central actions are the scene goals and less central actions the plan steps within the scenes. The more rapid retrieval of central actions in the membership decision task would result from the more direct links between the scene goals and the activity concept. Plan actions would have less direct relationships to the activity concept and, therefore, would take longer to retrieve.

There are two other possible explanations for the centrality effects. The first relies on the notion that some actions are more salient as members of their activities than others. The salience (or *distinctiveness*) of an action relates to how often the action is done in contexts *other* than the activity in question. If *every* instance of a given action is within the context of a certain activity, then that action is highly distinctive to that activity. If a given action occurs in many different activities, then the action is not very distinctive to any of those activities. The centrality effect may derive from a difference in distinctiveness among the actions in our activities.

A final possible explanation is that centrality is based on the frequency of occurrence of the actions in instances of the activity. Some actions are standard when doing the activity. Others are optional and not always performed. Centrality might reflect this difference in *standardness* among actions. This could derive from the repository function of knowledge structures. Those actions that often occur when the activity takes place might be represented in the knowledge structure as more strongly linked with the activity. Less standard actions might be more weakly linked.

In the next section, I describe experiments designed to evaluate these two explanations of the centrality effect.

EXPERIMENTS ON DISTINCTIVENESS AND STANDARDNESS

The Distinctiveness of Actions in Activities

Some actions are done in many different activities, e.g., *Stand in Line,* while others are done in only one activity, e.g., *See Head Waiter.* The action of standing in line is not nearly so distinctive to the activity of restaurant-going as is the action of seeing the head waiter. For example, if all you know is that someone is standing in line, you cannot make a very good guess as to what activity the person is engaged in. If, however, all you know is that a person is seeing a head waiter, you have a good guess that the context is restaurant-going. Since being able to supply the appropriate context for one's perceptions is so important to comprehension, distinctive actions may be very useful to the understanding process.

Quantifying the Distinctiveness Dimension

In order to examine the effect of distinctiveness on the latencies in the membership decision task, subjects' judgments were obtained on this dimension (Galambos, 1983). The norms in this and the next study came from *ratings* of action-activity pairs. In the ratings tasks, the stimuli were 18 pairs of three-word phrases, where one member of the pair was an activity name and the other was one of its component actions.

The 18 subjects making the distinctiveness ratings saw the actions at the left of the activities (e.g., POSITION THE JACK...CHANGING A FLAT), and at the top of every page was the question frame:

"When you _____, how
frequently are you in the process of _____?"

To the right of each pair was a line with 10 marks at equal intervals. The leftmost endpoint was labeled *never* and the rightmost endpoint *always.* Subjects circled one of the ten marks to record their rating. Each subject saw a different random permutation of the 360 pairs. The mean rating across subjects is taken as the distinctiveness value of the action in its activity. For example, in the activity "Painting a Room," some of the actions and their distinctiveness values were:

Action	Distinctiveness
Decide on Color	3.06
Move out Furniture	4.06
Cover the Floor	6.06
Mask the Woodwork	7.31

As in the norming studies of centrality and sequence, there was high intersubject agreement concerning the distinctiveness ratings.

The Standardness of Actions in Activities

The standardness of an action concerns the frequency of performing that action when doing a given activity. Some of the component actions in an activity are almost always performed when the activity is performed, e.g., *Get a Towel* in the "Washing Your Hair" activity. Others, such as *Get a Tripod* in the "Taking a Photograph" activity, may be less standardly included. Note that an action may be standardly done in some activity without its being necessary to the successful performance of that activity.

Standardness is similar to the notion of script *typicality* developed by Graesser, Woll, Kowalski, and Smith (1980), although their subjects made ratings of script actions on a scale labeled with varying degrees of typicality rather than frequency. The standardness norms make it possible to distinguish between two models of the retrievability of action concepts from the representations of activities. The first of these models maintains that action concepts are retrievable according to their frequency of occurrence in the activity. The second specifies that retrievability is a function of the role the action plays in the accomplishing the main goals of the activity. Thus, an action crucial to the accomplishment of the main goals of the activity might be more readily accessible than other actions that occur with equal frequency. Although clearly there will be a certain degree of overlap (since goal-related actions will occur with high frequency), the standardness dimension provides information that makes it possible to unconfound these two models.

Quantifying the Standardness Dimension

The stimulus packets were constructed in the same fashion as in the study of distinctiveness. However, for the subjects making standardness ratings, the pairs were arranged so that the activity was to the left of the action (e.g., CHANGING A FLAT . . . POSITION THE JACK). At the top of each page was the following question frame:

"When you are in the process of _____, how
frequently do you _____?"

The 18 subjects rated how frequently they did a particular action when engaged in the activity. As in the preceding study, subjects made their ratings by circling a number next to the activity-action pair on a ten-point scale marked *never* on one end and *always* on the other. The mean rating across subjects is taken to be the standardness value for the action. For example, in the activity "Taking a Photograph," some actions and their standardness values were:

Action	Standardness
Get a Tripod	2.00
Set the Exposure	4.44
Advance the Film	7.06
Press the Button	9.00

Correlations Among the Norms

Part of our interest in the two factors of distinctiveness and standardness was to examine whether they helped explain the centrality effect. One important question is the extent of overlap of the sets of norms. To examine this, Spearman rank correlation coefficients were computed for each activity for each pair of dimensions, using the ranks of the mean action judgments on the dimensions. The interpretation of so many correlations has its problems, and, of course, the actions cannot be presumed to be independent and randomly sampled. However, these correlation coefficients can at least indicate where there might be overlap between the three dimensions of centrality, standardness, and distinctiveness. (We do not here consider the relations between these three dimensions and sequence, but see Chapter 5 for sequence vs. centrality.)

The correlations over the 12 actions between centrality and standardness for the thirty activities ranged from −.326 to .883 with a median correlation of .482. This is the highest median correlation for any pair of dimensions. It indicates that, for at least some of the activities, the standardness judgments seem to approximate the centrality ranks. Highly central actions tend to be standard or frequent in their activities. There are some low centrality actions that are also standard (e.g., *Counting the Money* when "Cashing a Check," or *Disposing of Ashes* when "Smoking a Pipe.") The existence of this sort of action lowers the correlation and opens the possibility of experimentally unconfounding centrality and standardness effects.

The correlations between centrality and distinctiveness range from −.506 to .769 with median of .179. The median correlation here is not high, but the range of the 30 correlations is the widest of the six comparisons. For some of the activities (e.g., "Making a Campfire" and "Making New Clothes") the central actions are very distinctive to the activity and the noncentral actions are low in distinctiveness. For others (e.g., "Going on Vacation" and "Going to Restaurants") this pattern is reversed. This analysis indicates that these dimensions are fairly independent. Thus, an action that is distinctive to an activity can be either central to it (e.g., *Applying the Shampoo* when "Washing Your Hair") or not (e.g., *Putting Away Jack* when "Changing a Flat"). Similarly, central actions vary in distinctiveness. This pattern of correlations helps the selection of stimuli which covary these dimensions (Galambos & Black, 1982).

The correlations between distinctiveness and standardness ranged from −.639 to .550 with the median being .090. There seems to be little consistent overlap between these two dimensions. It is interesting that an action which is very diagnostic of a particular activity (i.e., one that is highly distinctive) need not be a highly standard action. Thus, a distinctive action in the restaurant activity is *See Head Waiter* but that action is not high in standardness. Conversely, a standard action such as *Eat the Meal* is not very distinctive to the restaurant activity since that action occurs in other contexts.

Distinctiveness and Standardness in Retrieval

The results of the correlational analyses indicate that distinctiveness and standardness can vary orthogonally. This permits the design of a membership decision experiment which pits the two variables against one another in an attempt to predict decision latencies.

Experiment 4

As in the earlier experiments, the stimuli consisted of an activity name and an action, and the task was to indicate whether the action was part of the activity. In this experiment, however, the action and the activity were presented in succession rather than simultaneously. A trial consisted of a fixation field followed by a one-second presentation of either the activity or the action. At the end of this interval, the first phrase was erased from the screen and the other element of the pair was immediately presented. On half of the trials the action was presented first, followed by the activity; on the other half the presentation order was reversed. Latency until a button press response was measured from the onset of the second part of the stimulus.

This modification in procedure was undertaken because of the possibility that the presentation order used in Experiment 1 differentially favored the standardness factor. Since in Experiment 1 the activity was always presented on the top line and was presumably read first, the activity concept would be the starting point for the search of the knowledge structure. This strategy would tend to be sensitive to differences in standardness if these differences reflect relative distance or strength of associative links originating at the activity concept and directed toward the action. With this strategy, the distinctiveness factor might have little or no effect on reaction time if distinctiveness involves (oppositely) directed links originating at the action.

The predictions must take into account the modification in the task described above. For "activity-first" stimuli, the standardness factor should have a greater effect than with "action-first" stimuli. The reverse should be the case with the distinctiveness factor. Thus, the main focus in this experiment is on the interactions of the two factors, each with the order of stimulus presentation. Such interactions would indicate that the task modification influenced the order in which the knowledge structure was searched (i.e., either bottom-up, with the action first stimuli, or top-down with the activity-first stimuli).

From each of 19 activities, nine actions were chosen which represented a complete crossing of three levels of each of the two factors. The primary finding was that the distinctiveness of an action influenced the membership decision latency when the action was presented before the activity. The pattern of reaction times shows this distinctiveness by presentation order interaction:

Distinctiveness Level	Action First	Activity First
High	726	882
Middle	755	869
Low	790	885

As these data show, the distinctiveness of an action had an effect when the actions were presented first. In contrast, there was very little difference among the actions at the different distinctiveness levels in the activity-first trials. Thus the distinctiveness of an action appears to exert a clear influence on the retrievability of its activity concept, but only when the action cue comes first. This distinctiveness effect appears quite different from the centrality effect, which appears most strongly in an activity-first sort of experiment (as Experiment 1).

The standardness factor exerted a small effect in the predicted direction. The interaction of standardness and presentation order was not significant using the conservative quasi-F statistical test. The standardness results were:

Standardness Level	Action First	Activity First
High	732	854
Middle	766	872
Low	772	910

There is a retrieval latency advantage for high (854 msec) as opposed to low (910 msec) standardness actions, when they are presented in activity first trials. Although this effect is statistically weak, it is not unlike the centrality effect found in Experiment 1 (that is, if we consider that the subjects in that experiment began their retrieval process with the activity concept).

The Representation of Standardness Information

Standardness was introduced as a possible explanation for the centrality effects we observed in Experiments 1, 2, and 3. The notion was that actions frequently performed in an activity might be more prominent in its representation than those occurring in fewer instances of the activity. Experiment 4 provides some weak evidence that this is the case. The question is whether the effect of standardness is merely a proxy for centrality in that experiment. If so, then differences in retrieval latency for different levels of standardness may be due to an underlying correlation of standardness with centrality. As shown earlier, the correlations between the centrality and standardness norms for actions in the 30 activities showed a moderately high positive relationship in general.

To examine this, an analysis of covariance was performed on the mean response latencies in Experiment 4, using the centrality ranking of the action in the stimulus as the covariable. The result is that the F for the standardness main effect decreases from 2.91 to .28 when the effects due to centrality are covaried. This supports the idea that the main element in the standardness effect in this experiment was really centrality. The marginal effect of this factor in Experiment 4 was clearly gone when the contribution of centrality was removed.

Of course, the same argument might be made about the centrality effect in Experiment 1 (i.e., that it is really due to an underlying correlation with standardness). To examine this possibility, I performed an analysis of covariance on the data in Experiment 1, using the standardness of the actions as the covariable. There was a decrease in the F for the centrality main effect from 7.94 to 3.43. This reduced F is only marginally significant. This reduction indicates the presence of a standardness effect behind the scenes. However, the reduction here is much less than that in the covariance analysis of Experiment 4 data. There is some remaining centrality effect after all the standardness effect has been removed.

Taken together, these two analyses lend support to the notion that centrality is the more important variable and that standardness is more derivative. The (central) actions that are the main goals in performing an activity will usually also be the most frequently present in instances of that activity. In this way, the standardness of these actions is a result of their centrality. The clearest test of this view has not yet been performed. The relative importance of the two factors needs to be examined in an experiment which crosses standardness with centrality. The selection of stimuli for this would be difficult but not impossible.

The Function of Distinctiveness Information

The primary finding in Experiment 4 was the distinctiveness effect. Distinctive actions presented before an activity facilitated the membership decision as compared with less distinctive actions. The explanation for this facilitation appears quite clear. With distinctive actions (in action-first trials) subjects could more accurately predict the activity in which the action belonged. Because of this, subjects could prepare for the presentation of the activity name during the interval before its presentation. Thus, the process of recognizing the membership relation occurred in this interval and was not part of the response latency. When the activity phrase was presented, subjects merely needed to check that it named the activity they had predicted. This process is presumably faster than the processes associated with checking the membership relation between the action and activity. For those stimuli with nondistinctive actions, this membership decision process cannot begin until the timed part of the trial (that is, until after the activity phrase has been presented). This is due to the difficulty in predicting which of a number of potential activities might be presented following a nondistinctive action.

Distinctiveness is an important attribute of information in knowledge structures because distinctive information has the major function of helping the comprehension system activate the appropriate knowledge structure by which to understand a situation. It should be noted that there are probably a number of clues that can be used to access the correct knowledge structure. For example, the name of the activity might be present in the input. If the word *restaurant* appeared in text, the knowledge structure containing information about restaurants could be activated immediately upon decoding the meaning of this word (see Chapter 3). Alternatively, the context can be inferred from knowing the prior states or goals of the protagonists (for example, that they were hungry business people on a downtown street at approximately noon). There are no doubt many subtler ways, including being alert for distinctive actions, used by the comprehension system to obtain the correct context.

The basic point is that the contextualization function of knowledge structures has important implications for the organization of information within those structures. One of these implications is that information must be organized so as to make it possible to access the appropriate knowledge structure for a given situation. The representation of distinctiveness is one way in which this might be accomplished.

THE DIFFERENT FUNCTIONAL ROLES OF CENTRALITY AND DISTINCTIVENESS

Although the original conception of distinctiveness was that it might be a component of centrality, it appears that the two are quite different. They both serve the function of contextualizing a given situation, but in different ways. Central actions are those which are most readily available to the comprehension system when the appropriate knowledge structure has been selected. Distinctive actions help the comprehension system by accessing the appropriate knowledge structure.

Thus, upon encountering in a story the sentence

John walked through the door and saw the head waiter.

it would be possible to access the restaurant knowledge structure as context for subsequent sentences. But once the knowledge structure is available, how does it aid the comprehension system? Presumably one way is by providing a structure in which incoming information can be readily matched with information already present.

If all the information in that knowledge structure were simultaneously activated, however, this might strain the processing, or working storage capacity of the system. Rather, it might be better to activate selectively, or more strongly, those components of the knowledge structure most important to the activity. Such actions might be those more strongly associated with the goals of the activity. If part of the function of the knowledge structure is to set up expectations for subsequent input, then central actions are the most appropriate information to expect. Therefore, central actions may be more prominent in working memory after selection of the knowledge structure has occurred.

Distinctiveness and Centrality in Retrieval

Experiment 5

Stimuli. As we have seen from the correlations of distinctiveness and centrality, it is possible to select sets of actions for which these two factors can be orthogonalized. In a study conducted with John Black (Galambos & Black, 1982), four actions from each of 22 activities were chosen to sample the combinations of high and low levels of both centrality and distinctiveness. From each activity, one action (Hi-C/Lo-D) was high in centrality in the activity and low in distinctiveness; a second action (Lo-C/Hi-D) was low in centrality and high in distinctiveness. The third action (Hi-C/Hi-D) was high in both factors; and the fourth (Lo-C/Lo-D) had a low level of both. For example, the four actions selected in the activity of "Cashing a Check" were:

Action Type	Action
Hi-C/Lo-D	Write Your Signature
Lo-C/Hi-D	Record the Amount
Hi-C/Hi-D	Go to Bank
Lo-C/Lo-D	Wait in line

Twelve *pairs* of actions were constructed for each activity by combining the four types of actions in all pairs, varying order. For example, the action *Write Your Signature* was paired with each of the other three actions in the check-cashing activity, and those three pairs were presented in both orders of presentation (i.e., with *Write Your Signature* appearing both before the other actions and after them).

Paradigm.   The experimental paradigm was similar to the membership decision experiments, except that in this case the subjects were asked to report whether or not the two actions in a stimulus were part of the *same* activity. We did not want to present the activity name because we were interested in how the knowledge structures are activated in the absence of the explicit statement of the name of the activity they represent. The presentation of the two parts of the stimulus was successive (as in Experiment 4) rather than simultaneous (as in Experiments 1, 2, and 3). The first phrase was presented on a CRT for 1,500 msec. This phrase then disappeared and the second phrase appeared. It remained on the screen until the subject responded. The response latency was measured from the onset of the second phrase to the subject's response.

The Effect of the Distinctive Item Coming First.   A number of interesting comparisons are possible, given the design of this experiment. The first prediction was that responses to stimuli where the first action was high in distinctiveness would be faster than those for stimuli where the first action was not distinctive. Therefore stimuli such as:

Go to Bank   →   Write Your Signature

should receive relatively faster decisions that the two actions are part of the same activity. Compare the example above with:

Wait in Line   →   Write Your Signature

where the first action is not distinctive enough to permit activation of the appropriate knowledge structure.

This prediction was strongly borne out. The mean reaction time for stimuli with distinctive first actions was 939 msec, whereas the mean for nondistinctive first actions was 1,078 msec. It appears that distinctive first actions permit the retrieval of the appropriate knowledge structure before the presentation of the second part of the stimulus. Stimuli with nondistinctive first actions do not share this advantage.

The Effect of the Central Item Coming Second.   The second prediction was that once the activation of the knowledge structure has occurred, the more central actions would be more easily accessed than the less central actions. In terms of the experimental design, this translates into a comparison of two classes of stimuli, both of which involve a distinctive first action. The first class contains stimuli with distinctive first actions followed by central second actions. For example:

Record the Amount   →   Write Your Signature

In contrast are stimuli with distinctive first actions followed by noncentral second actions such as:

Record the Amount   →   Wait in Line

These should be slower, since the second action is not as strongly primed by initial activation of the knowledge structure. The mean response latency for distinctive first actions followed by central second actions was 906. The mean for stimuli with distinctive first actions followed by noncentral second actions was 973. This effect is smaller than the distinctive-item first effect, but it does provide some evidence that more central actions may be activated earlier than less central actions in the knowledge structure.

The Effect of Same Items in Different Order.   The design of the stimuli in this experiment permits some fine-grained comparisons of individual stimuli which differ only in terms of the order of presentation of the same actions. The purest test of our activation model can be obtained by comparing stimuli where Lo-C/Hi-D actions are followed by Hi-C/Lo-D actions with the stimuli reversing this order. For example, our prediction would be that this order of presentation of the stimulus pair:

Record the Amount   →   Write Your Signature
Lo-C/Hi-D   Hi-C/Lo-D

would yield a far faster response than the reverse order of presentation:

Write your Signature   →   Record the Amount
Hi-C/Lo-D   Lo-C/Hi-D

Since the first action in the latter ordering is not distinctive, the subject is unable to access the appropriate knowledge structure. The lack of centrality of the second action in the knowledge structure also slows the response. The results show a very large 160-msec advantage for stimuli with the optimal presentation order when compared with stimuli with the same actions presented in the opposite order.

Getting and Using Context

The results of this experiment indicate the presence of two functional constraints on the organization of knowledge about common activities. Representational efficiency requires that knowledge structures be quickly accessed when needed. When an isolated action is encountered, it is necessary to find an appropriate context. Organization in terms of distinctiveness would support this important context-finding function.

The distinctiveness of an action to an activity can be represented as a link to the superordinate activity concept. If a distinctive action is encountered, then this link can be traversed and the activity concept retrieved. The results of Experiments 4 and 5 demonstrate that distinctiveness is a relevant structural characteristic in the functional organization of knowledge structures for common activities.

A second functional constraint is that the knowledge structures must organize information in such a way as to generate predictions about subsequent input. If the comprehension system can keep only a limited amount of information about a context available for prediction, it would be useful if the most relevant information were the most easily accessed. Such relevant information might include the main goals of the activity and the most important actions in the performance of those goals. For instance, if the restaurant context is involved in a narrative, then it is a very good prediction that subsequent input will include something about the action of eating. Our results indicate that this more central information does benefit from a greater availability once the activity is accessed.

GOAL STRUCTURE IN ACTIVITIES

In discussing centrality, I mentioned how it may be related to the goal structure of the activity. In a "goal structure" representation, the actions are related or linked as a plan in the service of a goal. Typically, doing the activity will involve the accomplishment of a number of these goals. For example, in the "Changing a Flat" activity the action of removing the lugs is performed in the plan for achieving the subgoal of removing the bad tire from the wheel. Any representation that preserves goal structure (such as those discussed by Graesser, 1978, 1981; Lichtenstein & Brewer, 1980; Smith & Collins, 1981) would depict the goal-consummation action as a superordinate node in a goal hierarchy. The plan action would be lower in the hierarchy and would be dominated by the goal it serves. The activity name itself is the highest node in the goal hierarchy since it is the goal that organizes all the subgoals.

Scene Clusters

Our supposition here is that scenes within activities are units that represent the plans needed to accomplish the subgoals of the activity. The proposal is that central actions are the superordinate concepts (the goals) for these scenes. In order to provide evidence for this proposal, the following sorting experiment was performed using the 30 activities and their sets of 12 actions.

Action Clusters

Experiment 6

Subjects were asked to sort together the actions in an activity that they felt belonged together. They were permitted to make as many clusters as they wished as long as they ended up with fewer than 12 and more than one cluster in each activity. In addition, they were asked to write a brief name for each cluster they formed. They were free to use one of the actions in the cluster as the name for the cluster. Alternatively, they could make up their own short name.

In this experiment, I was interested in the extent to which subjects used central actions to name the clusters they formed. The hypothesis is that central actions will be more often used as cluster names than less central actions, insofar as a central action is a goal of a series of plan steps. A standard cluster analysis (Johnson, 1967) was performed on these data, using the maximum method for assigning higher-order clusters. In addition, I employed a method developed by Brian Reiser (see details in Reiser, Black, & Lehnert, 1982) to select from the subjects' responses the best (highest consensus) name for each cluster. Finally, in order to examine the hypothesis, I counted the number of times central actions were used as names for clusters.

Despite considerable heterogeneity in the types of names used for clusters, central actions occurred commonly. For 12 of the 30 activities, the most central action was also chosen by subjects as the name for one of the sets of actions they had clustered together. In 11 of the activities, the second-most central action was used as a cluster name. Each of these counts increases by six if we consider "clusters" with only a single action. These results for central actions can be compared with the counts for the least central actions in each activity.

Among the 60 least central actions in the 30 activities, only two were used by subjects as names of clusters of actions. In 13 more instances, very low centrality actions named single-action clusters. These were often cases where single actions were isolated from the main plans involved in the activity, for example, "completion" actions such as *leave the theater* or *leave the library.*

Central Actions as Goals

These results support the hypothesis that central actions serve to organize groups of actions within activities. Meanwhile, the general view that activities are organized according to their goals and plans has received support from other work in this area (Graesser, 1981; Lichtenstein & Brewer, 1980). Thus the centrality effects in our experiments and the typicality effects in Graesser's studies of reading are probably traceable to the same source, the goal-plan organization of the knowledge structures involved in processing. As discussed in Chapter 5, central actions are also heavily implicated in explanations for the failure of scripted plans.

I alluded previously to the notion that standardness was derivative from an organization according to centrality. This can now be reinterpreted in terms of goals. The standardness of an action in an activity can be roughly determined by its position in the goal structure. Thus an action is high in standardness if (1) it is one of the main goals in the activity, or (2) it is one of the main actions involved in accomplishing one of the main goals. The first part of this specification accounts for the high correlations between centrality and standardness. The second part accounts for the fact that some highly standard actions are not high in centrality. These actions are, however, important to the plan to carry out one of the main goals. Such actions might be considered "central" in a more local fashion—central to the performance of a lower-level goal. In other words, an action is high in standardness if it must be done in order to get any of the main goals in the activity done. On this model whatever functionality the standardness dimension might provide can be obtained from the goal-plan structure.

Sequence information can also be partly computed from a knowledge structure organized around goals and plans. Specifically, if action A is performed in order to accomplish action B then it can be inferred that action A precedes action B. This may account for the availability of at least some local sequence information. This sort of "plan sequencing" is much more flexible than a strict linear sequence from the beginning to the end of the activity. It can permit interposition (between A and B) of other actions which might not be temporally sequenced with respect to A or B. Nonetheless, the plan sequence does recognize and represent those sequence relations that are most reliable. Thus temporal order can be determined from the goal-plan structure of the activity.

Furthermore, plan sequencing provides for an ordering of actions that is not typically based on physical causality. Convention plays a very strong role in how actions are ordered in planned activities. Plan organization inside knowledge structures accounts for "conventional causality," where, for example, snapping my fingers may cause a waiter to hurry to my table to get my order. There is no sense of physical causality here, but the conventions involved in the restaurant activity make this a perfectly understandable (if gauche) plan sequence. Insofar as it is necessary to use the temporal order information relating these two actions, it can be determined from the plan relationships.

To summarize: Centrality can be understood in terms of a structure where the goals of an activity organize the plans to accomplish them. In addition, the same sort of structure can serve as a representation of standardness and sequence information.

SUMMARY OF EXPERIMENTS 1–6

Taken together, the results of the five reaction-time experiments demonstrate some of the significant features of the organization of information about common events. The strongest evidence is for distinctiveness and centrality effects. Distinctiveness is important information because it can help the comprehension system find the correct knowledge structure. It no doubt also serves a tracking or checking function even after the correct context is activated. Distinctive information which is encountered later in the input assures that the context has not changed and that the activated knowledge structure is still appropriate to the comprehension and representation of the situation. Chapter 3 further discusses the activation of script structures.

Centrality information is important because it efficiently provides the system with expectations that will make comprehension easier if those expectations are realized. Of course, central information will neither always be activated nor necessarily be the only activated information. Other features of the situation or of the state of the processing system will often lead to the generation of noncentral components as expectations. However, in the absence of these other features, the central components of a knowledge structure provide a set of default values that are subsequently most likely to be present in the input. Thus it is representationally efficient to organize information in knowledge structures according to its centrality. Even more importantly, centrality information tends to be coordinated with subgoal information in activities. Actions clustering together into scenes for achieving subgoals can be summarized with the name of a central action.

The other two factors examined in the reaction-time experiments— sequence and standardness—appear to be more derivative in nature. They are certainly aspects of the information present in knowledge structures. Subjects in the norming experiments agreed very highly about these features, and we did find some weak effects on membership decision latencies. However, on the basis of our experiments, it is difficult to conclude that these features figure importantly in the way actions in scripts are interrelated in knowledge structures. Rather, it appears that information about sequence or standardness generally can be computed from other information.

Goal and plan information is importantly implicated in at least three of the four features we have discussed. The central actions, as noted, are often the actions that achieve subgoals. Meanwhile, sequence information attaches to the steps in plans to achieve subgoals, and standardness is either redundant with centrality or represents a lower level of centrality, local to subplans. This heavy implication of goals and plans in the knowledge structures for activities is precisely what one would expect from a functionally efficient knowledge system.

3 A Model of Knowledge-Based Expectations in Text Comprehension

Noel E. Sharkey

We would claim that in natural language understanding, a simple rule is followed. Analysis proceeds in a top-down predictive manner. Understanding is expectation based. It is only when the expectations are useless or wrong that bottom-up processing begins.

Schank (1978)

INTRODUCTION

The script concept (Schank & Abelson, 1975; 1977) was created out of a need to solve difficult computational problems in text comprehension. One such problem arose when trying to model text coherence (Schank, 1975a). The difficulty is that writers tend to leave out information that they believe their readers already know (Grice, 1975). Thus, readers must often infer the information necessary to combine the meanings of successive sentences. However, Rieger (1975) found that a computational mechanism which tried to produce every conceivable inference to combine the meanings of two sentences produced an excess of computation—an "inference explosion."

One way around this problem was to give computer programs some of the mundane cultural knowledge schemas, or scripts, which people share. Schank and Abelson (1977) emphasized the systematic use of world knowledge in the construction of contextual hypotheses. For example, if we read a story about a restaurant, we can safely predict that a customer will sit at a table, look at a menu, be served by a waiting person, and will eat food. It

49

was by using such hypotheses that later programs were able to control the number of inferences considered by the system. This use of scripts as a computational necessity makes the theory associated with scripts a *functional* theory of text cohesion and inference (Sharkey & Mitchell, 1985), and is thus quintessential to the point of view advanced in this volume.

Of course, the use of a schema representation is nothing new in psychology. There are obviously close parallels here with the schema approach outlined by Bartlett (1932). However, the novelty of the Yale approach is in the concentration on the *contents* of the representation. For the first time researchers have begun to look *inside* contexts for specific knowledge we have about how people and objects are related in the real world. This specification of content assists us in the construction of experimental materials and enables us to make predictions with greater precision. In addition, the construction of the computer models throws up many problems for schema-based comprehension which might otherwise be overlooked. (See Sharkey & Mitchell [1985] for criticisms of the tendency for content to receive too little attention in experimental psychology.)

The first computer implementation of Schank and Abelson's theory was SAM (Script Applier Mechanism). In SAM, (Cullingford, 1978), appropriate scripts are indexed by the processor when contextual cues or script headers are noticed in a text. One type of header is the mention of a geographical location at which the goal of a protagonist may be satisfied, e.g., Pizza Hut, or Taco Bell. This allows the system to set up expectation frames in active memory. These frames comprise a sequence of script event templates ordered according to the usual sequence of actions obtaining in a real-world setting. Each event template is itself a smaller action-centered frame containing both predictions and default values for the actors and objects likely to fill in the frame slots. In their original formulation, Schank and Abelson (1977) proposed that when we read a script header, a pointer is set up to the location of that script in memory. When a second line is encountered which makes reference to the same script, that script is loaded up and used as a predictive mechanism.

The claim that script expectation influences the processes involved in comprehension has been investigated in a number of reading time studies (e.g., Bower, Black, & Turner 1979; den Uyl & van Oostendorp, 1980; Haberlandt, in press; Sanford & Garrod, 1981). All of these studies have relied on two simple processing assumptions. First, sentences that are expected require less processing than sentences not expected. Second, reading time increases as a function of processing difficulty. Accepting these assumptions, the experimental work bears out the expectation hypothesis. Typically the experiments have demonstrated that a sentence is read faster if it has been preceded by related script materials rather than by other controlled text.

However, as myself and others (Sharkey, 1982, 1983; Sharkey & Mitchell, 1981a; Sharkey & Sharkey, 1983) have pointed out, there is no way of telling from the sentence reading-time research at what point in processing expectations occur, what form they take, or how they are used. For example, expectations may be set up for particular script words in a text, or scripts may influence the processes involved in word by word integration within a sentence, or they may operate on integrating complete sentences with the preceding context, or on any combination of these levels.

My empirical research on these issues over the last few years forms the basis of this chapter. To begin, I describe some of the experiments that I carried out with Don Mitchell at Exeter in England. These were mainly concerned with how word meanings are affected and controlled by "active" scripts. In order to understand this work it will be necessary to examine briefly some previous psychological work on word recognition, in particular, work concerned with the lexical decision task.

In the later part of the chapter, I shall describe some of the research carried out at Yale with Amanda Sharkey. This research extended the lexical decision findings by looking at how long people dwell on script words during sentence processing. I make a distinction between the availability of knowledge and its utilization. The first four experiments reported in this chapter explore the privileged availability of certain subsets of knowledge. In Experiments 5 and 6, I examine how this knowledge is utilized in sentence understanding.

All of the experiments are discussed in terms of a parallel spreading activation Knowledge Access Network model (KAN). This has been partly developed elsewhere (Sharkey & Mitchell, 1985; Sharkey & Sharkey, in preparation). KAN combines the script concept (Schank & Abelson, 1977) with a spreading activation parallel associative network account of memory (Collins & Loftus, 1975; Anderson, 1983). The model is based on psychological evidence collected by myself and others. It has provided me with a convenient notational form with which to link my work with the general psychological literature on context effects.

CONTEXT EFFECTS ON THE AVAILABILITY OF MEANING

The first research to be discussed here concerns the effect of scripts on the availability of the meanings of script words. This research led me to a close examination of the English Language Interpreter (ELI) at the front end of the SAM system (Riesbeck, 1978). ELI serves to map English onto a language-independent conceptual representation, avoiding inference as much as possible (Schank, 1975a). In fact, in the SAM implementation there is little interaction between the parser and the Script Applier modules where most of the inference is done. The flow of processing runs mainly from the parser to the Applier. The only exception to this is that if mainly a single script context is anticipated in advance, certain verb senses are set on a priority list by the knowledge domain; e.g., within the restaurant script the action "serve" would not be mistaken for the sense of serve that is appropriate for "tennis" or "fighting in a war."

One psychological prediction which arises from the implementation of ELI particularly concerns the point at which scripts influence text processing. To spell out some of the relevant computational details, Riesbeck's system begins by using hash-coding procedures to access the entries in its relatively small lexicon. The possible meanings are then handed over to Active Memory where the context effects begin to exert their influence.

Accordingly, the word meanings in ELI's dictionary are entirely unaffected by semantic context or real-world knowledge. According to Riesbeck's program, the influence of scripts is introduced almost entirely after a sentence has been processed. It is difficult to say how much of this modularization was simply programming convenience. (In later systems such as BORIS and FRUMP, some attempts were made to integrate parsing with semantic context.) Nonetheless the idea of complete modularity is worth experimental evaluation.

The Lexical Decision Task

We (Sharkey & Mitchell, 1981a) used the lexical decision task to test whether or not scripts affect the availability of individual word meanings. This experimental technique that has been widely used to study the effects of context on word recognition (Becker, 1979; Becker & Killion, 1977; Fischler, 1977; Fischler & Goodman, 1978; Kleiman, 1980; Meyer & Schvaneveldt, 1971; Meyer, Schvaneveldt, & Ruddy, 1975; Neely, 1976, 1977; Schuberth & Eimas, 1977; Schuberth, Spoehr, & Lane, 1981; Schvaneveldt & McDonald, 1981). In this task, people are presented with a string of letters (usually on a computer screen) and are required to decide as quickly as possible whether or not the letters spell an English word (e.g., RABBIT) or a nonword (e.g., ASSINTART). A response key (yes or no) is pressed as soon as the decision has been made.

The premise underlying this task is that the response latency for a word is made up from the time taken to decide if a word has a meaning in memory (James, 1975), plus some constant response time. In this way the lexical decision task may be thought of as a *probe* that can be used to isolate and study the effects of context on the availability of a word's meaning. For example, Becker (1979), Becker and Killion (1977), and Meyer and Schvaneveldt (1971) have demonstrated that lexical decision time is speeded up when a word is preceded by a single, related word (e.g., when a target word such as DOCTOR is preceded by a context word like NURSE).

It follows from the previous paragraph that if script contexts affect the availability of word meanings, then the lexical decision time for a word would be facilitated by the prior appearance of a script context. That is, if a word names a default value for one of the script actions, then we would expect a prior script context to reduce the time required to make a "yes" decision. Such a finding would run counter to predictions based on the ELI program.

A further question to explore is whether script contexts replicate previous work on contextual effects in word recognition. According to Whaley (1978) and Gordon (1983), one of the strongest predictors of lexical decision time is the frequency of occurrence of a word in written English (Kucera & Francis, 1967). Word frequency has been shown to have a strong and reliable effect on the recognition processes in a number of different tasks (Forster & Chambers, 1973; Goldiamond & Hawkins, 1958; Just & Carpenter, 1980; Mitchell & Green, 1978; Rubenstein, Garfield, & Millikan, 1970; Schuberth et al., 1981; Solomon & Howes, 1951; Stanners, Jastrzembski, & Westbrook, 1975). The general finding is that decisions about high-frequency words are faster than for low-frequency words.

From my perspective, one of the most interesting things about word frequency is its interaction with context. The interaction effect is different for the two types of context that have dominated the field of visual word recognition. These contexts are the "single word," in which DOCTOR acts as a context for semantically related words such as NURSE, and "incomplete sentence" contexts in which sentence fragments such as THE CAT SAT ON THE . . . act as a context for words such as MAT. Single-word contexts have been shown to interact with word frequency, i.e., the frequency effect is markedly reduced for words which are sematically related to prior contexts (Becker, 1979; Becker & Killion, 1977; Meyer & Schvaneveldt, 1971). By contrast, the decision times for words following incomplete sentence contexts are additive with frequency, i.e., decision speed for very likely words is facilitated but the actual magnitude of the frequency effect is the same regardless of contextual strength (Schuberth & Eimas, 1977; Schuberth et al., 1981).

Experiment 1.   In our first experiment, we had people make lexical decisions for pronounceable nonwords, script words, or script-unrelated words. The script words were collected from a free associative script norming procedure similar to that used by Bower et al. (1979) and Graesser, Gordon, and Sawyer (1979). We used only the object nouns (props) from actions which had been mentioned by at least half of our informants. Each decision was preceded by either a two-sentence script context (see example 1 below) or a row of 'X's (neutral context). In addition, half of the decision words were high in word frequency and half were low. Thus, there were two primary factors in the experiment: Frequency (high and low) and Context (script, unrelated and neutral):

Example 1

The children's birthday party was going quite well.
They all sat round the table prepared to sing.
Decision word: CANDLES

The mean lexical decision times for Experiment 1 are shown in Table 3.1. There were two main findings of interest. First, the results showed a clear-cut pattern of facilitation for script words in comparison with both unrelated and neutral words. Second, there was also a marked reduction in the word frequency effect for script words (10 msec) compared with unrelated or neutral words (100 msec). These differences produced a significant Context X Frequency interaction. Overall, the findings suggest that scripts do influence the availability of word meanings. Furthermore, the virtual elimination of the frequency effect suggests that script context effects are parallel with those produced by single word contexts (Becker, 1979; Becker & Killion 1977; Meyer & Schvaneveldt 1971). A model to combine these findings from the word recognition studies with our experimental results is taken up below.

Our results run counter to predictions based on the ELI parser. As I mentioned earlier, all of the words in ELI's lexicon have approximately equal access time. There is no provision for frequency of occurrence of words. However, even from a purely functional point of view, it makes sense to have a system that learns to grant greater accessibility to its most frequently used items. Furthermore, the SAM system allows very little word by word interaction between the script domain and ELI. This is inconsistent with the data obtained from our experiment. One compromise solution, which we shall take up later, is to have word meanings represented

TABLE 3.1
Mean Lexical Decision Times for Experiment 1

	Related	*Unrelated*	*Neutral*
Target Word:			
High Frequency	664	701	698
Low Frequency	672	784	798

as nodes in a parallel spreading activation network. In such a network, activation may be used to order the importance of lexical items according to their contextual relevance. The procedures of ELI could then utilize this knowledge during the process of parsing.

Parallel Spreading Activation

Initially Don Mitchell and I (Mitchell, Sharkey, & Fox, 1983; Sharkey, 1983; Sharkey & Mitchell, 1981b) discussed the connection between ELI and word recognition in terms of the "logogen" model (Morton, 1969). Briefly, in this model, meaning access operates through a system of word-detector units or logogens. Each word in the mental lexicon has its own logogen, which may be thought of as an evidence-collection device. Logogens collect evidence both from the contextual system and from featural information coming in from words. Thus, when a word is input into the system, every appropriate logogen gradually accumulates information until one of them reaches a preset threshold. When this occurs, the logogen fires and the address of the word meaning becomes available to the processor. Both context and frequency are thought to affect the resting level of a logogen. However, as Schuberth and Eimas (1977) have pointed out, the logogen model predicts additivity of context and frequency. This is not what we found in our experiment.

More recently we (Sharkey & Mitchell, 1985) proposed that the influence of script-based contexts on word recognition could be described in terms of an associative network spreading activation model (Anderson, 1983; Collins & Loftus, 1975). Such a model can provide a common notational form with which to combine our script findings with other context research. The network model has many similarities with Morton's (1969) system. Essentially the logogen model is a forerunner to the whole notion of parallel production systems. With the increase of interest in computer simulation, however, such models of word recognition (McClelland & Rumelhart, 1981) have become more computationally sophisticated. (One major difference between the logogen model and Rumelhart and McClelland's system is that the latter emphasizes the use of facilitory and inhibitory links between the different levels of evidence collection.)

In the basic network account, illustrated in Fig. 3.1, related word concepts are represented as a set of interlinking nodes. For example, a word like DOCTOR would have a direct link with the word NURSE. DOCTOR would also be associated with the word WIFE but more distantly, i.e., there would be more intervening nodes on the path between doctor and wife than between doctor and nurse. This has implications for response time measure as we shall see.

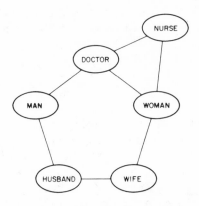

FIG. 3.1. A simplified portion of a possible semantic network configuration.

As a word is read, activation accumulates on its concept node. In addition, activation spreads across the arcs emanating from the activated concept node to associated nodes such that the various meanings of the word become available for further processing (Swinney, 1979; Seidenberg, Tanenhaus, Leiman, & Bienkowski, 1983). Consequently, if a word that is related to the previous word is read, it will need less activation to reach threshold and so lexical access will be faster (Meyer, Schvaneveldt, & Ruddy, 1972). It is assumed that lexical decision time is proportional to the amount of activation on a concept node.

One important aspect of the network account is how it can handle the combined effects of word frequency and context. Schuberth et al. (1981) have suggested that differences between incomplete sentence and single-word contexts may be attributable to differences in the size of the semantic sets generated by the two types of context. We assumed that activation at associated nodes is inversely related to semantic set size (Anderson, 1983). Thus, with a large set size, associated activation should combine additively with base level activation as suggested by the findings of Schuberth and Eimas (1977) and Schuberth et al. (1981). However, when the semantic set size is small, the activation level on associated nodes should reach a maximum level (see McClelland & Rumelhart, 1981, for a discussion of asymptotic levels). A "ceiling" of this type would eliminate the detection of base-level differences in activation. In this way, frequency effects should be virtually eliminated for words presented in the presence of a strong context, as Becker & Killion (1977) and Becker (1979) have demonstrated.

Sharkey and Mitchell (1985) translated Schank and Abelson's (1977) script construct into a parallel spreading activation network model. This has led to the development of a Knowledge Access Network (KAN) model which is described in more detail later. Sharkey and Mitchell proposed that a script may be viewed as a region of an associative network. In this way, when enough evidence accumulates to activate a network region corresponding to a script, the meanings of words related to that script have inflated activation levels. Such an account can explain both the speedier decision times and the reduction in frequency effects for script words.

The Control of Script Priming

I suggested, in discussing our word-recognition experiment, that the results allowed us to align script contexts with single-word contexts. One major problem in doing this concerns the time characteristics of the single-word contexts. There is evidence from a number of studies that the effects derived from word contexts are both very short-lived (Loftus, 1973; Meyer & Schvaneveldt, 1971; Warren, 1972) and can be disrupted by as little as one unrelated intervening item (Foss, 1982; Gough, Alford, & Holley-Wilcox, 1981; Meyer & Schvaneveldt, 1971). Such a rapid decay time presents problems for the notion of a functionally significant script context. If the influence of script context only affects meaning availability for a maximum of a few hundred milliseconds, it is difficult to see *how* this type of context would influence natural language processing. Furthermore, it is difficult to see *why* contextual effects with such limited scope would be of use to a reader.

Experiments 2 and 3.   We investigated the longevity and control characteristics of script activation in two further lexical decision experiments. In the next experiment, we broached two related issues concerning the longevity and control of the priming effects reported in the previous experiment. First, we asked whether script activation lasts beyond the next word in a text or whether a small amount of intervening material will destroy the effects. We tested this by employing a basic script context (Example 2a) and a target word, sometimes changing the context by adding neutral filler material (2b). If the scripts are like single-word contexts, then their influence should be disrupted by a filler sentence:

Example 2

(a) The restaurant was quite empty when we got there.

(b) The restaurant was quite empty when we got there. It had been quite a good journey.

(c) The restaurant was quite empty when we got there. We left quickly and went to an animal park.

(d) The restaurant was quite empty when we got there. We sat down at a vacant table.

Decision word: MENU

The second question we asked concerned how the network region corresponding to script contexts is deactivated, if not through rapid decay. Schank and Abelson (1977) have proposed that there are a number of different control signals that indicate an exit from one script and the beginning of another. According to their theory, the strongest exit signal is an action that changes the geographical location of a main protagonist. Thus, we tested the notion of textually cued script deactivation by interposing a script exit sentence between an initial script sentence and its related decision word (2c). We predicted that an exit sentence should destroy any facilitation effects for decision words related to the initial script. A comparison condition in which the script context was continued with a second sentence was also used.

The mean lexical decision times for Experiment 2 are shown in Table 3.2. The results from this experiment replicated the finding that decision times were faster for script words than for unrelated words. Also, the neutral filler materials (2b) did not significantly reduce the influence of scripts. This means that scripts are not simply displaced by intervening material. However, the "exit" findings were something of a surprise to us. The exit materials *did not* deactivate script influence (that is, priming in cases like 2c was no less than in cases like 2d). Recalling that single-word contexts may be disrupted by as little as one intervening unrelated item, this means that script contexts are a lot more robust to interference than single-word contexts. It also means that we were still left with the question as to how scripts *are* deactivated.

The latter question formed the basis of Experiment 3. We reasoned that one possible explanation for the deactivation failure in Experiment 2 was that more evidence is needed to establish that the initial script is no longer useful. It could be that a decision has to be made about whether new goals

TABLE 3.2
Mean Lexical Decision Times for Experiment 2

	Context Sentences			
	1 Script	*Script + Filler*	*Script + Exit*	*2 Script*
Target Word:				
Script-Related	624	617	622	599
Unrelated	719	723	713	706

initiated by an actor are a temporary detour from a current script or whether they represent a shift to a new script. Alternatively, we thought that the active influence of a script may simply decay over time since last mention. This decay period would have to be relatively long in comparison with the decay period observed for single-word contexts, as shown above. However, it is possible that if an active script has not been referenced for a longer period, say three sentences, then its influence might exhibit decay.

In Experiment 3 we extended all of the contexts used in the preceding experiment to be five sentences long. The first two sentences of every context were script sentences, and the final three were either more sentences from the same script; three neutral filler sentences; or an exit sentence followed by two sentences in the new situation (see Example 3). We hypothesized that if script activation simply decays over time since last mention, then three filler sentences would be enough to promote deactivation. On the other hand, if deactivation is textually cued then it should only be picked up by three exit sentences.

Example 3

All-script:
    The record store didn't seem to have what I was after.
    I looked through most of their selection.
    I asked the assistant for some help.
    But she couldn't find it either.
    Then I looked through the same selection.

Script + Filler:
    The record store didn't seem to have what I was after.
    I looked through most of their selection.
    Then I heard something outside.
    I looked out of the window.
    There was a parade marching past.

Script + Exit:
    The record store didn't seem to have what I was after.
    I looked through most of their selection.
    Then I went to the library.
    The poetry section was upstairs.
    But all the Wordsworth was out.

Targets: CASHIER STIRRUP

The mean lexical decision times for Experiment 3 are shown in Table 3.3. Indeed there was fairly clear-cut evidence that script contexts were

TABLE 3.3
Mean Lexical Decision Times for Experiment 3

		Context Sentences	
	Script	Script + Filler	Script + Exit
Target Word:			
Script-Related	772	787	850
Unrelated	899	941	851

deactivated only by cues from the text alone. There was no evidence of either decay over time or straightforward interference by new words. Taken together, the results from the preceding two experiments demonstrate that the control of script activation differs radically from what would be predicted from the fast decay function of single-word primes. In one experiment we found that a single script sentence was sufficient to facilitate related decision words. Furthermore, a single exit sentence did not disrupt this priming. In contrast, when we used three exit sentences we observed a clear reduction in priming effects.

Experiment 4. In a further experiment we tested two explanations to account for the combined results of Experiments 2 and 3. On the one hand, both the initial script and the script indicated by an exit sentence are activated at the same time. Accordingly, both scripts could simultaneously facilitate their associated decision words by an equal amount. On the other hand, it is possible that only one script can be active at a time. That is, it may be that in order to begin to activate a second script, enough evidence must first be accumulated to deactivate the existing one. From the latter account it is predicted that after a single exit sentence only the decision words associated with the initial script would be primed.

In order to test these alternatives we carried out an experiment in which script words could be related either to an initial script or to a script indicated by a later exit sentence. This is illustrated in Example 4 below:

Example 4

Script + 1 Exit:
    Colonel Jones got up early this morning.
    He went to the bathroom.
    He walked down to the station.

Script + 3 Exits:
    Colonel Jones got up early this morning.

He went to the bathroom.
Then he walked down to the station.
He strolled along the platform.
The train had not arrived yet.

Initial-script word: WASH
Exit-script word: BENCH

The mean lexical decision times for Experiment 4 are shown in Table 3.4. It turned out that when there was one exit sentence both the initial-script word and the exit-script word were primed. This implies that both the initial script and the exit script were simultaneously active. However, after three exit sentences only the exit script was active. Thus, the overall pattern of data from Experiment 4 supports a parallel activity explanation of the script and exit findings from Experiments 2 and 3. This is taken up in more detail below.

THE KNOWLEDGE ACCESS NETWORK (KAN) MODEL

The findings from the preceding experiments suggest that knowledge structures such as scripts are activated and deactivated by contextual cues. In order to explain the experimental results, I turn to a Knowledge Access Network (KAN) model. This was heralded by the subnode competition model of Sharkey and Mitchell (1985) and is being further developed with the help of Richard Sutcliffe, a graduate student at Essex. KAN is mainly concerned with access to script concepts in a currently active script. The core of the model is a spreading activation network. Scripts are represented as a collection of interrelated concepts within the network. Some concepts such as "eat," "food," "plate," and "table" all co-occur in most contexts involved in eating food. Other concepts are associated only through the mediation of a script, e.g., "waiter," "tip," "menu," and "check."

TABLE 3.4
Mean Lexical Decision Times for Experiment 4

	Context	
	Script + 3 Exits	*Script + 1 Exit*
Target Word:		
Exit Word	792	819
Script Word	900	799

In brief, I am proposing that a script can be represented as a interrelated region of a parallel spreading activation network. Essentially, this region is governed and controlled by a script subnode. A subnode represents a connecting station between the concept nodes which collectively make up a script (and its extended associations). A simplified portion of a network region is illustrated in Fig. 3.2. In the KAN model, when information comes in from a text, activation begins to accrue in a network region like that shown in Fig. 3.2. (This has been simulated using a slightly modified version of McClelland and Rumelhart's [1981] spreading activation formula.) As nodes are activated in KAN, they broadcast activation to all their related nodes (Anderson, 1983). The amount of activation which one node receives from its neighbors depends upon its strength of connection with that neighbor.

In the current implementation of KAN, the network is configured such that when a wave of activation spreads throughout the network, it sums on associated script subnodes until one of them reaches threshold. When the activation level of a script subnode reaches threshold, the address of that subnode is placed in a focus register (F-register). The function of the F-register is to sustain the activation level of the script subnode whose address it contains. The network region governed by this subnode (i.e., the script) is then said to be "in focus." The system has now focused on the relevant part of the knowledge database (Grosz, 1977; Sidner, 1978). The F-register contains only one address at a time and this is displaced (or deactivated) only when another subnode reaches threshold. Because the

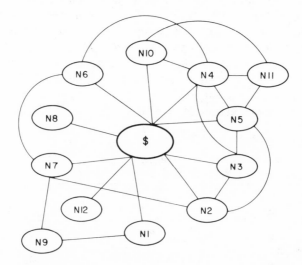

FIG. 3.2.   A network region corresponding to a script. $ Represents a subnode, and N represents a node.

level of activation of the subnode in the F-register is sustained at a constant level, activation is also maintained in the corresponding network region.

Once a script has been thus displaced from focus, the nodes in its network region decay back to levels indistinguishable from their resting levels. This provides us with an explanation for some of the findings from Experiments 2 and 3. Since a subnode can be displaced from the F-register only when another subnode reaches threshold, it follows that neutral filler sentences will not deactivate a script. This is because the activation emanating from "neutrals" does not converge on a particular network region. Thus, they do not push another subnode to threshold.

In order to make the flow and control of processing clearer, it will help to examine the simplified network illustrated in Fig. 3.3. Now, suppose that concept 6 and concept 9 are activated. Activation courses around their associates but accumulates fastest on the subnode ($1) where they converge. The activation level on $1 increases exponentially until it reaches the threshold, whereupon its address is placed in the F-register and the script is said to be in focus. Now the activation level of $1 will be sustained at a constant level. This means that activation will also be maintained in the network region which it governs. (It should perhaps be noted here that activation may come from other sources such as active goals [Sharkey & Bower, 1984]). If, in the meantime, another subnode reaches threshold (say $2), it will take over occupancy of the F-register. That subnode will now be sustained while $1 and its corresponding network region decay (or leak) back to resting level.

Of course, it is important to note that there is a "handover period" where one subnode takes over occupancy of the F-register from the other. This handover period may best be thought of as comprising two time slices. In the first, $1 is in the F-register and $2 has risen almost to its threshold level. In the second, $2 has reached threshold, replacing $1 in the F-register, and $1 has just begun to decay back to resting level. During this handover period, both network regions have fairly indistinguishable activation levels (the duration of "handover" is mainly determined by the magnitude of the decay parameter).

Now we can explain some more of the experimental results. Recall that, in Experiment 4, it was found that two scripts appeared to be simultaneously active for a short time. This can be explained in terms of the handover period where focus is being passed from one script to the other. While parts of KAN are speculative from a psychological perspective, it indicates fruitful avenues for future empirical research. In addition, KAN provides us with a psychologically plausible processing account of how mundane world knowledge is controlled in memory. The model may also fit data from other areas, such as word recog-

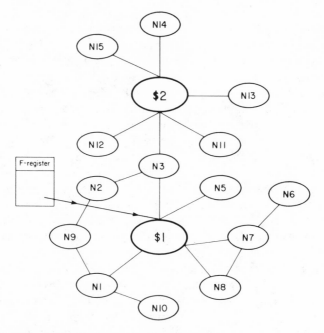

FIG. 3.3.   A simplified network with two scripts.

nition and fact retrieval. However, this is not the place to go into such details.

SENTENCE PROCESSING

So far I have said quite a lot about how psychological processes may operate on a network representation of knowledge. The lexical decision task is a useful way to probe the differential availability of word meanings in such a network. However, I have said very little about how the procedures involved in text comprehension could operate on this network. In the rest of this chapter, I shall discuss two experiments which Amanda Sharkey and I carried out at Yale to test the influence of scripts on sentence processing.

Three Hypotheses About Script Influence

We (Sharkey & Sharkey, 1983; Sharkey & Sharkey, in preparation) investigated three alternative hypotheses about script influence during sentence processing. The first hypothesis was that scripts facilitate the reading times for individual words in a sentence. That is, in the presence of an active script, there would be a reduced reading time for every script word in a sentence. Such facilitation is predicted from the increased availability of the meanings of script words as reflected by the lexical decision task. This would be useful to the system, for example, if the words in a sentence were individually integrated with the preceding context as they were read. Such a view was tentatively put forward by Sharkey and Mitchell (1985).

A second hypothesis is that script influence is confined to integrating entire sentences with prior context. In this way scripts may be seen as having an interpretive function in reading, rather than being seen as setting up expectations for particular words. Don Mitchell and I have already demonstrated that scripts affect the availability of word meanings in lexical decision tasks, but we did not know how this would affect a task more closely approximating normal reading. The third hypothesis was a mixture of the first two. That is, scripts exert an influence on both a word-by-word basis and on the integration of entire sentences within prior context.

Experiments 5 and 6.   We investigated these alternative hypotheses by examining the priming influence of script contexts upon words at different sites within a sentence. In the next two experiments, we presented subjects with short script vignettes. Each sentence was divided into two parts, which were read one at a time. The initial part of a sentence would appear on the screen (e.g., He picked up) and then, when the subject pressed a bar, this would be replaced by the final part (e.g., the tip). This technique enabled us to time the reading of targets (e.g., the tip) either in the initial or final position of a sentence. For example, the sentence "The tip pleased the waiter." enabled us to time the target "The tip" in the initial position, while the sentence "He picked up the tip." enabled us to time the target "the tip" in the final position.

We reasoned that if scripts operate during word-by-word integration, the targets should be primed in both the initial and final sentence positions. However, if scripts are simply influencing the process of sentence integration with prior context, only the final target should be primed. This integration with the prior context occurs at the end of the sentence. If, however, scripts influence both word and sentence integration, then differences should be observed in both the initial and final sentence positions.

In both Experiments 5 and 6 the materials for all of the conditions were identical except for the final critical sentence of each vignette. These contained the targets. The target was always either an article plus a script word or an article plus a control word. The only difference between Experiments 5 and 6 was in the choice of control words.

In Experiment 5, we were concerned that the reading times for final position targets would be influenced by the initial parts of the sentences in which they occurred. For example, the initial part of the sentence would be highly predictive of the target as in "The cat sat on the ... MAT." This could mask out any effect of the script contexts. In order to overcome this problem, we collected sentence completion norms for the critical sentences in isolation. We gave subjects the critical sentences with the final word deleted (e.g., He looked at the ...) and asked them to generate the five most likely single-word alternatives to complete each sentence. On this basis, we chose control words which were more likely completions than the script words. In fact, none of the script words were generated in the sentence completion phase.

As a second precaution, we asked subjects to generate five alternative single-word completions to the script vignettes. None of the control words were generated in this phase. However, three judges chose control words which were reasonable completions of the vignettes. A typical story along with the four types of critical sentences and words is illustrated in Example 5. The targets are in italics:

Example 5

The customer was in an irritable mood in the restaurant. But the service was very fast and efficient. His mood began to mellow. The dessert really cheered him up. He smiled and thanked the waitress as he walked out.

Script word final position: She picked up /*the tip.*
Script word first position: *The tip/* pleased the waitress.
Control word final position: She picked up /*the mess.*
Control word first position: *The mess/* displeased the waitress.

The experimental predictions may be summarized as follows. First, if scripts influence the reading times for individual words only, then script targets will be read faster than control targets in both the initial and final sentence positions. Second, if scripts influence only the integration of a sentence with its preceding context, differences between script targets and control targets should only show up in the final sentence positions. Third, if scripts exert an influence upon both the individual words in a text *and* integration of a sentence with prior context, then differences should appear in both the initial *and* the final positions. However, because of the extra help from scripts in the final positions, the magnitude of the difference should be greater there. That is, we would predict a statistical interaction between type of target and sentence position (see also Anderson, 1983, 1984) for a discussion of the interaction between level of activation and computational complexity).

The mean reading times for Experiment 5 are shown in Table 3.5. What we found was that subjects took longer to read the control words than the script words in the final sentence positions. However, there was no reliable difference between targets occurring in the initial sentence positions. This runs counter to the view that scripts exert their influence upon individual words during sentence processing. Instead, we suggested that the meanings of the initial targets are being buffered until later in processing. We investigated this possibility further by examining the reading times for parts of the sentences which contained initial targets. These analyses also revealed significant differences. Thus it seems that differences between the initial script and control words were being picked up at the ends of sentences.

A different interpretation of the findings is that there *is* a word-by-word linking with prior context which does not concern meaning availability. Instead, the overall findings supported the hypothesis that scripts facilitate only the speed of sentence-by-sentence integration. If this is the case, differences between initial targets should show up at the ends of the sentences in which they occurred. We investigated the possibility that differences in initial target sentences show up later by analyzing the relative reading times for their final portions; i.e., if the sentence was "The tip pleased the waitress." we would examine the reading time for "pleased the waitress" in comparison with the final phrase for the control-word sentence. These analyses revealed significant effects. Thus, it seems that differences between the initial script words and control words were being picked up at the ends of sentences. This adds further support to the notion that scripts facilitate the integration of sentences with prior context.

Thus it appears that in Experiment 5 we have not found evidence that scripts set up expectations for particular words in a text. This contrasts with the strong evidence from the lexical decision experiments reported earlier. However, before any conclusive statements can be made to the effect that scripts only serve an interpretive function and do not set up expectations, we must first examine an alternative explanation of our findings.

TABLE 3.5
Mean Reading Times in Milliseconds for Experiment 5

Context	Control			Script	
Position	Initial	Final		Initial	Final
Mean RT	686	860		655	728

Although we did not find a statistically reliable difference between the control targets and the script targets in the initial sentence position in Experiment 5, the main response time for controls was 31 msec slower than that for script targets (see Table 3.5). It is possible that this 31 msec reflects a real difference in activation levels which our task was not sensitive enough to detect. Such an account would provide us with an easy way to explain the seeming incompatability of the sentence findings and the lexical decision findings. Remember that in the lexical decision task, subjects not only have to read the target words, they also have to make yes/no decisions about them. This task would obviously be computationally more complex than the task of reading a word and moving on. The added complexity could thus magnify any differences in activation levels at concept nodes (see Anderson, 1984, for a similar account of the interaction between complexity of mental computation and level of activation). The complexity notion may also explain why we detected statistically reliable differences at the ends of sentences and not at the beginnings. Again, the computational processing for sentence wrap-up (Just & Carpenter, 1980) would be more complex than that for simply reading a word at the beginning of a sentence and moving on. For example, at the end of a sentence a reader would also have to integrate the individual word meaning to build a conceptual structure which is appropriate for the context. If such sentence wrap-up involves some iterative procedures, then any observable differences would be magnified on each pass.

In Experiment 5, the control words were not script-based, but they were nonetheless rated as reasonable completions of the stories. It seems likely then that although these words were not generated by the subjects in the story-completion norms, they received some activation from the script texts in Experiment 5. In Experiment 6, then, we attempted to magnify the initial sentence-position effects by using control words which were unlikely completions of the stories. Note that if network activation only affects sentence processing at sentence boundaries, then any manipulation at initial positions will only show up at the ends of sentences.

The only difference between Experiments 5 and 6 was in the choice of control words. In the latter experiment, we replaced the control words with words that were incongruous completions of the script-based texts. Each incongruous word was matched with a script word for word frequency and number of letters. Thus the target *the mess* in Example 5 above was replaced with *the hen.* The mean reading times for Experiment 6 are shown in Table 3.6. As in Experiment 5, we found significant differences between script targets and controls in the final position condition. We also found, as before, a significant interaction of position by target type. However, this experiment differed from the preceding one in the initial position findings.

Contrary to the previous experiment, Experiment 6 yielded statistically reliable reading time differences between the script targets and the incongruous controls in the initial position condition.

These results suggest that scripts do more than influence the integration of sentences with prior context. They support my earlier suggestion that differences between targets in the initial position condition of Experiment 5 were too small to be detectable by using the reading time technique. Such a conclusion brings the current findings into concord with the lexical decision results. It seems that scripts serve both to set up expectations for words in a text and to help interpret incoming sentences. However, these combined findings also suggest that a lot more information may be active than would be predicted from theories based on the notion of scripts as discrete memory packages. The findings could be more easily accommodated by a system which treated memory as a continuum in which associated information is clustered together but is continuous with the rest of memory. The KAN model provides us with such a system. It combines the structural benefits of script systems with the benefits of distributed processing. Thus, memory access is not restricted to the particular script under active consideration. With the addition of an interpretive parser, the KAN model could easily account for the findings from Experiments 5 and 6.

DISCUSSION

The aim of this chapter was, in part, to assess the claim that understanding proceeds in a strongly top-down predictive manner. The findings from the lexical decision experiments presented at the beginning of the chapter suggested that there was considerable interaction between knowledge structures such as scripts and the meanings of words. That is, world knowledge appears to affect the availability of lexical items prior to the operation of the parser. This led Sharkey and Mitchell (1981b) to propose that the word recognition mechanisms of the Riesbeck's ELI parser should be more influenced by top-down information. This proposal has been further supported by the results from the sentence-processing experiments

TABLE 3.6
Mean Reading Times in Milliseconds for Experiment 6

Context	Incongruous		Script	
Position	Initial	Final	Initial	Final
Mean RT	755	1284	688	788

reported here (Experiments 5 and 6). It appears that during parsing, there is a facilitatory influence of "active" knowledge on reading time for individual words.

In summary, what I have attempted in this chapter blurs any clear distinctions between a strict top-down and a strict bottom-up philosophy of understanding. I have proposed a knowledge access network model (KAN) which is driven by parallel spreading activation. This provides the comprehender with knowledge-based expectations. However, I have proposed that activation originates from both perceptual and contextual information. In this account, a parser such as Riesbeck's (1978) ELI may be an adequate model of human conceptual processing, given a greater degree of interaction between its lexicon and a parallel spreading activation knowledge access network similar to the one used in KAN.

We have already developed a simply conceptual parser NELI (Nearly an English Language Interpreter) at Essex, which interfaces with the KAN system. However, NELI was built primarily to enable us to use natural language to access the network and not to model human processing. Thus, it simply passes complete conceptual structures on to the network. We are currently converting NELI to interact with KAN on a word-by-word basis. I am optimistic that this completed model will provide us with further detailed empirical predictions about the structure and use of human knowledge in text comprehension.

4

The Encoding and Retrieval of Memories of Real-World Experiences

Brian J. Reiser

In other chapters in this volume we have described the use of knowledge structures to make sense of the world around us. An event is understood and explained by finding the knowledge structure or combination of structures that best fit it, and building a causal explanation of those aspects of the event that deviate from the fit. In addition to this knowledge-structure based understanding, an important source of information for these prediction and explanation processes is also found in the individual instances of a type of event. In the following examples, a particular experience retrieved from memory provides information not available in the generalizations encoded in a knowledge structure:

1. "Let's try the Hunan Wok again. Last time we went there, the food was really good, especially the fried dumplings."
2. A: "Oh no, the line at the ticket booth is really long, we might miss the train."
   B: "Don't worry. I remember once before when the line was this long, someone told us we could buy the ticket on the train and it worked out okay."
3. "This is the same error message I got on that program I wrote yesterday. I better check to see that I updated the counter correctly."

Knowledge structures are constantly changing. When an event doesn't exactly fit an existing knowledge structure, it may be useful to keep it around in memory for future reference. Deviations from prototypes may be used to explain similar deviations, to avoid problems encountered in the past, and to form new generalizations to incorporate into a knowledge structure (e.g., Hammond, 1983; Schank, 1982). The function of knowledge structures, therefore, is not only to catalog general information to predict and explain events, but also to organize individual events that were processed using those structures and deviated from its predictions. In this chapter, I will discuss how individual events are stored in memory and their relation to general knowledge structures. Most research on memory for individual occurrences or "episodic memory" has centered on information learned in the laboratory, such as memory for a list of words or sentences (see Tulving, 1983). The goal of our research is to examine how people process and store real-world episodes. A complete model of the use of knowledge structures in cognitive processing must address how individual items are understood using those structures, how the items are stored in memory, and how processing individual items may change a knowledge structure. Thus a model of the organization and retrieval of individual episodes has implications for a theory of comprehension, memory organization, and a theory of how knowledge structures are learned and modified.

THE CONTEXT–PLUS–INDEX MODEL

In previous papers, I have described a context-plus-index model of autobiographical memory organization (Reiser, 1983; Reiser & Black, 1983; Reiser, Black, & Abelson, 1985). This model builds upon work by Kolodner (1983, 1984) and Schank (1982) who argued that individual experiences are connected in memory to knowledge structures. At the time experiences are encoded, knowledge structures have been accessed to guide the cognitive processing required in the event. These structures are used to plan a course of action that achieves the goals of the actor, and to understand the behavior of other actors in terms of their goals and plans. Therefore, the mental context during an event is a configuration of knowledge structures guiding planning and comprehension, and as a result the representation of that event will be stored in memory connected to those knowledge structures. For example, as a consequence of accessing the *Going to a Restaurant* knowledge structure while actually dining in restaurants, individual restaurant experiences become associated with that knowledge structure in memory.

The link between a knowledge structure and an individual experience consists of a description of the features on which the individual event deviated from the prototype in the knowledge structure. The basic idea for this scheme dates back to Bartlett's (1932) "schema-plus-correction" model, in which a new event is understood by finding the closest fitting knowledge structure and noting the deviations of the item from the general information. Similarly, Schank and Abelson (1977) proposed that the memory for a story episode consists of a reference to a script, the particular details that instantiate the script's variables, plus causal chains connecting any events not predicted by the script. Graesser (1981) has investigated a schema-plus-tag model for scripts and other types of knowledge structures. In the models of Schank (1982) and Kolodner (1983, 1984), experiences are linked by *indices* specifying the deviations or unique aspects of the event that differentiate it from the general information in the knowledge structure.

Two types of search processes are employed to retrieve an experience in this organization. An individual episode in memory is retrieved by accessing the context in which it was encoded (Tulving, 1983). Thus, the first step in retrieving an individual experience is to specify the knowledge structure that contextualized the encoding of the original experience. This knowledge structure serves as the general event category to which search will initially be constrained. The next step in retrieval is to specify the deviations from the prototype that discriminate the target experience from the others associated with that context. For example, the chosen search context might be the knowledge structure *Going to a Restaurant,* and the particular index found might be "the time when I ate too much lasagna and felt sick."

The rest of this chapter is concerned with four issues that have guided our work in developing this context-plus-index model:

1. What type of retrieval mechanisms are used to search for autobiographical memories?
2. What types of knowledge structures are accessed by these mechanisms?
3. What type of knowledge do those structures provide for these processes?
4. What determines the accessibility of experiences associated with a knowledge structure?

In addressing the first issue, I will provide a general characterization of the retrieval mechanisms used to access individual experiences. I will argue that retrieval of experiences from memory cannot rely solely on automatic processes, but instead draws upon a directed search process. The types of strategies in this directed search will be described. The second issue concerns the nature of the knowledge structures used in autobiographical memory retrieval. The use of these structures for planning and comprehension places important constraints on the type of structures used in retrieval. Evidence concerning several types of event knowledge structures will be presented. The third issue concerns the type of information organized by the structures used in retrieval. It is important to characterize how retrieval strategies utilize the information made available by these knowledge structures. Finally, the fourth issue concerns the accessibility of individual experiences. Characterizing the nature of the knowledge structures and links connecting individual experiences should enable predictions about the differential accessibility of experiences based on the type of deviations each has from the prototype experience.

DIRECTING MEMORY SEARCH
FOR INDIVIDUAL EXPERIENCES

Let us first consider the type of retrieval mechanisms that guide the search for an individual experience in memory. Evidence suggests that this memory search is a *directed search* rather than an automatic retrieval process (Reiser, in press; Reiser et al., 1985). Retrieval of an experience is typically directed by search strategies that use general information in order to elaborate the original retrieval description so that it is specific enough to discriminate a target experience. These strategies draw upon information contained in knowledge structures to predict which paths in memory are likely to lead to the target event. As in the other tasks described in this book, a focus on the *information content* of knowledge structures is therefore an essential component of the memory model. Characterizing how search strategies are used to direct retrieval requires a model of the type of knowledge structures used by the strategies and the type of information contained in those structures on which the inferences necessary for retrieval can be based.

Retrieval Strategies Direct Search

Directed search can be contrasted with an automatic process in which the representation of an item in memory is accessed when a cue is presented, and then associated paths in the memory network are followed until the target node is reached. For example, in spreading activation models, associated information is accessed by spreading activation to connected nodes in a memory network, thus extending the search to other nodes until a target is accessed (Anderson, 1976; Collins & Loftus, 1975). In these models, the strength of activation decreases as a function of the number of links it travels, and increases when it converges upon a node from multiple sources. If multiple cues are presented, the search can intersect on a node with sufficient activation to retrieve it. An important distinction between this type of model and our directed search model is in the use of information associated with a search cue. Directed search entails a *selective use* of associated information in order to determine which paths to follow in memory. Reasoning mechanisms are employed to use associated information in order to construct a likely scenario for an event with the target characteristics. This type of search is thus "controlled" rather than "automatic" (Schneider & Shiffrin, 1977).

The following protocol from Reiser (in press) provides an example of this type of reasoning during retrieval:

[1] **Experimenter (E):** Think of a time when you felt cold at an exam.

Subject (S): Cold at an exam . . . Wow, I keep thinking how most of my exam rooms have been really well heated! I remember being really hot in exams but never really cold, which I guess is pretty lucky. 'Cause most . . . I mean, at Christmas it's usually been really well heated.

E: What's going through your mind now . . . what can you think of?

S: Um, I was trying to start thinking through the exams I've taken at Christmas. Um, going through the different classes but they're not really coming . . . I think maybe my Bio exam freshman year I was cold 'cause I had to walk all the way up to Science Hill to go take it, but the room was heated. But they gave us lollipops in the exam, which I thought was kind of nice! But it was a long walk and it had snowed.

Strategic direction may be required in both stages of memory search, selecting a context and discriminating an experience within the context. First, a strategy can be used to focus search on a particular context, in this case, "taking exams" rather than "feeling cold." The subject was queried about both a feeling and an activity, and yet appears to have focused on the activity, since he recalled experiences matching the activity that didn't fit the state and not vice versa, even though we may reasonably assume there were more "feeling cold" experiences than "exam" experiences in memory. As we shall see, scripts such as *Taking an Exam* are more effective cues than mental or physical states, hence strategies focus the search on these more profitable contexts.

In general, the initial search context is sometimes provided in the query, as when one is asked to recall an experience involving a particular common activity, such as going to movies or dining at restaurants. However, more typically a search is initiated in response to an incomplete cue. For example, one may be trying to remember an argument, a taxi ride, running into an old friend, or some other event that might occur in many different contexts. Given such cues, it will be necessary to use the information in the original description to construct a more useful context. This reformulation of the search context tends to occur when the original description does not enable very specific predictions about features of the events. For example, questions about feelings are often transformed into more specific questions about common activities. Many of our subjects, asked to think of a time when they felt ambitious, first mentioned that they sometimes feel ambitious at their job or studying for an exam, and then tried to pin down a specific experience in the chosen context. Interestingly, these reformulations result in a description that is not only more predictive, but is also easier to mentally "picture" or image. Protocol results suggest that subjects tend to focus their search on common activities rather than feelings or more general event descriptions (Reiser, in press; Reiser, Black, & Kalamarides, in press). Activity structures are essential in many types of planning and provide a great deal of information about the motivations, behavior, and consequences in common situations. Retrieval strategies have developed to take advantage of this organization, directing search to access activity categories and then utilizing information contained in those structures to guide further search. Protocol [2] from Reiser et al. (in press) demonstrates how a subject elaborates the cue in order to restrict the search to an activity. In this protocol, the subject proposed "school" situations a likely context for feeling ambitious, considered school work, and then other school activities, finally focusing on a school election.

[2] **E:** Think of a time when you felt ambitious.

S: What I'm thinking is this could be tough—ambitious is just not my style. I'm sure there must be something.

E: What's going through your mind?

S: I'm trying to think along school lines, because that is where I would be ambitious, like work or something, doing school work. I'm trying to think of exactly what I have done . . . ambitious. Um, I think probably since I can't find anything for school I'd say getting signatures. When I first went to school in the 10th grade I wanted to be class president, so I went and the first day of school . . . I chased people around and got signatures and got in a half a day 150 signatures from people I didn't know, and that was relatively ambitious for me.

This protocol demonstrates a frequent type of evidence for the incremental nature of the directed search process. The subject described a new elaborated context in general terms before a particular experience had been found. These cases are more illuminating of the subject's reasoning than retrievals in which the subject simply recounts an experience in answer to the question. Features present in a recalled experience are not very strong evidence that those features were involved in the retrieval strategies, because they may have merely been components of an experience retrieved by focusing on other features.

The next use of strategies occurs when searching within the chosen context. Frequently the search cue does not contain enough information to discriminate an experience from the others in the context, and thus retrieval strategies must be employed to elaborate the description of the target event by inferring additional plausible features. These retrieval mechanisms rely primarily on general information represented in the knowledge structure in order to make these inferences. For example, in protocol [1], the subject added the plausible constraint that the exam took place at Christmas rather than spring term. Strategies are required to decide which dimensions (e.g., participants in the event, reasons for engaging in the event, time of year, varieties of an activity) are relevant in finding the particular target experience, and then to generate plausible values for the chosen dimension. In order to predict effectively the circumstances that would include an event with the target features, strategies must utilize social knowledge about the causes, motivations, and results of behavior. Thus, an important role of the directed component is to find the type of associated information that will be useful for predicting further features of the target event. Such strategies are called "elaboration strategies" (Kolodner 1983, 1984). If one is trying to remember a conversation that occurred with a business associate, one could first use knowledge about the interactions of business associates to generate a candidate list of contexts, e.g., cocktail parties, business meetings, and business lunches. After selecting one of these contexts, say business lunches, general knowledge contained in that context could be used to restrict the search further, considering "Fancy Restaurants," rather than "College Bars," as a more likely context for the target experience. Then, the information in that more specific context can be used to direct further probes of memory. It is important to note that the relevance of a particular dimension for retrieval depends on the nature of the target features. In some cases, the type of restaurant may be the salient detail necessary to find the experience, while for other types of targets this feature may not be predictive, and instead, the participants might be the crucial, discriminating feature.

The directed search process is summarized in Fig. 4.1. Search strategies are applied sequentially to build a successively more detailed description of the desired event. An initial context is selected, and then information associated with that context is examined to find a more specific version likely to be the setting for the target experience. For example, the activity context *Eating in Restaurants* can be constrained to *College Hangouts* or *Restaurants in New York*. Information from the more specific structure is added to the retrieval specification, and the structure becomes the new search context. Further inferences about the experience can be based upon the information in the new context, until finally enough general information has been accumulated to pick out an experience with the target features. As in Norman and Bobrow's (1979) descriptions model, partial retrievals provide information that can be used to constrain further probes of memory. In our model, the partial retrievals consist of general information adding to the characterization of the target event features.

Support for the Directed Search Model

Why are these types of elaborative strategies necessary? There are several types of arguments and evidence for the directed nature of autobiographical memory search (Reiser, in press). The first difficulty for an automatic search mechanism is that there are simply too many paths to follow in memory for such a search to be successful. Most contexts contain rich sets

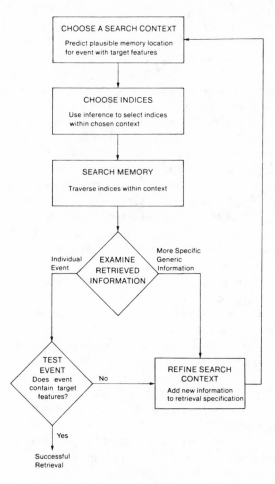

FIG. 4.1. The retrieval mechanisms used to search for an individual experience in memory.

of general information and many associated experiences. For example, retrieving the *Going to a Restaurant* structure provides access to information about the motivations for the activity, standard varieties of restaurants, likely participants of the experience, larger contexts in which going to a restaurant might occur (e.g., a vacation), etc. All of these are features that might be involved in indexing a particular experience (Reiser, 1983; Reiser et al., in press). Yet not all these types of information are relevant in each retrieval. If all possible values for each of these various dimensions were considered, a prohibitive number of paths would be generated for testing. In fact, when different values on these dimensions are combined, a combinatorial explosion of possibilities results. The role of retrieval strategies is to constrain the search to likely paths by considering the attributes of the target event and selecting the type of information salient for that retrieval description.

In fact, retrieval protocols often reveal that subjects have elaborated the description by adding plausible features as constraints. For example, the subject in protocol [1] inferred the additional constraint "winter semester" in searching exams, and the subject in protocol [2] restricted the query about ambition to school situations. Many of our protocols demonstrate subjects considering several subclasses of an activity, then selecting the one most likely to be the setting for the target experience. These elaborations are particularly evident in "false starts" and "near-misses." In the cases of false starts, a subject articulates a new category for search elaborated from the original description, and then after considering that category, decides it does not contain a suitable event. For example, one subject transformed a question about being served the wrong item in a restaurant into a search of experiences involving a particularly hectic restaurant, but then failed to recover an experience matching the original question. In a near-miss, a subject recalls an experience that doesn't match the presented description but is similar in some respects to the target. The additional elaborations suggest features that may have been added to the retrieval specification. For example, a question about not having identification at a bank led a subject to recall an experience where she was unable to take out money for a completely different reason. Thus, presenting a particular type of situation led to inference of the problematic result of that situation, which when used as a search cue recovered an experience with the same result, but a cause different than the original specification.

Another factor requiring directed search is the differential effectiveness of retrieval features. Some cues are of low salience or occur in a wide variety of contexts, and may not enable very specific predictions. Thus, strategies are necessary to generate or focus search upon an activity rather than a physical or mental state cue. Furthermore, the importance of a particular type of feature will depend on the nature of the target information.

In protocol [1], the time of year in which the exam occurred was relevant because of the constraint added by the "feeling cold" feature, yet for other types of questions the other participants involved in the event or the time period of the person's life may be more predictive. When a dimension has been selected, strategies are employed to refine the context to include a particularly plausible value on that dimension. The following protocol from Reiser et al. (in press) demonstrates this type of successive refinement. Here the knowledge about the activity is used to select from several alternative subclasses. In particular, after considering different types of shopping experiences, the subject decided that shopping experiences in Connecticut were more likely to satisfy the "couldn't pay for the item" constraint than shopping experiences in Massachusetts, first accessing successively more specific knowledge structures (*Grocery shopping in Connecticut, Grocery shopping at Pathmark*), and then isolating a specific instance.

[3] **E:** Think of a time when you went shopping and couldn't pay for the item that you wanted.

S: Um, it happens when I go grocery shopping in Connecticut because I don't have any check-cashing privilege cards. Like, for example, Pathmark will have a special card that they issue. And so I have to pay with cash and I don't always calculate exactly what's in the carriage. So I'll have to put back, like, yogurt . . . usually, yogurt's what goes. But otherwise I usually pay by check when I'm in Massachusetts, so I don't have to, you know, worry about putting anything back.

E: Can you think of one particular experience?

S: Uh, yes. Pathmark in East Haven, I often do that.

E: Can you describe one time?

S: Yes, when I was in East Haven, I was—didn't have enough so I had to put back. I think, three yogurts. And the girl was very nice and I thought to myself, "Oh, I should ask for a subtotal next time."

This protocol demonstrates another function of retrieval strategies. Most cues are incomplete in their original form and must be elaborated. Retrieval strategies use information in the knowledge structures that have been accessed to construct a more complete picture of the target event. In some cases, the original cue underspecifies the experience and a subclass of experiences is retrieved. Such cases are apparent in protocols in which a new elaborated context is described in general terms before a specific experience has been isolated, as in protocol [3]. A second type of incompleteness occurs when the cue describes a constraining event feature that cannot be used until a more specific context is constructed. For example, subjects queried about common feelings such as impatience often consider situations in which they would experience that feeling, and then try to pin down an experience involving that situation, rather than focusing on other information associated with the feeling such as related emotions or common behavioral responses to the emotion. Another aspect of this incompleteness is that the features described in the original retrieval specification may not correspond to the features used to index the target experience. Many protocols contain cases where subjects apply reasoning strategies to go from the information given to features presumably more suited as search cues. For example, in this protocol from Reiser (in press), the subject asked about feeling hungry recalled an experience that included an event that was a likely consequence (buying food), yet did not include the specified feeling:

[4] **E:** Think of a time when you felt hungry on the train.

S: I remember the last time I was on a train. Have I ever been hungry on a train? I usually feel sick to my stomach on a train. Yeah, I was visiting my friend Chris coming back early with her friend Ann to get to work on time. We bought breakfast so I must have felt hungry, but I don't recall ever feeling hungry on the train.

Directed Search and Causal Reasoning

These considerations lead to a conception of autobiographical memory search as a process of *reunderstanding* the target experience. Retrieving an event requires constructing a plausible scenario for an occurrence of that type of event. Finding plausible connections to other features that elaborate the original description is essentially the process of *explaining* this hypothetical event. In order to find a target event in memory, retrieval strategies consider the event's motivations, the behavior of others that would have provoked it, larger episodes in which it may have occurred, new states resulting from the event, or other events motivated by it. These types of connections correspond to those constructed during comprehension, and can thus rely on the same type of inference processes.

An important issue to consider in evaluating the psychological validity of this model is the parsimony of a complex array of retrieval strategies that rely on such a rich indexing and organizational scheme for experiences. First, it is important to note that the data generally support this complex indexing scheme. Examinations of autobiographical retrieval protocols reveal a set of reasoning mechanisms employed to direct search that rely upon a rich representation of general world knowledge (Kolodner, 1983, 1984; Reiser et al., in press; Whitten & Leonard, 1981; Williams & Hollan,

1981). Second, the parsimony of this model must be considered in the context of the other psychological phenomena discussed in this book. We have not proposed these complex structures solely to account for autobiographical memory phenomena. Instead, this memory organization is motivated also by considerations of the use of these same knowledge structures for planning and performing actions, comprehension of texts and real-world events, and being reminded of general and specific information learned from texts or experience. As described in other chapters, knowledge about the motivations and results of behavior in common situations is used in order to plan, understand, and explain behavior. Therefore, the context-plus-index model of autobiographical memory organization and retrieval is *more* sensible and parsimonious than models that rely on different knowledge structures, memory organizations, and inference processes for different cognitive tasks.

An important feature of the retrieval strategies we have discussed is their reliance on causal reasoning. As discussed in Chapters 6 and 7, representations of events are causally based. The structures accessed in order to act in a particular event are likely to be those knowledge structures containing planning information required to select actions and activities to achieve the desired goals. Furthermore, it is typically necessary to understand the actions of the other people involved in a situation by inferring motivations for those actions, and this comprehension relies upon the planning knowledge contained in these same structures. Causal explanations appear to be a central component in comprehending both text (Black, 1984; Reiser & Black, 1982), and real-world events (Nisbett & Ross, 1980).

As a consequence of the central role that causal representations play in comprehension, the memory representation for an experience is constructed using causal inferences and is connected to planning structures in memory. Thus, the features of experiences that are most relevant in their organization are the motivations of the people involved, the actions undertaken to achieve their goals, the outcomes of the goals (whether they were achieved, thwarted, or motivated new subgoals), the consequences of the actions for the states of the participants, and the effects on their future behavior. Furthermore, the type of planning structures that serve as contexts in autobiographical memory are rich in predictive power, containing information useful for constructing a plausible scenario for an event. The directed search mechanisms, like planning and comprehension mechanisms, can draw on this general knowledge for causal reasoning.

A summary of the different types of retrieval strategies found by Reiser et al. (in press) is shown in Table 4.1. Strategies are employed first to find a context. Search may focus on an activity mentioned in the query, or it may be necessary to infer a plausible activity context. After a general context has been selected, strategies are employed to further refine that context and pin down an individual experience. Subjects employ strategies to enumerate various subclasses of an activity and then to select among them to focus on a likely subclass. In many cases, knowledge external to the activity may be employed to refine the context. For example, knowledge about important participants or geographical or temporal maps may be employed. In addition, many types of strategies entail reasoning about the motivations or causes of an event or its plausible consequences.

KNOWLEDGE STRUCTURES USED IN RETRIEVAL

I have argued that autobiographical retrieval proceeds by using information in the cue to find a search context, then using information in that context to elaborate the original description until an individual experience is discriminated. In this section, we consider the type of structures needed to guide this retrieval process.

TABLE 4.1
Strategies Exhibited in Protocols

I. FINDING A CONTEXT.

    A. Activity-Based Search: Search activity mentioned in query.
    B. Find Related Activity:
        1. Employ causal reasoning to predict activity leading to given state.
        2. Use situational definition of concept to infer plausible activity.

II. SEARCHING WITHIN A CONTEXT.

    Activity Subclass Strategies
    A. Activity Subclass Selection: Focus search on a subclass of the activity.
        1. Find a specific variant of the activity, such as college eateries.
        2. Find specific instance, such as a particular restaurant, library, or store.
    B. Activity Subclass Enumeration: Use a strategy to enumerate classes of the activity so that one can be selected for search.

    Access External Knowledge
    C. Participant Selection. Find plausible participant.
    D. Map Search: Iterate through mental map of geographical area, a time line (of semesters at school), etc.
    E. Select Time Era: Find a part of your life likely to be the setting for the target event.

    Causal Chain Reasoning Strategies
    F. Infer Motivating Goal: Infer reason for performing target event.
    G. Infer Event Cause: Infer event or state that would lead to target event.
    H. Infer Event Results: Infer result of target event.

(from Reiser, Black, & Kalamarides, in press)

Functional Distinctions Between Knowledge Structures

Let us first consider the constraints upon these structures. There are two types of considerations concerning the use of knowledge structures in this organization: (1) the role of the structure at the time the experience is encoded, and (2) the later role of the structure when searching for the experience in memory.

Retrieval of episodic information requires accessing the context active when the event was encoded in memory (Tulving, 1983; Tulving & Thomson, 1973). As discussed earlier, the encoding context for experiences consists of the knowledge structures brought to bear in planning the behavior of the actor and in understanding the behavior of the other participants in terms of their goals and plans. Although many different types of knowledge may be accessed during comprehension, the structures providing the principal "scaffolding" for the episodic representation will supply the principal access into the experience. Thus, characterizing the knowledge structures that drive these inferences will suggest the central contexts used to organize experiences in memory. The second consideration is the use of the information in a knowledge structure during the retrieval process. Search requires elaborating the original cue, considering the information associated with the structure to generate further plausible features. Therefore, an effective retrieval context will be one that provides access to information useful for predicting features of a target event.

These two considerations, utility in planning/comprehension and inference capabilities during retrieval, can be combined to characterize the knowledge structures used in the retrieval of individual experiences. First, experiences are stored in memory with the knowledge structures active at time of encoding, that is, those that served as the principal source of inferences for planning and understanding behavior. Second, experiences must be retrieved by directing search to appropriate memory contexts, then typically using information within those contexts to elaborate the features used to describe the target event. Therefore, this process will be directed by structures that are most effective in making predictions about the causes, results, and associated contexts of events. Both constraints suggest that knowledge structures rich in predictive power are used to direct the retrieval of experiences and organize them in memory.

We argued in previous papers that event knowledge structures are maximally useful in directing search for experiences, since the information encoded in autobiographical memory is a set of experiences, and experiences are certainly events rather than static facts or propositions (Reiser, 1983; Reiser et al., 1985). One contrast, for example, is between event descriptions and static descriptions such as emotions. If emotions were organizing contexts, then experiences would be indexed according to the type of emotion associated with the experience, and information associated with emotions would be used to direct retrieval. Emotions can be used as a source of inferences about the causes and results of a given psychological state (e.g., Lehnert, 1981; Roseman, 1984), but these states are experienced in such a wide diversity of situations that information from other sources is usually required to discriminate experiences involving a given emotion. Consistent with this lack of predictive power, Robinson (1976) found emotion cues to be inferior to activity and object cues for autobiographical retrieval, and subjects in our protocols often reformulate questions about feelings into searches for experiences with a particular type of situation.

Another important source of information is knowledge about people. Schemas organize knowledge about the attributes and behaviors of people possessing a particular trait or personality (Cantor & Mischel, 1977; Hastie & Kumar, 1979). These schemas are very predictive of general information, but may not contain sufficient information to discriminate individual experiences because one encounters exemplars of a particular stereotype in many different situations. In fact, Cantor, Mischel, and Schwartz (1982) have shown that situational knowledge (i.e., common activities) appears to contextualize the retrieval of person information, so that person information is more accessible if a situational context is also provided. Another candidate type of structure represents information about the central figures involved in a person's life, such as a parent, sibling, spouse, roommate, etc. Barsalou (1985) has demonstrated that cues of this sort may be as effective in retrieving general information and experiences as event cues. One explanation for this finding is that the knowledge structure for such a figure not only organizes general information about the figure's personality, appearance, and themes involving the person (Schank & Abelson, 1977), but also is linked to subcategories of events that are highly predictive. For example, the knowledge structure for a particular college roommate may contain links to activities commonly performed with the person, e.g., *Going to Chinese Restaurants with Scott, Going to Science Fiction Movies with Scott,* etc. Such connections are frequently found in our retrieval protocols (Reiser et al., in press), and may be necessary for person information to be an effective cue. Accessing information about a person could lead to a large wealth of possible scenarios for experiences, so it may be necessary to discriminate an event by pinning down other characteristics, such as the contextualizing social situation. Thus, although person information is clearly important in reasoning during memory search, its utility may lie in connections with event knowledge structures. More research is necessary to explore precisely how these types of information are used in retrieval, but knowledge about common events appears to be an important source of inferences during retrieval. Prototypes for social situations are very rich structures, including substantial amounts of information about typical people, behaviors, and feelings associated with the situation.

For these reasons, our research strategy has been to focus our initial investigations on knowledge structures encoding information about common events, in particular knowledge structures well studied in recent work on text comprehension and planning. In a series of experiments, we investigated the effectiveness of several types of autobiographical memory cues in an attempt to characterize the type of event knowledge structure principally accessed during retrieval (Reiser et al., 1985; Reiser, Galambos, & Black, 1982). Reiser et al. (1985) investigated *activity* and *general action* knowledge structures. These structures are heavily used in both understanding and planning behavior in many common experiences and are therefore reasonable candidates for directing autobiographical memory search. Common activities are represented as a stereotypical sequence of deliberate actions undertaken to achieve one or more goals (Schank, 1982; Schank & Abelson, 1977). For example, the activity *Eating in Restaurants* achieves the goal of satisfying hunger, and is often performed to satisfy goals of entertainment and socializing. Artificial intelligence investigations of these knowledge structures have included work on scripts (Schank & Abelson, 1977) and Memory Organization Packets (Schank, 1982). Each component of the activity is an action that accomplishes one of the activity's subgoals, and is itself an important source of knowledge. These actions are often performed with variations in several different activities. *General actions* (called *generalized scenes* in Schank, 1982), encode the generalizations about an action common to all the activities that contain that action. For example, the activity *Eating in Restaurants* includes the actions *Make Reservations* (sometimes optional), *Enter, Be-Seated, Order, Eat, Pay,* and *Exit.* The general action *Make Reservations* is also a component of other activities such as *Going on Vacation, Playing Indoor Tennis,* and *Going to Nightclubs.*

An important functional distinction between activities and general actions is that activities are "self-contained" knowledge structures (Reiser et al., 1985). Activities describe a sequence of actions in service of a goal, and contain information about how each general action is modified for that particular context. A general action is a situation-free description of the common attributes of the manner in which a subgoal of activities is achieved. Consider answers to the question "Where were you earlier today?" An activity-based event summary sounds reasonable ("I went grocery shopping."), while a description comprised of one or more general actions is too abstract to serve as a sufficient summary or explanation ("I paid for some items and transported them home."). Similarly, one never experiences paying or making reservations in the abstract, but instead performs the action in the context of a particular activity that provides more concrete fillers for inferences such as "what was paid for?", "why was it bought?", and "what was reserved?", "what will the reservation enable us to do?", "why was the reservation necessary?", etc. To return to the observation made earlier, retrieval strategies tend to be employed to develop the retrieval description into an event that can be concretely imaged. It is difficult to image "paying" in the abstract, but "paying in a restaurant" can be imaged quite easily. Adding the restaurant information to the paying general action enables inferences about the presence and physical appearance of actors and props in the situation.

The self-contained nature of activities should make them more useful in autobiographical retrieval. There are two lines of argument supporting this role of activities during retrieval, corresponding to the two types of functional constraints presented earlier. First, consider the issue of the structures active at encoding. Because of the inference-richness of activity structures and the context-free nature of general actions, general action structures will be insufficient to guide comprehension, and instead, activity structures will be accessed. Events are not typically perceived at the level of abstraction represented in general actions. For example, the general action *Paying* is never experienced in its "pure" form. Instead, events involving this action are seen as components of activities such as *Eating in Restaurants* and *Shopping in Department Stores*. Thus, activities provide more of the information at the level at which it tends to be originally represented, suggesting that general actions will be effective retrieval cues only when they direct search to an appropriate activity.

Second, it is necessary to consider the utility of each of these types of structures for inferences during retrieval. Accessing an activity enables an important class of inferences to be made, including the reason for executing the actions in that sequence, and concrete expectations concerning the types and appearance of the social roles and physical objects involved in the activity. For example, accessing the *Shopping in Department Stores* activity provides predictions about salespeople, customers, merchandise, a cash register, a counter, music, elevators, etc. General actions do not enable the same type of concrete predictions. Consider the example from Reiser et al. (1985) comparing the utility of the *Restaurant* activity and the *Paying* general action in predicting features of a *Restaurant-Paying* experience. The general action provides the information that a monetary transaction occurs, but the probable appearances of the recipient of the money and the physical surroundings, the nature of the purchased items (food), the reasons for the event (hunger, entertainment, socializing), other related events (a date, a movie, a celebration), and many other features can only be predicted using knowledge specific to the *Restaurant* activity. The importance of predicting plausible features of the target event during retrieval suggests that accessing an activity will lead to more successful retrieval of an experience than trying to focus search on a general action.

Empirical Support for the Central Role of Activities

We examined the role of activities and general actions in autobiographical retrieval by comparing the effectiveness of activity and general action cues in eliciting recall of experiences. In a first experiment, subjects were given cues composed of an activity (*had your hair cut*) and a general action (*paid at the cash register*) and were required to recall a specific experience from their own past that matched the presented description. On half the trials, the subjects saw an activity and then, after a 5-second delay, saw a general action phrase; on the other half of the trials, the presentation order was reversed. If activities provide the crucial information for retrieval, then presenting the activity first should enable subjects to get a "head start" relative to the action-first condition, in which subjects must wait until the second cue to receive the useful information. As expected, subjects were much faster to recall a matching experience when the activity was presented before the action cue.

A second experiment further demonstrated the facilitative nature of activity information. Subjects received three different types of cues: a single activity, a single general action, or an activity-general action combination. Subjects were told to recall a specific personal experience that matched each presented description. If activity structures provide information useful in retrieval, then a general action cue will become more effective when paired with an activity. However, the activity cue should not be improved by augmenting it with a general action, since the additional information is not very useful and may add extra constraints slowing the search. The results confirmed the predictions. First, subjects were able to recall experiences much faster when presented with an activity than when given an action. More importantly, when an action cue was paired with an activity, the time necessary to retrieve an experience was substantially faster than for the action presented alone. No such facilitation occurred when an activity was augmented with an action, instead adding the action elicited slower retrievals than the activity alone trials. The results of these experiments suggest that the activity provides the crucial information for the retrieval process. Search from a general action must first access an activity in order to find an experience. General actions are much like the emotions used as cues in the protocols described earlier, in that they may contain information useful for accessing an activity which can then guide search, but are not themselves effective in eliciting experiences.

Interestingly, the type of general action used also affected the difficulty of retrieving a matching experience. Activity-action pairs were slower when the action described the failure of a goal (e.g., *didn't get what you asked for*) rather than a normative action (e.g., *picked out what you wanted*). Since activities provide the principal contexts for memory retrieval, each action description describes additional attributes to consider in searching within the activity context. The normative and failure actions provide different amounts of constraint on the choice of experiences associated with the activity, and thus differ in the difficulty of finding a path within the context leading to an experience possessing the target features. Failure actions are more unusual, and thus more extensive inferencing is required to predict the types of circumstances that would result in the specified goal failure. Consequently, the failure action cues require more elaboration to find the indices among the available paths that lead to a matching experience.

Activities, failure actions, general actions, and combinations of these cues vary in terms of the amount of *constraint* they place on the memory search. These results can be viewed as characterizing the optimal amount of constraint to be placed on a memory retrieval description. More constrained cues place more specific requirements on the nature of the target experience, and thus reduce the number of experiences in memory that could be produced to match the cue. On the other hand, some amount of constraint is necessary. Cues that do not specify enough information require more inference to refine the context and find a knowledge structure to guide search. The activity cues used in these experiments provide more constraint than the general actions, because the actions can occur in several different activities. Adding an action to an activity cue increases the constraint, because it specifies a particular portion of the event sequence that the target event must contain. The type of action also affects the amount of constraint placed on the search. Failure actions provide more constraint because they specify an unusual (and less frequent) variant of the normative form of the action.

These results demonstrate that activities provide an optimal amount of constraint during retrieval. Underconstrained cues (general actions) do not provide enough information to direct retrieval, hence retrieval is slowed by the extra processing to find an appropriate context. Cues that are more constrained also elicit slower retrievals. These additional requirements made on the target experience are not particularly useful for elaborating the description. Instead, they place extra requirements on the target, causing even more inference to be required to find an event with the right set of features. Thus, in this experiment, subjects were slower to recall an experience satisfying an activity-action cue than one that satisfies only the activity cue, and the addition of a failure action to an activity slowed the search more than the addition of a regular action.

Other experiments (Reiser, Galambos, & Black, 1982) support these conclusions. We investigated how the amount of constraint provided by the action in an activity-action combination would affect retrieval. The actions used in these experiments varied in how general or how *distinctive* they were. The distinctiveness of an action may be viewed as measuring how diagnostic an action is of a particular activity (Galambos, 1983, Chapter 2, this volume; Galambos & Black, 1982). An action high in distinctiveness enables easy inference of the activity of which it is a component. For example, the action *See head waiter* is understood as a particular action in the *Eating in Restaurants* activity. Understanding this action carries along with it the retrieval of the activity itself. An action low in distinctiveness is involved in a greater number of activities, and is typically understood by accessing only a general action representation. For example, the action *Stand in line* is a relatively low distinctive action that might be involved in the activities *Cashing a Check, Shopping for Groceries, Going to Movies*, etc.

Retrieval descriptions were constructed by pairing each activity with a high distinctiveness action, a medium level distinctiveness action, and a low distinctiveness action. In addition, presentation order was varied as in the first Reiser et al. (1985) experiment. We predicted that the distinctiveness of the action would affect retrieval time, but only when the action was presented before the activity. If activity information is central in retrieval, then the effectiveness of an action cue will be determined by the extent to which it makes a plausible activity context available. As predicted, an activity cue plus a high distinctiveness action elicited faster retrieval of an experience than the same activity combined with a low distinctiveness action, but only when the action was presented before the activity. When the activity was presented first, the distinctiveness of the action had no effect. This result is consistent with the idea that the activity provides the essential information. When the activity is presented first, the differential predictiveness of the action has no effect, because the activity is already guiding the retrieval process. Thus, these experiments support the central role of activity information in retrieval.

It is important to point out that it is difficult for a simple structural model to account for the pattern of results in these activity-action experiments. The slower retrieval times for cues both less and more constrained than simple activities demonstrates that the retrieval time differences are not due to activities simply providing a more precise specification of an experience than general actions. For example, attempting to quantify the cues in terms of the amount of information contained in the cue will not lead to a simple model of the results. More information is not always better—what is crucial is the type of information provided in the cue. Of course, one could quantify the results and plot retrieval time as a function of the amount of information in each cue, and argue for the resulting U-shaped curve as a good summary of the data. In fact, the curve would be a good summary of the results, but any explanation of *why* such a curve exists would have to rely on the nature of the information provided in the various types of cues. A general point we are trying to make in this book is that complete theories of complex cognitive processes will necessarily include a theory of the *content* of knowledge structures. A full explanation of this U-shaped curve must include a model of the types of information provided by various knowledge structures and the manner in which that information is used. Thus, the optimal point on the tradeoff is the type of cue that provides enough information to contextualize retrieval for an experience, but then allows search to utilize whatever paths within that context are the most accessible.

These results suggest that people categorize the world in terms of the behaviors (of ourselves and others) that take place in physical or social settings. Activities are the optimal-level descriptions of these events, applying to as many varieties of experiences as possible, while losing little in richness compared to their subordinates (i.e., compared with more specific versions of the activity). Since activities contain information about people, behaviors, and perceptual features associated with a type of event, they are heavily used in comprehension and planning, and therefore are useful in predicting features of target events during retrieval.

These experiments have only compared activities to general actions. Further research is needed to explore the relation of activities to other types of information used in comprehension. Barsalou (1985) has found person, location, and time information to be effective retrieval cues. It is important to determine whether these cues are effective because they provide access to activity subcategories (e.g., *Museums in New York, New Year parties*), or can be used to direct search without accessing activity information. It is also important to examine why accessing activities is effective. The next section explores the types of information accessed when activities are processed during retrieval.

EVENT FEATURES ACCESSED DURING RETRIEVAL

In the previous section, we considered some types of knowledge structures accessed during the autobiographical retrieval process. In this section, we examine in more detail why retrieving these structures is effective. In particular, what types of information become available when these retrieval contexts are accessed? This is the part of the retrieval process labeled "Refine Search Context" in Fig. 4.1, in which information found in a knowledge structure is used to elaborate the retrieval specification in order to form a more complete description of the target event. The protocol evidence demonstrates that this information is successively added during search. That is, information is available not only from the activity first chosen as a context, but also from other knowledge structures organized by those activities. The access of these additional structures is evident in retrieval protocols in which subjects describe experiences as more specific versions of the general activity with which they initiated the search. For example, the subject in protocol [3] described in general terms what typically happens to her in the *Grocery Shopping at Pathmark* activity in response to a question about shopping, then continued and was able to discriminate a specific experience. In general, after an activity has been accessed, retrieval may continue by recovering more specific versions of that activity to further refine the description of the target (Kolodner, 1983, 1984; Reiser et al., in press). For example, after the *Restaurant* context has been accessed, search may consider motivating goals for the experience, and thus access the contexts *Dinners at Conferences, Romantic Dinners, Celebrations,* etc. It is important to characterize the types of information used to refine the context and access these more specific structures. As in much of our work, the issues of organization and retrieval are tightly interwoven. Retrieval strategies are tailored to the organization of knowledge structures and their subclasses. Thus, the features that subjects add to their descriptions of the target event during retrieval will be those used to discriminate subclasses of activities and link an activity to other structures.

One approach we took to investigating these features was to examine the types of information mentioned in subjects' remembered experiences (Reiser, 1983). In the retrieval time experiments described earlier, subjects pressed a response button when they had successfully recalled an experience, and then wrote down a brief description of the experience. This experiment focused on the contents of the remembered experiences. The basic premise was that if a feature was useful in retrieving an experience, it would be reused in later memory searches. Information generated while retrieving an experience should be available in memory and thus accessed by the retrieval processes during later memory searches. This provides a method for discerning the features important in retrieval. Demonstrating that a particular feature can be used in later searches indicates that a search strategy was able to use that feature in both retrievals, perhaps because the two experiences were both indexed using that feature. If elements of the same context are used in a subsequent search, this should be observable by noting commonalities between the two remembered experiences.

In order to make different types of information available, we used a priming or cue-repetition methodology. Subjects in the experiment were asked to recall experiences matching cues that in some cases repeated some type of information from the preceding cue. In other cases, no information was repeated from the immediately preceding cue. In this way, we can observe what types of event features can be reused in an immediately following retrieval when the question concerns a similar or a different type of event. The best situation for reusing features should be when search is required to stay within the same context. Information generated during the first retrieval involving that context should be able to be used again in later searches of the context. To evaluate this condition, cues were constructed using an activity and general action (e.g., *went shopping—stood in line*). Each target trial either (1) repeated the activity from the preceding trial with a different general action, (2) repeated the general action with a different activity, or (3) concerned a different action and activity. Subjects were required to recall a *different* experience from their own past in response to each trial. The dependence of the retrieval process upon information organized by activities suggests that repeating an activity cue should facilitate retrieval relative to repeating an action cue. Repeating an activity cue enables search to reuse salient information generated on a previous search, while information accessed by processing the same action on a prior trial should be less useful. Thus, repeating the activity cue should enable more repetition of features than repeating a component general action, and should lead to faster retrieval times.

Subjects' remembered experiences were examined to find commonalities between the features mentioned in each experience and those from prior recalls. Only those features that did not correspond directly to information in the cue were analyzed. Any feature mentioned in an experience that was explicitly mentioned in an earlier trial was counted as a repeated feature. This included features such as particular person, a location, a common goal, etc. As expected, more experience features were repeated when the cue repeated the activity; repetition of the general action elicited no more repeated features than a different action and activity. Thus, repeating the activity phrase enabled more features of the remembered events to be reused on the next memory search. This supports the claim that accessing an activity structure provides access to information used to elaborate the retrieval description. When a later trial includes the same activity, some of that information can be used again in this subsequent search. The retrieval times also supported this conclusion. Repeating the activity cue led to significantly faster retrievals than repeating the general action cue. The retrieval time results suggest that the greater number of repeated features are due to the facilitative effect of reaccessing the activity knowledge structure.

We classified the repeated experience features in an attempt to characterize the particular components of experiences used to discriminate them during retrieval. There were three types of information repeated in later retrievals: information contained in an activity, information from a knowledge structure not mentioned in the query, and general or nonactivity specific features of events. A brief description of these classes of information follows. (These representations are described in more detail in Reiser 1983.)

1. Activity-Specific Features.   First, the most frequent type of repeated information was activity-specific information. In these cases, the repeated information was contained in the activity knowledge structure. This type of feature repetition would occur when information available in the activity accessed earlier was still available and hence was reused in a subsequent search.

Activity Variant: Whenever activity-specific information was repeated, it could be considered an Activity Variant repetition, i.e., the repetition of a particular subclass of an activity mentioned earlier. For example, one subject recalled two haircuts involving the same barber, while another recalled two shopping experiences at the same store. The activity subclass strategies found by Reiser et al. (in press) listed in Table 4.1 are consistent with this type of feature repetition. Subjects refine the search context to a particular subclass of an activity, such as haircuts involving a particular barbershop, Chinese cooking, or shopping experiences at the Yale Coop. Then, when queried later with the same top-level activity, this subclass is more available and the subject tries to search again within this more specific context, rather than generate a different context. If the search is attempted and successful, the remembered experience would share the features with the previous recall that discriminated this particular subclass from the others organized by the activity.

2. Features Referencing Other Knowledge Structures.   A second source of repeated information involves an additional activity or some other context outside the activity provided in the cue. These cases would occur when a cue is reformulated to access another knowledge structure which is also found to be relevant in a later query.

Other Activity: In these cases, an activity is used in combination with a second activity not mentioned in the query. This typically occurred when two activities combined to form a salient subclass of experiences. For example, one subject, queried twice about cooking meals, each time recalled an experience involving Boy Scout campouts. In other cases, the activity utilized in a previous question contained a connection to the activity in a later trial. For example, one subject recalled an experience involving shopping for food at a grocery store in response to the cue *went shopping— stood in line.* Although the next trial concerned a bookstore (*waited for service—went to a bookstore*) the subject retrieved an experience where the object sought at the bookstore was not books, but chocolate cheesecake. (The particular bookstore mentioned by the subject contains a coffee and desserts concession.) The causal chain reasoning strategies found by Reiser et al. (in press) would produce this result. If the retrieval mechanisms considered goals that would motivate the bookstore activity, the less conventional reason of buying food would be available from the activity accessed in response to the previous question, and thus would immediately index a subclass of bookstores concerned with buying food at this unusual bookstore.

Larger Context: This was the most frequent type of other knowledge structure used in retrieval. In these cases, subjects recalled two experiences with a common larger context or setting in common. For example, subjects recalled two experiences that took place during the same vacation, a school break, or a trip. Here again the causal chain reasoning strategies would account for this result. For example, given the cue *went to a museum* these strategies might retrieve the fact that one often attends museums during vacations or trips to other cities. When a later query is presented, that vacation or trip is still active in memory and the retrieval mechanisms may try to use that setting information to refine the context in that later query.

Causally Connected Events: In this third type, subjects recalled two experiences that were causally linked. For example, one subject recalled an experience involving the purchase of a book, and then later recalled an experience where she returned that book to the store. In these cases, the previously recalled experience is presumably still very available when the later query mentions the same activity, and a second experience linked to the previous one can be easily recalled.

3. Nonactivity Specific Event Features. In this third class of feature repetitions, subjects repeated features that are not specific to a particular activity, but refer to attributes that may be filled by the same value for a number of different activities. These types of repetitions are consistent with the "access external knowledge" strategies found by Reiser et al. (in press). Knowledge external to the activity, such as particular participants or a location, was accessed in order to refine the context, and then this feature was successfully incorporated into a different context in a later search.

Location: In these cases, subjects recalled two different experiences set in the same location, such as a particular university or city.

Participants: Here the subject recalled two experiences involving the same participant, such as a sibling, roommate, or friend.

Topic: In these cases, the subject recalled two somewhat related events concerning the same topic or object. For example, one subject recalled taking a math exam after previously remembering an experience involving the purchase of a math book for the same course.

In another experiment described in Reiser (1983), we used a second methodology to examine the features used during retrieval. We asked subjects to recall experiences involving a particular activity and then to sort those experiences into groups of similar experiences. The subjects' labels for those groups were used to infer the event features salient in discriminating these experiences. Most of the event features found in the cue repetition experiment were used by subjects to determine the clustering of their experiences. For example, two frequent types of groups of experiences were determined by common Activity Variants (e.g., a group of museum experiences, all involving museum libraries) and common Participants (e.g., a group of museum visits, all involving the same school friends). The clustering experiment also indicated the importance of abstract commonalities between experiences, such as emotions and goal relationships and outcomes (e.g., a group of experiences in which a similar type of goal failure was experienced). These abstract commonalities were difficult to observe in the short descriptions of experiences produced by subjects in the cue repetition experiment.

The features of experiences found to be important in these two experiments are consistent with the types of retrieval strategies found by Reiser et al. (in press). Taken together, these results suggest that experiences are indexed and retrieved according to those features that are causally relevant to the goals and course of action taken by the person in the activity. Experiences concern deliberate actions, and thus both the comprehension and planning involved in an experience entail considering the interacting goals of one or more participants. It is therefore reasonable to expect that features relevant to these goals and their outcomes will determine how the experiences are represented and stored in memory. For example, when one decides to perform an activity, one must decide on particular goal objects or standard varieties of the activity. Thus, considering the type of food desired in a restaurant, the type of atmosphere desired for going out drinking, or the type of movie desired, would each result in the selection of a particular Activity Variant. The other "choice points" in an experience represent discriminations on goal-relevant features such as Participants or Location. Other goal-related features concern the reason for performing the activity (a motivating goal), and the relation between the goals and outcomes of the experience, including associated emotions. Thus, experiences are indexed using features that represent choices about the goals in the event, relationships among goals, descriptions of outcomes, and their effects on goals, and connections to other experiences (including larger contexts) that motivated or resulted from the experience. Autobiographical retrieval can be generally characterized as a type of causal reasoning process, where the inference mechanisms also used in comprehension are used to construct a picture of an event by connecting motivations and plausible results with the behavior of these involved.

ACCESSIBILITY OF EXPERIENCES

Thus far, we have considered the nature of the retrieval mechanisms that search memory for individual experiences, and have characterized retrieval as a causal reasoning process that accesses information in planning and comprehension knowledge structures in order to predict features of the target experience. We have seen that representations of knowledge about everyday activities appear to play a key role in this retrieval process. These structures provide access to knowledge concerning the causal relationships between the motivations and behavior of interacting participants, which is then used by the retrieval strategies to refine the context further. In this section, we consider how properties of the target experiences themselves affect how accessible they are in memory. If reasoning about the causes and motivations of actions is required for retrieval, then characteristics of the target experiences that affect this inference process should determine the type and amount of search necessary to retrieve these experiences. Here we are concerned with the component of retrieval labeled "Choose Search Indices" in Fig. 4.1. What characteristics of experiences affect the amount of processing necessary to select a successful index?

Factors affecting this inference difficulty were explored in two additional retrieval time experiments presented in Reiser (1983). First, we demonstrated that the difficulty of retrieving a target event from memory is partly determined by the relative number of different circumstances within an activity in which such an experience tends to occur. If a particular type of experience occurs in many different varieties of an activity, then the retrieval process can use whatever features are available in order to direct search successfully to such an experience. If an experience is more unusual and the retrieval specification does not provide the features indexing those unusual features, then more detailed inferencing is necessary to select the right path. The search mechanisms must access the set of causal relationships contained in the activity in order to predict carefully the circumstances in which that unusual experience would occur. Search is less constrained when looking for a highly standard type of experience, and can use whatever salient features are most available to find more specific contexts (e.g., particular participants, locations, and motivations involved in the activity). This observation was suggested by the slower retrieval times for trials involving failure actions in the Reiser et al. (1985) experiments. We attempted to replicate this result by asking subjects to recall experiences involving activity-action descriptions that varied in how frequently such an event tends to be performed. Frequency was varied by using actions that ranged in "standardness," a rating that measures the likelihood of performing the given action in the activity (Galambos, 1983, Chapter 2, this volume). Each activity was paired with a high standardness action and a low standardness action. For example, subjects rated that they would be more likely to perform the action *Tip the Waiter* than the action *Order Some Drinks* in the activity *Eating in Restaurants*. As predicted, subjects were slower to recall experiences matching the low frequency cues than the high frequency cues, supporting the claim that the magnitude of causal reasoning required to predict a setting for the target experience determines its retrieval difficulty.

In addition, the causal importance of the target experience should affect its retrieval difficulty. If each experience is indexed according to causally relevant features and is internally represented as a causally connected set of components, then the causal relevance of any particular component should affect its ease of retrieval. Cues that describe highly central components of activities provide more of the required information for the inference mechanisms, because they provide access to features used to index experiences. Cues describing low salience details do not provide sufficient direction for retrieval, because these features do not correspond to those used to encode experiences. Greater elaboration of the retrieval specification is therefore necessary, and the retrieval mechanisms must search for other information in the context to assemble features necessary to select indices leading to an experience. We tested this prediction by pairing an activity with a high "centrality" action and a low "centrality" action. The centrality of an action is a measure of the action's importance to the goals of the activity (Galambos, 1983, Chapter 2, this volume). High centrality actions describe components causally linked to the central goals in the activity, while low centrality actions describe more peripheral components of the activity. For example, the action *Receive the Money* was rated a more central action than *Write Down Date* in the activity *Cashing a Check*. The high and low centrality actions chosen for this experiment were balanced for standardness. As predicted, an activity paired with a high centrality action elicited faster retrievals than one paired with a low centrality action. Retrieval is a causal reasoning process, therefore providing information more important to the goals of the activity will be more useful for the retrieval strategies, and will better correspond to the features used to encode experiences. The results of these studies of accessibility of experiences support the claim that the principal component of the strategic retrieval process involves causal reasoning to select the right path to an experience.

CONCLUSIONS

We have tried to characterize the types of structures and mechanisms used to retrieve experiences from memory. We began with the premise that if knowledge structures are used to understand the world around us, then traces of one's experiences should be connected in memory to those structures. Attempting to characterize the processes that search memory for an experience revealed a directed search process. Searching memory for an experience begins by selecting an appropriate context for search, which may necessitate accessing additional knowledge structures than those mentioned in the query. Searching within that context proceeds by elaborating the original retrieval description until enough information is generated to discriminate a unique experience with the target properties. This process can be seen as a causal reasoning process, drawing on the same store of world knowledge that comprehension and planning utilize.

Given this type of retrieval process, we considered two constraints that govern the use of knowledge structures in retrieval: utility in planning/ comprehension and predictive power during retrieval. These considerations were used to argue for the central role of activities in the retrieval process. Information from other sources may be accessed during retrieval, but activities provide the principal scaffolding for the inferences necessary during search. Protocol evidence and retrieval time experiments supported this role of activities. When retrieval is initiated using more abstract situation-free knowledge, such as general actions or emotions, strategies are utilized to infer a plausible activity and then use that to guide the search.

Further experiments demonstrated the types of knowledge these structures make available during retrieval. A rich set of causally relevant features is typically used to connect experiences with other experiences and with structures in memory. Finally, we have begun to consider the factors that affect the accessibility of experiences associated with these structures in memory. Results concerning the frequency and causal relevance of events indicated that the difficulty of retrieving a target experience is determined by the amount of causal reasoning required to assemble a set of circumstances in which an event with the target features was likely to have occurred. This reasoning may be facilitated by information available from other contexts or previously recalled experiences. Taken together, these results form the basis for a model of the nature of the organizing contexts and the type of information used by the directed search mechanisms in autobiographical memory.

II

GOALS AND PLANS

The boundary between scripts and plans is not altogether sharp. Both types of knowledge structures encode purposive sequences of actions. The main distinctions between the two are that scripts are more stereotyped, consensual, and societally institutionalized. One can refer to *the* restaurant script, or doctor-visit script, etc., in reasonable confidence that much very concrete detail is thereby communicated. The experiments reported in Part I in fact took advantage of this stereotyping in their stimulus materials and task demands, and were rewarded with very coherent results.

Plans are coherent in a looser, more abstract way than are scripts. One does not speak of *the* plan to win the heart of someone, or even of *the* plan to get from New Haven to Indianapolis. The activity of planning implies that there is a choice among alternative overall plans, and often that subplans will need to be developed as well. In experimental explorations of plans as knowledge structures, therefore, we cannot rely much on prepackaged materials and tasks. Approaches must be more varied and indirect.

Despite their flexibility, plans as knowledge structures are nevertheless highly constrained. They are rule-bound. Understanders appreciate the relevance of particular methods to the achievement of particular goals or sub-

101

goals. If the goal of an actor is known, certain actions will seem sensibly interpretable as parts of a plan for its achievement; conversely, otherwise cryptic actions may be explicable by assuming the presence of some goal they serve. The structured relationships between goals and plans, therefore, have implications for the processes of comprehension, of inference, and of explanation.

In Chapter 5, Robert Abelson and John Leddo investigate some factors involved in the choice among competing explanations for events. Their stimulus materials pose various *script failures,* and solicit explanations from subjects. Script failures recruit planning knowledge above and beyond script knowledge—the failure of occurrence of expected events forces the understanding process to move to a more abstract level involving the plans that scripted actions serve.

Chapter 6 presents a review by Valerie Abbott and John Black of the role that knowledge of goals and plans plays in giving coherence to story materials. An alternative coherency analysis in terms of the repetition of concepts across text sentences appears to be far less satisfactory. The contrast between the two coherency models is especially sharp in the data from Abbott and Black's own experiment, presented at the end of the chapter.

5

The Nature of Explanations

John Leddo
Robert P. Abelson

INTRODUCTION

How people explain events is a standard topic in social psychology. It goes under the name "attribution theory," referring to how people make attributions of causation. Such theorizing in social psychology has grown up as an independent body of propositions, rather unconnected with other ideas in cognitive social psychology. From our point of view, this is unfortunate. As outlined in our introductory chapter, we emphasize flexibility of function in the application of knowledge structures. It seems cognitively inefficient (and implausible) that there should be specialized structures and processes solely for the purpose of explaining events. Rather, "explanation" may be more profitably conceived as a special case of the general process of understanding. The same knowledge structures used in understanding ought to be implicated in explanation.

Of this, more later. First, though, we try to give a bit of the flavor of standard attribution theory by presenting a brief outline of the most popular attribution framework, that of Kelley (1967). Kelley posits that causal attributions for a given event depend upon a matrix of bits of information about related events. In the simplest version of the system, the major distinction is between "person attributions" and "stimulus attributions," and the attributor is disposed toward one or the other depending on "consensus" and "distinctiveness" information in the matrix. Here is how it works:

The event is represented as person P performing a given behavior associated with stimulus S. Distinctiveness information concerns how person P behaves with other stimuli; consensus information concerns how other people behave with stimulus S. Thus if the event is "Harry fails a history test," distinctiveness concerns whether Harry fails other tests, too (a pattern with low distinctiveness), or only the history test (high distinctiveness). Consensus concerns whether other people also fail the history test (high consensus) or whether other people generally pass the history test (low consensus). Low distinctiveness and low consensus each dispose toward a person attribution: If Harry fails other tests and other people pass this test, then Harry's failure on this test must be due to something about him (he's not smart enough). On the other hand, high distinctiveness and high consensus each dispose toward a stimulus attribution: if Harry passes other tests and other people fail this one, then it's the test that causes Harry's history failure (the test is too hard).

To take another example, in explaining why according to these attribution principles "Mary avoids the dog," one would conclude that it was something about Mary if Mary also avoids other dogs and/or no one else avoids this dog. However, if Mary does not avoid other dogs and/or others also avoid this dog, then the explanation involves something about the dog.

While there is some evidence that people can use this formal attribution logic (e.g., McArthur, 1972), several criticisms can be directed at the approach. (See Leddo, Abelson, & Gross, 1984.) We have already mentioned one, namely, that it is too specialized a system, operating only for explanations. Furthermore, it seems a rather abstract way for people to reason about concrete events, and questions can be raised about the utility of the abstract categories of "person" versus "situation" attributions.

In particular, there is the issue of how the individual goes beyond the general category to focus on particularities. When people are asked to give event explanations in their own words, they give quite concrete responses that go well beyond a general dichotomy into person vs. situation (Lalljee, Watson, & White, 1982). Often these responses are difficult to classify as personal or situational attributions (though defenders of the attribution paradigm rely also on combination categories such as "person-by-situation interaction" [Jaspars, Hewstone, & Fincham, 1983]). In any case, even when responses can be simply categorized, the attribution paradigm does not explain how the specifics arise. For example, in explaining "Mary avoids the dog" (and many other dogs) as being due to "something about Mary," how does the individual arrive at an articulation such as, "Mary is scared of animals," or "Mary is a nervous child"?

It might be argued that whatever search mechanisms are needed for specifying further detail (such as picking out "nervous child" as the something about Mary explaining her avoiding dogs), at least the attribution paradigm narrows the search to features of the person or of the stimulus. This argument implies an "abstract first, concrete later" processing model.

But this in turn implies that an abstract conclusion (e.g., "something about the person") could be reached more quickly than any concrete conclusion (e.g., "a nervous child"). This prediction was in fact tested by Druian and Omessi (1982) and was not verified. Subjects much more quickly gave concrete than abstract explanations for events.

Another doubtful aspect of the standard attribution paradigm is its implication for information search behavior. To behave according to the Kelley model, a subject seeking to explain why "Person P behaved in a certain way toward Stimulus S" would primarily want to know whether other persons behaved in a certain way toward S, and whether P behaved thus toward other stimuli. But in many cases this seems quite implausible. A slyly chosen example will make this clear.

Several years ago the newspapers carried the item, "Jewish Defense League sends Passover matzohs to Soviet Embassy." Now, how might someone seek to explain this odd event? Would they ask whether the Jewish Defense League sends matzohs to other embassies on Passover—or whether other organizations send matzohs to the Soviet Embassy? Not likely. Rather, the line of inquiry would want to explore possible motives for the behavior, implicating knowledge about the relations between Jews and the Soviet Union. A motivational inquiry might hit upon an explanation such as the package being sent in ironic protest over Soviet emigration policies. This explanation would be, as it were, internal to the event involving the two actors, and would not implicate other actors involved in hypothetical parallel episodes. It can always be argued that implicitly the individual already knows the answers to questions about other embassies and other matzoh-senders, and doesn't need to ask. But this is a rather weak defense of the standard paradigm, since at best it still leaves out the interesting part of the analysis of the example.

Finally, we appeal again to a point made earlier, namely that the event explanations people give in their own words are difficult to classify as person-versus-situation attributions. Thus the reason why Mary avoided the dog could be that "she was afraid it might bite her," or "she didn't like its loud bark," which invoke properties of *both* Mary and the dog. This is very common.

In several ways, then, the standard analysis seems unnatural. What would be a "natural" scheme for providing explanations? Our contention is that the natural way to explain events is in terms of the major knowledge structures used in understanding, specifically scripts, goals, plans, themes, etc. A large class of very natural explanations for why a person did such-and-such is in terms of intentional action: it served some purpose to do such-and-such. Thus Mary is plausibly seen to have a purpose in avoiding the dog (to avoid its aversive bite or bark, for example). When we appeal to the knowledge structures of goals and plans—and scripts, too—we center our analysis directly on intentional action.

Lalljee and Abelson (1983) have further discussed the contrast between traditional social psychological views of explanation and the knowledge structure view. In their analysis of the knowledge structure position, a distinction is made between constructive explanation and contrastive explanation. In constructive explanation, the individual must embed the given event in an appropriately selected or constructed schema. In certain mundane cases, constructive explanation would simply involve reference to an appropriate script. Thus, "Why did John phone the restaurant?" could plausibly be answered with "to get a reservation." In contrastive explanation, the individual must account for departure of an event from what might normally be expected; i.e., what needs explanation is why something did not happen. For example, the question "Why did George stay seated during the playing of the national anthem?" is tantamount to asking, "Why didn't he stand up?".

Most AI programs designed to answer questions about the causes of behavior have emphasized constructive explanation. In Wilensky's (1978a, 1978b) "Plan Applier Mechanism" (PAM), fragments of a plan are input, and the program in accounting for the actor's behavior may need to fill out more of the plan in relation to its initiating goal. Thus, PAM might be given the input text, "John needed money. He got a gun and went to a liquor store." The program then links these fragments by hypothesizing a particular robbery plan. When asked, "Why did John get a gun?", PAM replies, "To threaten the liquor store owner."

Occasional attention has been given to contrastive explanation in AI question-answering programs. For instance, Lehnert (1978) gave a method of searching the input text in script-based examples to answer questions such as why John, who ordered a hamburger, didn't eat a hamburger. (The waitress said they didn't have any.) In general, however, a systematic analysis of contrastive explanation has not been done. It is a hard task, in part because explanations for the nonoccurrence of expected events involve failures, and failure can occur in a large number of ways in most intentional activities. How individuals select among plausible alternative causes of script or plan failure has been an unsolved problem.

Lalljee and Abelson (1983) have proposed a possible categorization of types of "failures" which can be invoked for contrastive explanations. These are given below, using the illustrative example, "Why did John leave his bike unlocked when he was downtown?". When judged by the standard goal of wanting to preserve one's property against theft, this behavior violates expectation.

Goal absence: He was naive and didn't realize the risk.
Goal conflict: He was desperately late for an important appointment.

Goal reversal: He wanted to get rid of the lousy bike anyway.
Goal satisfied: The bike was safe because a friend was watching it.
Plan failure: He forgot to bring the lock.
Interference: Thieves stole the bike before he could lock it.

How do individuals prioritize these types of explanations? Clearly, contextual cues can make one or another type more salient. For example, if the problem were phrased, "Why did John leave his rusty bike unlocked when he was downtown?", the appeal of the explanation that he wanted to get rid of it would probably be enhanced. But what determines the relative appeal of explanations in the absence of such clear, focusing cues? This chapter represents a modest beginning exploration of this area.

Explanations and Knowledge Structures

We begin by constraining the type of knowledge structure within which explanations are to be sought—our examples come from scripted activities. Further, we do not attempt to pit all six of the above types of explanations against each other. Instead, we expand the category of "Plan failure" into finer detail, and examine explanatory preferences among different possible plan failures, occurring at different points in the script. The reasons for this strategy are twofold: First, scripts have sequential structure, and choice of explanation may depend on sequence (in ways we will indicate later); second, norms are available on various attributes of script actions (see Chapter 2), and perhaps the explanatory priorities given to failures of different actions can be associated with these norms. We report three studies, respectively based on the first, the second, and both of these strategic reasons.

DESCRIPTION OF STUDIES

Study I

In our first study, we wanted to explore ways in which the sequential positions of events within a script might relate to the relative plausibility of different explanations for the failure of script execution. For example, suppose we know that John went to a particular restaurant, but came home without having eaten there. We might explain this failure in terms of something going wrong immediately, such as the restaurant being closed; or something amiss later on, say, the restaurant not having what he especially wanted to order; or as a failure well into the script, such as an angry rejection of the food served him. Averaging results from this example with those from other scripts, is there any preference for explanations in early vs. middle vs. late positions? Or is sequential position quite irrelevant to choice of explanation—or perhaps merely a surrogate for some more content-relevant variable?

We used two types of probes into the effects of sequence. The simplest was to present bare statements of script failures, for each offering several explanations varying in sequential position, as sketched above. This constituted a base-line control ("0") condition.

Additionally, we were interested in the effects that the elimination of certain explanations would have upon the relative credences given to remaining explanations. This is related to script sequencing in the following way. Suppose the event context specifies that the character reached a certain point in the script sequence, but then somehow failed to complete the script; for example, "John went to a restaurant and was seated at a table, but came back later without having eaten there". Such a context implicitly rules out explanations for failure located before the script point reached by the character (e.g., that the restaurant was closed).

How, though, might such a context affect the relative strengths of explanations coming after the script point? There are several possibilities. All remaining explanations might benefit equally—or proportionately. Alternatively, explanations immediately following the critical point might gain the most in strength, and explanations farther away in the script sequence gain the least, as though the script were being searched in a forward direction from the critical point. Or perhaps the script is searched in the backward direction, with explanations near the end being favored the most. To test these various possibilities, we created stimulus contexts in which the character had implicitly achieved two steps in the script sequence (the "2" condition), and other contexts in which the character had implicitly achieved four steps (the "4" condition). Likelihood ratings were elicited for all explanations, as in the "0" condition, thereby including explanations both before and after the critical script point.

Here is one of the stimulus arrangements as given to subjects in the "0" condition:

Bill entered the library.
He left without a book.

Please rate how likely you think each given explanation is to account for what happened:

1. Bill didn't want a book.
2. Bill couldn't find the card catalog.
3. There was no card for the book in the catalog.

4. Bill couldn't find the stacks.
5. The book wasn't on the shelves.
6. Bill forgot to take his card, and couldn't check out the book.
7. Bill forgot to take the book with him.
E. He met a friend who agreed to lend him the book.

The item labeled 1 is a negation of the standard goal of the script, items 2 through 7 are obstacles or errors in the execution of successive steps of a standard library script, and the item labeled E—which could occur anywhere in the sequence—is an external intervention making script execution unnecessary. In the actual stimulus presentation, a nine-point scale of likelihood accompanied each alternative explanation, the above identifying labels were not attached to them, and they occurred in a random order on the page.

In the "2" condition, the same explanations were presented, but the event statement was expanded so that the character had apparently proceeded to a script point beyond item 2. In the stimulus example above, the statement was:

Bill entered the library.
He approached the card catalog area.
He left without a book.

Presumably the effect of the statement, "He approached the card catalog area," is to eliminate the first two failure explanations ("He didn't want a book" and "He couldn't find the card catalog area"), leaving the field to the other six explanations. Of course, with imaginative subjects and inevitable stimulus ambiguities of one sort and another, the first two explanations might not end up totally eliminated, but the degree to which they are weakened can be checked from the subjects' ratings.

In the "4" condition, the event statement placed the story character at a point implicitly beyond item 4:

Bill entered the library.
He approached the stacks of books area.
He left without a book.

Presumably here the first two items are weakened, as well as the third and fourth: ("There was no card for the book in the catalogue" and "Bill couldn't find the stacks").

Each subject rated eight explanations for each of 10 scripts (Library, Motel, Movie, Restaurant, Bank, Locking a Bike, Fixing a Flat Tire, Subway Ride, Barbecue, and Phone Call), arranged in a fixed order on the questionnaire. One-third of the subjects received all scripts in the "0" condition, one-third all in the "2" condition, and one-third all in the "4" condition. Ratings were made on a nine-point likelihood scale, with 1 representing the least likelihood, and 9, the greatest. Thirty-six subjects were recruited from the Yale undergraduate psychology pool, and assigned at random to conditions. Subjects were run in small groups, and the questionnaire took about 15 minutes to complete.

Results

Table 5.1 presents the likelihood ratings for the eight explanations in the three conditions, averaged over subjects and scripts.

Several things are noteworthy about this display. First of all, the mean likelihoods of the eight explanations differ rather sharply even in the Control (0) condition. In that condition, there is a significant main effect of explanation position, over both subjects and stimuli ($F' = 4.62$, d.f. = 7,15; $p < .01$). There are peaks in likelihood at sequence position 3 and again at 5 and 6. We return later to an interpretation of this sequential position effect.

The main focus of the study, however, was on the differential effects of the 2 and 4 conditions, compared to the 0 condition. These differential effects are given in the bottom part of Table 5.1. The first two explanations in the 2 condition and the first four in the 4 condition should be rated lower in likelihood than they were in the 0 condition, if our basic reasoning about the implicit weakening properties of those conditions is correct. Indeed, this manipulation check is successful. Although the disconfirming tendencies are incomplete (the lowest possible rating being 1.0), nevertheless in all six cases of predicted weakening, some drop in likelihood occurs. The high statistical reliability of this tendency can be inferred from the signifi-

TABLE 5.1
Mean Likelihoods in Study I

Condition				Explanation				
	1	*2*	*3*	*4*	*5*	*6*	*7*	*E*
0	3.71	3.71	5.55	4.24	5.23	5.14	3.75	4.24
2	2.76	3.40	6.45	5.29	5.25	5.28	4.26	4.15
4	2.14	2.45	3.14	3.99	5.58	5.83	4.55	4.19
Condition Differentials								
(2-0)	– .95	–.31	.90	1.05	.02	.14	.51	– .09
(4-0)	–1.57	–1.26	–2.41	– .25	.35	.69	.80	– .05

cant overall Conditions × Explanations interaction ($F' = 6.92$, d.f. = 14,152, p < .01), as well as from the high consistency of the drops.

Having established that the 2 and 4 conditions operate more or less as expected in weakening early explanations, we can examine the results for late explanations. We see that in the 2 condition, explanations 3 and 4 show substantial gains in likelihood, with explanations 5, 6, 7, and E in general gaining trivially. This result seems superficially consistent with a process of "forward search" for a failure explanation, starting from the last given point in the script (event No. 2). The statistical reliability of the differential gain attaching to explanations 3 and 4 can be assessed by the interaction of conditions (0 versus 2), with explanations (contrasting 3, 4 versus 5, 6, 7). This test yields $F' = 4.64$; d.f. = 1, 10; p < .10.

The results in the 4 condition, however, are of a different character. The sizes of the differential gains for later explanations 5, 6, 7 are relatively constant; if anything, the gain is greater the later the explanation in the script sequence (setting aside explanation E, which is not properly in the sequence at all). Statistically, a "constant gain" model is supported, because a test of the interaction of conditions (0 versus 4) with explanations (5, 6, 7) gives a value of F' less than one.

Thus the outcome is a mixed one. When the first two items in a script sequence are presupposed, search for script failure explanations seems to focus on the events immediately following; when the first four items are presupposed, search is fairly evenly distributed over the remaining items. "Forward search" as such seems not to be the general rule. In order to understand this unusual result, it is important to examine the content of stimulus items occurring at various sequence positions. Sequence position itself is a rather diffuse variable, and could function differently, depending on the content with which it is realized. Below are several instances, more or less typical, of failure explanations occupying the No. 3 and No. 4 sequential positions. The introductory stimuli from the 2 condition are indicated in parentheses:

> (Jeff entered the motel.
> He checked to see if there was a vacancy.
> He didn't stay there that night.)
> 3. There were no rooms available.
> 4. The price of the rooms was too high.

> (Jill went to the movie theater.
> She arrived at the ticket window.
> She didn't see the movie.)
> 3. There weren't any tickets left.
> 4. She didn't have enough money for a ticket.

(Mary went to a restaurant.
The waitress handed her a menu.
She left without eating.)
3. What Mary wanted wasn't on the menu.
4. When the waitress came to take the order,
   she was rude to Mary.

(Sam went to the walk-up withdrawal teller
outside the bank. The machine asked for his
ID number. He left without money.)
3. Sam forgot his ID number.
4. The machine read his ID incorrectly and rejected it.

What these stimuli have in common is that they refer to the making of a contract between the individual and the institution named by the script. At the motel, there must be a room available for which the customer can pay; at the movie, there must be payment for a seat; in the restaurant, a willingness to order something available; at the bank, an acknowledgment that a withdrawal is legitimate. The No. 3 and No. 4 items refer variously to failures of these contractual arrangements, because one or the other party is unwilling or unable to make them. Thus in the 2 condition the differential gains in the likelihoods of these items might well be interpreted as a stylistic focusing effect: The stimulus introduction leads the reader right up to the point at which arrangements for script participation are to be made, and then it is revealed that script performance failed. ("Jill arrived at the ticket window. She didn't see the movie.") The style of this presentation seems to imply that the impending arrangement (buying a ticket) failed, rather than something later on in the script.

The script failures captured by these No. 3 and No. 4 items we refer to as *failures of arrangement*. In the 0 condition, such failures are already considered rather likely (especially the No. 3 item—see Table 5.1); the hypothesized enhancement effect of the 2 condition makes them even more likely. Meanwhile, the No. 5 and No. 6 explanations are also initially likely in the 0 condition. Why doesn't the 4 condition, which leads the reader to the just preceding time point, exert a special enhancement or focusing effect on these explanations? Again, we look to the stimulus content; some samples are given below:

(Jill went to the movie theater.
She bought some popcorn.
She didn't see the movie.)
5. She couldn't find a free seat so she left.
6. The film projector broke down.

(Mary went to a restaurant.
Mary told the waitress she wanted a steak.
She left without eating.)
5. The cook said they were out of what Mary wanted.
6. The food was burnt.

(Sue went to the subway.
She passed through the turnstile.
She didn't ride the train.)
5. Sue didn't know which train to take.
6. The train didn't come and she got tired of waiting.

In these stimuli (and others not shown here), the impression is of somewhat miscellaneous conceptual relationships between the lead-in statements and the failure explanations to follow. This contrasts with the situation in the 2 condition, where the No. 3 and No. 4 statements almost always referred directly to the "arrangement" implied by the lead-in. Thus, the lack of a stylistic enhancement effect focused on the No. 5 (and No. 6) explanations in the 4 condition is not surprising. It is hard to construct stimulus materials which maintain constant abstract meaning across scripts for the events in given sequence positions. (We do, however, attempt this in Study III below, for a somewhat different purpose.)

What have we learned from Study I? The study was designed to explore what happens to relative preferences among several alternative explanations for script failure, given a statement of the script situation in which the actor is known to have reached a certain point in the script. At least three phenomena are manifest in our data.

First, it is apparent that readers are responsive to the presupposition that if the actor has reached a certain point, then he or she must have performed the actions preceding that point. This in turn implies (and the data verify) that script failure is not likely to be attributable to failure of those preceding actions. (If one gets to the popcorn stand in the movie theater, it is not likely that there were no tickets left.) While this result is fairly straightforward, it is nevertheless worth adding to the list of "gap-filling" phenomena associated with script processing (Abelson, 1981a; Bower, Black, & Turner, 1979), that is, ways in which the reader exposed to mention of a script is readily able to fill in gaps in what is explicitly stated.

Second, we have found that explanations following the critical script point gain in likelihood more or less equally, with some exceptions. Again, this is a reasonably straightforward result. It is plausible that when some explanations are infirmed, the remaining explanations should gain in likelihood. The likelihood that an explanation is true depends in part upon the viability of alternative explanations (Einhorn & Hogarth, 1983). However, it was not obvious at the outset how the gain in likelihood would be distributed over the remaining explanations. Our evidence speaks against certain exotic possibilities, such as "forward search" from the critical script point, or "backward search" from the end of the script.

Third, and most interesting, is the pattern of results in the condition where the critical script point occurs just before the actor is about to make arrangements for entry into the main body of the script. Here we find that failure explanations tend to focus differentially on events immediately following the critical point, and that these events concern failures of arrangement. This result we interpreted as a stylistic focusing effect. Such an effect, incidentally, is one which classical attribution theories would not be able to handle at all, because it does not in any way evoke the information matrix associated with the event. Many interesting types of stylistic or semantic focusing effects on the prioritization of explanations are no doubt demonstrable; however, they are beyond the scope of this chapter. One further result of Study I, the large differences in the likelihoods of the various explanations in the 0 condition, called for further interpretation, leading us to Study II.

Study II

What might account for the pattern of likelihoods for the various failure explanations in the 0 condition? Each explanation refers to the failure of some standard script event, and it could be that some differential property of those standard events could account for the differential popularity of the failure explanations. The availability of the Galambos norms (Chapter 2) for a large number of scripts is helpful in investigating the role of different properties.

Two properties seem especially relevant: "centrality," the degree to which an event is rated to be "important in the performance" of the script; and "standardness," the rating of the relative frequency of occurrence of the event in repeated performances of the script. Perhaps script failures are more likely to be attributed to more central or to more standard events. Centrality is especially interesting as a possible factor, in view of the Galambos and Rips (1982) finding that in a verification task on whether an event belongs to a script, more highly central events are verified faster. (For example, "putting on the spare" is more quickly verified than "putting away the jack" as part of "fixing a flat.") As it were, the script primes or first calls to mind its more central component events. A corollary of this result might be that when told a script has failed, a person first examines as explanations those events most central to the script.

To investigate these conjectures, we chose 10 scripts for which Galambos' norms were available, and selected four events from each, covering the four combinations of High and Low ratings of Centrality (C) and Standardness (S). A fifth event, Medium on both factors, was also selected. These five events were each negated in a plausible way, to produce five failure explanations. Here is an example:

	Bill went to the library to check out a book.
	He left without the book he wanted.
(HiC,HiS):	The book he wanted was not on the shelf.
(HiC,LoS):	Bill didn't get the call numbers of the book he wanted.
(MeC,MeS):	Bill noticed there wasn't anyone at the checkout desk.
(LoC,HiS):	Bill didn't have his library card at checkout time.
(LoC,LoS):	There was no one to inspect the books when leaving the library.

It is both central and standard in taking a book out of the library that it be taken from the shelf. The stimulus negating this event was the assertion that the book was not there. It is a highly central action to look up the call numbers of the book; however, this is low in standardness. This was negated by simply asserting that Bill didn't get it done. And so on.

In this way, five failure explanations were constructed for each of 10 scripts. Subjects (N = 25) were asked to rate the likelihood of each explanation on a nine-point scale, as in the Control condition of Study I.

Results

The mean ratings over subjects and scripts are presented in Table 5.2.

Failure explanations pertaining to events high in both centrality and standardness are especially preferred; next highest rated are explanations based on high central, *low* standard events. Low event centrality yields low ratings of likelihood. Statistically, the main results may be summarized by analyzing the 2 × 2 table in the corners of Table 5.2, yielding a highly

TABLE 5.2
Mean Likelihoods in Study II

		Standardness		
		High	Medium	Low
	High	6.06	—	4.68
Centrality	Medium	—	3.87	—
	Low	3.29	—	3.19

significant main effect for Centrality (F' = 18.82; d.f. = 1, 9; p < .01), but not for Standardness (F' = 1.23), and marginally for the interaction (F' = 3.53, d.f. = 1, 9, p < .10).

In explaining why a script has failed, then, subjects give preference to reasons based on the failure of highly central events. These are events rated by judges as highly important to script performance, events which also prove in a reaction-time task to be more rapidly identifiable as properly belonging to the script. Without a further experiment, however, we do not know whether speed of "popping to mind" is directly implicated in the failure explanation preference for central events.

Nor do we know, actually, exactly what it is about the "centrality" or "importance" of an event that gives it priority in explaining script failure. Certainly if an event is "important" to a script, then a script failure seems readily attributable to a failure of that event. But what does "importance" mean? One notion might be that importance simply means "causal necessity"; i.e., that the script can't be completed without the occurrence of the event (for example, you can't take a subway ride without entering the subway). Causal necessity is often mentioned in discussions of the logic of making attributions (e.g., Kelley, 1972).

As plausible as causal necessity might be as a candidate for the operative factor underlying our centrality effect, it does not prove adequate. A causally necessary event would certainly be maximally high in Standardness— every completion of the script would include this event. But our results show that Standardness does not account for failure explanation likelihoods. One critical cell is for High Centrality, Low Standardness, containing events such as looking up the call number of a book in the card catalog. (The very existence of such events argues against the interpretation of centrality as nothing other than causal necessity.) Such events are not strictly necessary, but they are "important" in the sense that if they occur, the chances of successful completion of the script are enhanced. Furthermore, an event could be causally necessary but so much taken for granted that it is not considered important. Such events lie in the Low Centrality, High Standardness cell, for example, showing your library card at checkout time. Events in this cell are not good candidates for failure explanations.

We speculate, then, that the importance (centrality) rating of an event is based on a pair of considerations: (a) The event is at issue in the performance of a script: It requires effort or thought, or may sometimes not occur; (b) when it occurs properly, it makes a big difference to the successful completion of the script. Events of this nature are the prime candidates for providing likely explanations for script failure. This analysis still leaves open a question about sequential position effects. Why should explanations at positions Nos. 3, 5, and 6 in the Control condition of Study I have been especially favored? Event centrality relates highly to likelihood, as we have seen, but why should central events tend to fall at these sequence positions? It is to this question that we turn in Study III.

Study III

The "0" condition of Study I showed that there were typically two main locations of explanation preference: In the beginning of the script, around the contractual stage, and toward the end, around the actualization of the main script action.

Study II showed that explanations based on items previously rated as most important (central) to the script are favored in explaining script failures over explanations based on noncentral items. We can attempt to connect the two studies by graphing centrality as a function of script sequence from the Galambos norms, as in Fig. 5.1. As can be seen from the figure, there are two places in the script which seem to be highly central: in the beginning around the contractual state and near the end, toward the actualization of the main script action.

This graph shows how Study II can offer a possible interpretation of the "0" condition of Study I. The differential preference of items in the "0" condition of Study I may be partly explained by their differing importance to the script. One may ask the further question "What makes an item important (central)?" As previously noted, items that subjects rated as most

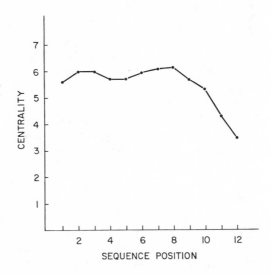

FIG. 5.1. Mean centrality of script actions as a function of position in script sequence (from Galambos norms).

central seemed to share similar content, e.g., the aforementioned contract initiation and main action actualization. This suggests that the function of an action to a script might determine its importance and preference for utilization in explanation.

In Study III, we systematically replicated the "0" condition of Study I, using script function as the basis for generating candidate explanations for subjects to rate. This study presupposes the interesting theoretical argument that all scripts are made up of functionally comparable events. In addressing this issue, Schank (1982) has argued that all scripts (he terms them memory organization packets, or MOPs) can be abstracted into a set of generalized scenes, which are indeed similar in function regardless of the script they came from. Schank terms this set of generalized scenes the "universal MOP." In generating candidate explanations for Study III, we borrowed Schank's concept of the universal MOP and its generalized scenes. Before outlining the study any further, we present these generalized scenes, noting modifications we made for the purposes of our study.

Before a script can typically be entered, there is often some *Preparation* that needs to be made. In a restaurant, this may involve making a reservation. Other typical preparations may be buying tickets in advance, checking locations, etc. All scripts typically involve some *Entry* scene (Schank terms this enablement). Physically this may involve nothing more than simply walking inside whatever place one is going, but entry may sometimes be blocked, preventing the script from proceeding. Once the script has been entered, there may be some *Precondition* before things can get under way. This may involve such actions as waiting in a restaurant, filling out forms in a bank, etc.

The next set of actions Schank terms side conditions, which refer to actions of no necessary intrinsic value, which are done in order to get one to the main action. We refer to this package of actions as an "instrumental plan." An example of this might be the order–serve sequence in a restaurant. For the purposes of this study, instrumental plans are broken down into three more specific components leading up to the main action of the script. The first is the *Instrumental Precondition,* an action required for the instrumental plan to begin (in the restaurant example this might refer to getting a menu, which is typically a precondition for ordering); *Instrumental Initiation,* an action which initiates the instrumental plan (in the restaurant case, ordering the meal); and *Instrumental Actualization,* which refers to the completion of the instrumental plan and hence the arrival at the main action (in the restaurant case this occurs when the waiter serves the meal).

Next, there is the *Doing* of the main action. This is the purpose for being in the script in the first place (e.g., eating in a restaurant, seeing the movie, etc.) After the main action, there are *Postconditions* which relate to unfinished business of cleanup required before the script can be exited. This may include such things as paying checks, returning script props, etc. Finally, after everything has been completed (or occasionally even when the script hasn't been completed), there is an *Exit* scene (which Schank terms disenablement) where the person leaves the script context. These nine actions: Preparation, Entry, Precondition, Instrumental Precondition, Instrumental Initiation, Instrumental Actualization, Doing, Postcondition, and Exit, form the functional bases for generating the explanations used in Study III.

We used 10 scripts (Grocery store, Painting a room, Cashing a check at a bank, Serving wine, Building a campfire, Buying a car, Pitching a tent, Seeing a museum exhibit, Going to a ball game, Riding a roller coaster) in this study. Each script was presented as a vignette where a main character intended to perform the script but failed to do so. For each script, nine explanations, based on the nine generalized scenes presented above, were presented to account for why the script failed. Each was followed by a nine-point likelihood scale. Below is a sample script vignette, the explanations given and the script actions to which the explanations correspond.

There are two things to note about the previous example: In the introductory vignette, no specific mention is made about the character entering

TABLE 5.3
Bill went to the grocery store. He left without groceries.

Function	Script Action	Failure Explanation
Preparation	Make list	Bill forgot his grocery list
Entry	Enter	The store was closed
Precondition	Get shopping cart	Bill couldn't find a shopping cart
Instrumental Precondition	Get to food aisles	The aisles were too crowded
Instrumental Initiation	Select items	The store didn't have the items he wanted
Instrumental Actualization	Checkout items	The checkout lines were too long
Doing	Pay for items	The store wouldn't accept Bill's check
Postcondition	Bag items	On the way out, Bill's bags broke and he lost his groceries
Exit	Leave	The store closed before he could finish shopping

the context, lest this logically contradict some failure explanation based on entering or preparation. Second, the exit-based explanation (and sometimes also the postcondition-based explanation) is phrased so that its occurrence is before the doing action even though it typically occurs afterwards. This was done intentionally, since to say that the reason someone fails to bring his groceries home is because the store closed after he was through paying for them seems absurd. Rather it seems as though exits interrupt a script when they are forced to occur prematurely.

The explanations occurred in fixed randomly determined order for each story across subjects. Stories themselves were presented in a fixed randomly determined order across subjects. Subjects were 32 Yale undergraduates who were paid for their participation. They were run in small groups and the time for filling out the questionnaire was approximately 15 minutes.

Results

The mean likelihood ratings for each of the nine explanation categories across stories and subjects are presented below:

Preparation	4.23
Entry	5.35
Precondition	4.54
Instrumental Precondition	4.17
Instrumental Initiation	4.64
Instrumental Actualization	4.03
Doing	5.62
Postcondition	2.91
Exit	3.63

In general, Entry and Doing explanations received the highest ratings. A contrast of Doing versus the four explanations occurring after Entry and before doing yielded a significant effect, $F' = 24.85$, d.f. $= 1, 11, p < .001$. The contrast of Entry versus the same four explanations yielded an effect that approached significance, $F' = 4.64$, d.f. $= 1, 9, p < .10$.

This finding is consistent with the findings of Study I and Fig. 5.1, showing two favored locations of explanations. Events of the Entry and Doing types are perceived as highly central and they occur in the favored locations.

The other finding of note in this study regards explanations lying outside the main body of the script, namely Preparation, Postcondition, and Exit explanations. In general, as might be expected, scenes occurring after the doing scene were the least favored of all, in spite of our attempts to make them more plausible by presenting them as interruptions, $F' = 12.98$, d.f. $=$

1, 10, p < .01. However, Preparation explanations were not rated significantly higher than Postcondition or Exit explanations, $F' = 1.94$, n.s., suggesting that it is not the fact that Postconditions and Exits occur after the main part of the script that infirms their plausibility but rather that they occur outside of the main part.

DISCUSSION

We have been seeking the determinants of preference among different possible explanations for script failure. In the absence of contextual factors that might cue other alternatives, the most-favored explanations concern failure of the most-central actions. These in turn occur most often in particular script sequence positions, and serve particular script functions. These privileged functions we label Entry and Doing; the former occurs early in the script, and the latter near the end.

Entry presupposes the success of script entry arrangements. For scripts using public facilities, such as Shopping or Movie, these concern whether the facilities are available to the script actor. For scripts involving private object use, such as Barbecue or Fix Flat, "entry" depends on having the objects in question. All the scripts we used in our studies were of these two types. However, it is interesting to note that entry arrangements might be even more of an issue for private social scripts such as Business Appointment or Date. There, script entry may depend crucially on a favorable attitude toward the actor.

"Doing" presupposes the actor's willingness and the ability to carry out the action serving the main goal of the script. With scripts involving public facilities, factors of taste or style may control the Doing (for example, the actor may not like the food or the movie). For object-use scripts, rudimentary technique might be at issue (e.g., being able to barbecue a steak without burning it). For private scripts, the actor's social technique matters (e.g., closing the deal may depend on one's persuasive skill). Entry and Doing are the focal actions where something might go wrong. They are the prototypical problem points of scripts. They are the aspects an observer might query in wanting an account of a script performance ("Was the library open? Did you find the book?" "Did you get an appointment with Smedley? Did you close the deal?"). They are the actions most requiring anticipation and planning lest difficulties be encountered, and thus the most likely candidates for the explanation of script failures.

We cited early in this chapter an analysis by Lalljee and Abelson (1983) that there are at least six categories of explanation for why a seemingly intentional action might contrast with normal expectation: Goal absence, Goal conflict, Goal reversal, Goal satisfied, Plan failure, and Interference.

Our three studies focused mainly on the Plan failure category, using scripts as standardized plans with inexplicable failure. Our main finding can be construed as showing that the Plan failure category should be subdivided into Plan arrangement failure (problems of Entry) and Plan consummation failure (problems of Doing). This seems quite reasonable, even compelling. But what about the prioritization among these two categories and the other five? Are we simply left with the same general problem as before, but with seven categories rather than six?

No, we think that further progress can now be made more easily, by using the preference rating procedures of the present chapter, among other methods. Preference for plan failure explanations can be compared with other explanations. In fact, a modest beginning was made on that in Study I. The explanations given as sequential No. 1 in each script were generally of the Goal absence type, and explanations labeled "E" were generally of the Interference type. The relatively low ratings in the 0 condition given these alternatives relative to the main Plan failure options suggests that without special cueing these explanatory categories are prioritized below Plan failures. A larger set of systematic comparisons would be welcome among all seven categories (or however many categories there turn out to be after cleaning up ambiguities in the formulation of the present list).

Beyond simple extension of the present method to more failure categories, however, there is need for greater attention to contextual cueing. We have a hint of the importance of context in the 2 condition of Study I, where the style of posing the scenario enhanced preference for Entry failure explanations. Certainly there must be ways in which preference for any category of explanation can be enhanced by contextual hints. Without any such hints, the explainer really faces an underdefined, difficult problem in choosing an explanation. What form these cues might take for each category is important to determine. Indeed, our content-based orientation toward knowledge structures makes such an analysis imperative.

6

Goal-Related Inferences in Comprehension

Valerie Abbott
John B. Black

INTRODUCTION

Functional Motivation for the Use of World Knowledge in Comprehension

Memory and inferences derived from memory are essential to the study of language understanding. Even such low-level tasks as resolving ambiguity illustrate the critical role of memory in understanding. Because of this critical role, it seems desirable that the understanding process should, in turn, affect memory in a way that would increase its usefulness in successive understanding tasks. For this, it is critical that new information that is understood using some prior information in memory be related to that prior information so that it, in turn, can be used in the future.

Understanding, whether of stories or experiences, is necessarily based on what we already know of the world. Every new event is analyzed, not in isolation, but in the context surrounding its occurrence, in light of our memory of similar events and with respect to our semantic knowledge of such events. This knowledge may have been acquired through direct experience or through reading accounts of similar events. We use prior knowledge to connect related events, create explanations of what has occurred, make predictions about what might come next, ignore irrelevancies, interpret the motivations of characters, or identify with a character's affective state. The events in a story should be interconnected in a way that will permit later retrieval and use of the information contained therein to understand future events, and explanation of the events described. The formation of these kinds of connections depends upon the knowledge utilized in understanding the text.

The fact that new knowledge is linked to the memory structures that were used to understand it is indicated by the fact that people are reminded of old information while reading new information on the same subject. Schank (1980, 1982) has noted that people seem to recall, without conscious effort, previous experiences similar to the situation in which they find themselves, and use the memory of these experiences to guide their actions and expectations in the current situation (Schank, 1980, 1982). This cannot be explained simply by using the same memory to understand separate incidents entirely separately, leaving the memory unchanged. Quite apart from the inefficiency of this procedure, we tend to be surprised and annoyed when it is pointed out that we have had an experience that would have helped in interpreting a recent event. The usual situation is to automatically call to mind relevant prior experiences in the understanding process.

It is not necessary to have personal experiences of situations; people can utilize information they acquire in other ways to guide actions and expectations. Anyone who has had any dealings with policemen will know that it is unwise to drive too fast in their presence. However, even if one's only information about policemen came from stories about them, it would be easy to use knowledge gained from reading to guide one's actions in the same way. Essential to this ability is the capacity to recognize potentially useful information in text and to store it in a way that will facilitate retrieval in another situation. Useful information about policemen includes, for example, the idea that it is their job to enforce the law. They typically have the goal of thwarting people who do not obey the laws, and the plans they invoke to achieve this aim are often inconvenient for the lawbreaker.

The psychological literature has provided empirical evidence that people are able to use their knowledge of the world to impose organization on information they receive, and that this organization facilitates its retrieval at times when it might become useful. Johnson and Kieras (1983), for example, have shown that familiarity with the subject matter of a text predicts study time and recall of prose. A subject with prior knowledge of the subject matter of an experimental text is at an advantage in understanding the text. Prior knowledge, applied to experimental prose passages, can speed reading. It seems that in such cases, the subject does not have to construct new memory representations from scratch, but has merely to modify existing ones. Recall is also enhanced because information is not lost through failure to connect new knowledge appropriately into the memory representation. This might happen either because of a lack of appropriate knowledge on the part of the reader, or because his or her cognitive capacity was strained by the need to take in new information and organize it at the same time.

People's ability to skim text provides yet another reason to believe that understanding must proceed under the control of information stored in memory. Often, a large portion of the text is skipped without significant loss in understanding. Readers are looking for certain information in the text which their memory informs them will be important and thus they pass over the rest. This idea has been applied with some success in work in artificial intelligence. For example, FRUMP (DeJong, 1979) is a program that skims text on the basis of memory structures called sketchy scripts. It searches for concepts that indicate which script is appropriate. Once that has been accomplished, it searches only for details that will fill in what the selected script indicates needs to be known.

Another artificial-intelligence program, IPP (Lebowitz, 1980), takes advantage of FRUMP's skimming strategy in that it does not read every word of a story, but rather looks for words referring to interesting concepts. It then devotes considerable processing resources to the context surrounding these words. However, its primary theoretical interest is in the fact that it actually alters its memory structures on the basis of what it reads. If two stories are read about similar incidents containing some additional facts in common, IPP will store those facts with the memory structure used to understand both stories. Those facts will then be used in the understanding of further stories on the same subject.

The Study of Story Understanding

The study of story understanding in the psychological and artificial-intelligence literature has been extensive. The purpose of these studies has been to discover the memory structures and cognitive processes that enable linkage of text into a cohesive memory representation. However, the processes people use in understanding and remembering stories are likely to be the same as those used in understanding real-world experiences. The situations depicted in stories are similar to those encountered in everyday life. This is simply a statement of what stories are. They give us a glimpse of behavior in situations that the author believes will interest us. There may be a motive for choosing the particular piece of life we are shown in a story—to convey a moral, or to give insight into the internal processes that lead to overt behavior, or to give an understanding of a different time and place. However, the thought and behavior of characters in stories is intended to be believable to us as something that might indeed have happened. If this fails, the story fails. So stories present in words the same sorts of situations we could encounter in life. They allow us to vary our experience to include things we might not experience directly. It would thus be strange if we did not utilize the same knowledge and strategies (apart from the initial perception processes) to understand

and remember stories as we use in understanding events in everyday life.

We need to understand how the pieces of information contained in a story are connected in memory after the story has been understood, and what this implies about the kinds of knowledge structures used in understanding the story. The organization of mental representations of discourse has been the subject of several theories in the psychological and linguistic literature. Some theories relate only to the internal cohesion of individual sentences. These will not be considered here because, regardless of their virtues in understanding text, they are very unlikely to be generalizable to understanding events in the world, tied as they are to the linguistic context of the sentence. Of those theories that attempt to deal with larger portions of text, one group relies on bottom-up processes, utilizing only information that is contained within the text to explain cohesiveness or coherence. In predicting the organization of a mental representation of some text using these theories, it can be assumed that the reader needs access only to the meanings of words in the text or rules of grammar to connect parts of a text. Most linguistic theories of coherence fall into this group (e.g., Halliday & Hassan, 1976) as well as the theories of concept repetition (Kintsch, 1974; Kintsch & van Dijk, 1978). Another group of theories appeal to the top-down application of world knowledge people bring to the task of reading to account for cohesiveness in text. This knowledge may be in the form of associations acquired prior to reading the passage or to knowledge about the world that leads to the forming of connections between parts of the text. These theories may be further divided into those that are intended to encompass knowledge intended solely for understanding stories (e.g., Mandler & Johnson, 1977; Rumelhart, 1975a, 1975b) and those intended to have wider application (e.g., Schank & Abelson, 1977; Schank, 1982). In this chapter we provide evidence that, when the two are directly contrasted, the reader's use of world knowledge can be a more powerful factor in organizing mental representations of text than explicitly stated information processed without reference to world knowledge.

TYPES OF COHERENCE RELATIONS

Coherence Connections Not Requiring World Knowledge

The psychological study of the organization of mental representations of text is closely related to the study of text coherence by linguists. The coherence of a text is its tendency to seem to hang together as a whole rather than as a set of unrelated sentences. It is not farfetched to expect that those qualities that contribute to the coherence of a text would be those which assist in the organization of a mental representation of the text.

In the linguistic literature, characteristics of text such as anaphora and grammatical coordination have been explored in an effort to account for the fact that, intuitively, some texts seem more coherent, or organized, than others (Halliday & Hassan, 1976). When a pronoun is used to stand for a person or thing mentioned earlier in a text, the text tends to appear more coherent. Presumably, this aids the reader in constructing a mental representation of the text by signaling that a connection exists between the information grammatically connected to the pronoun and to its referent. Similarly, such grammatical constructions as conjunction can explicitly signal connections between parts of a text. Empirical support for some psychological role for such linguistic theories of coherence was found by deVilliers (1974), who showed that when linguistic signals encourage the formation of inferential links (by the use of definite rather than indefinite articles), the resulting text was better remembered.

Referential Coherence

One of the major proposals in the psychological literature concerned with the organization of mental representations of text has much in common with linguistic theories that depend on co-reference to establish coherence in text. A minimal requirement for the coherence of a text is that reference be made to the same objects, people, or concepts in the sentences of the text. Utilizing such repetition of concepts within a narrative to form the links in a connected representation of that narrative has been suggested by Kintsch (1974) and elaborated by Kintsch and van Dijk (1978). According to the concept (or argument) repetition hypothesis, a text is represented as a series of propositions, each proposition consisting of a single predicate and one or more concepts which serve as its arguments. When a newly parsed proposition shares an argument with a proposition which is already included in the representation of that text, the new proposition is linked to that prior proposition. Connections formed by concept repetition in a text, coupled with information about the order of the propositions in the text, can be used to form a hierarchical representation of its meaning (Kintsch, 1974). Experimental evidence that links have been formed between repetitions of the same concept within a text has been collected in several ways. False recognition of propositions not seen in a presented version of a text, better memory for propositions connected by links, and recognition speedup of connected propositions are all empirical evidence for the concept repetition hypothesis.

For example, recognition priming due to concept repetition has been observed by McKoon and Ratcliff (1980a). They gave subjects a story made up of simple sentences, some of which referred to the same objects, and some which did not. Those that did primed each other in a sentence-recognition task, even when they were separated in the text by other sentences.

Within Kintsch's theory, concepts repeated in later parts of a text are linked upward to their first mention. Thus, after a whole text has been processed, a hierarchy has been formed with early instances of a concept higher in the hierarchy than later instances (Kintsch, 1974). Items high in the hierarchy are better remembered and recognized more quickly than those lower in the hierarchy (McKoon, 1977). This indicates first, that a hierarchy based at least in part upon concept repetition has been formed, and second, that a search process starting at the top of the hierarchy is being utilized.

Connecting all the occurrences of a given concept in a text is a first step toward sensibly clustering the information in the text. All information concerning a given concept that is derived from the text would be available through access of the concept in the text representation. However, this organizational scheme alone does not seem sufficient. In a more recent elaboration of the argument-repetition hypothesis, Guindon and Kintsch (1984) have shown that the *macropropositions* of a text may be accorded a special place in the memory representation of the text. A macroproposition is a summary statement of the information in a text. It is not conceived of as being derived from the world knowledge of the reader, but rather as coming from the information within the text. After a reader has organized a text hierarchically, based upon the repetition of arguments, the representation is further processed to produce the macroproposition. Therefore, it is not a knowledge structure used in the comprehension process. It does not contribute to uncovering coherence in a text, but is rather a result of, and a means of representing, the coherence of a text.

Causal Knowledge

Referential links alone are not enough to make stories coherent. A text may have them in abundance and yet be incoherent. For example, consider the following text fragment:

> John's wife comes from Texas. The boss called John. John has blond hair.

Furthermore, even when there are no explicitly mentioned referential connections in a text, it may seem coherent. For example:

> The road was icy. The truck was speeding. Many people were injured in the accident.

What the second example seems to possess, and what the first lacks, is a sense that the propositions in the text are causally related. When knowledge of an episode is organized for later use, certain organizations are likely to be of more general use than others (Black, 1983). A representation organized according to the causal relations among events—i.e., a causal chain—is likely to be useful because it allows for prediction of later events from earlier ones. If a person correctly abstracts the causal connection between a vase's falling to the floor and the vase's then breaking, he can modify his future behavior with respect to vases. The causal relationships between events in a text serve to tie the representation of that text into a coherent whole rather than a series of unrelated statements. These relationships make the difference between reading a sequence of sentences and reading a story.

Schank (1975b) has proposed the use of causal chains in representing events. His theory of conceptual dependency embodies a system of representing simple actions, states, and the causal relations connecting them, that can be used in representing linguistic input. The complexity and shades of meaning in language are reduced to a few primitives which can be combined to represent the gist of a linguistic communication. This theory was successfully employed in the (Schank, 1975b) MARGIE program to produce paraphrases and make inferences from text by computer. There are many sources of empirical support for Schank's proposal that causal links confer coherence in a text. For example, it has been demonstrated that children show better memory for story episodes that are internally connected by causal relations than for episodes without these interconnections (Mandler & Johnson, 1977). Black and Bern (1981) have shown that sentences in narratives that are causally connected, as compared with those that simply form a temporally connected sequence, are better remembered, both in free recall and when cued by a related sentence. Causally connected sentences were also found clustered together in recall.

In some stories there is a causal chain leading from the beginning to the end of the story. But even in such cases there may be branches from these chains that do not lead to the final resolution of the story. Several experiments have established that items on the main causal chain are better remembered than those on side branches (Black & Bower, 1980).

Analogous to Haviland and Clark's (1974) work on referential cohesion, Haberlandt and Bingham (1978) have found that the presence of explicit causal relations between sentences in a text causes them to be read faster than sentence sets for which subjects must try to infer causal connections to make sense of the sets of sentences. It has also been shown that setting information given at the beginning of a story is much better remembered if it can be causally connected to actions later in the story (Black, 1980).

Coherence is maintained when there is a consistent point of view. Who the main character is, and the perspective of the narrator with respect to that character both help to determine that point of view. When there are inconsistencies in point of view, sentences take longer to read, stories are rated as less comprehensible, and are misremembered as having a consistent point of view. Point of view also influences which causal inferences are made. People identify with the main character and make inferences consistent with attribution theory on this basis (Bower, 1978; Black, 1982; Jones & Nisbett, 1971; Kelley, 1967; Owens, Bower, & Black, 1979).

Schematic Knowledge

In any given text, there are likely to be many sequences of causally connected events. Some will be related by simple physical causation, such as the example of the vase. Others are related by the motives of characters. It is unlikely that all should be considered equally in forming a representation of the text.

Some causally related knowledge may be clustered together into a schema (Bartlett, 1932; Rumelhart & Ortony, 1977). These schemas often contain specific content pertaining to a particular domain (Black, Wilkes-Gibbs, & Gibbs, 1981). Scripts, plans, and goals have been developed (Schank & Abelson, 1977) to embody the kind of world knowledge necessary to infer causal relationships between isolated facts in a text. A script is a schema for mundane knowledge about stereotyped sequences of actions. The specific actions are a part of this schema. A plan is a series of actions one would perform to attain a particular goal state. For standard goals, such as using an object, a set of common plans can be set out: approaching the object, gaining control over it, and using it. The power of conceptual dependency was increased greatly by the development of such knowledge structures. They allow access to information about possible problems which could arise in activities, enable explanation of that which has occurred, and give predictions about what is to come.

Scripts

Sometimes having recourse to knowledge of a standard sequence of events, the reasons for which we have already determined to our satisfaction, is useful in the understanding process. When a waitress comes to our table with food in a restaurant it is not necessary to figure out what caused her to arrive. It is sufficient to have knowledge of the usual sequence of events in restaurants to allow us to behave appropriately. This knowledge leaves more cognitive capacity available for use in more interesting tasks. It also allows a certain amount of ellipsis in textual accounts of situations that have a commonly recognized sequence of events. These standard sequences of events have been termed scripts (Schank & Abelson, 1977)

The SAM system (Cullingford, 1978) is a computer program designed to take advantage of the script concept in understanding stories. SAM matched input sentences (represented in conceptual dependency terms) to actions that could be expected to happen in the script. If some actions were left out of the account, SAM inferred them, filling them into its representation of the story it was reading. The result was a representation containing information read by the program and additional knowledge inferred from schematic world knowledge supplied to the program. The additional notion of using the script to assist in the understanding of the actual sentences of the text as each was read was not a part of the SAM system.

Evidence for the use of scripts in understanding stories was found by Bower, Black, and Turner (1979), who demonstrated with script-related stories that subjects showed confusions in memory between actions that were explicitly stated, and those that could be inferred based on the script. This confirms that inferences are made from world knowledge about stereotyped situations and that such inferences are included in text representations. Bower, et al., and Abbott, Black, and Smith (1985) also show that the need to infer script actions occurring between those explicitly mentioned in a text affects reading speed. The number of script actions omitted between stated script actions was directly related to reading times for the stated actions.

Story Grammars

One kind of knowledge specific to reading stories is knowledge of the structure of the story itself. This may not apply to sophisticated stories or longer texts such as novels. However, people do seem to have some expectations about the structure of simple folktale-type stories. The attempt to capture this knowledge is the motivation for story grammar theories (Mandler & Johnson, 1977; Rumelhart, 1975a, 1975b; Stein & Glenn, 1978; Thorndyke, 1977). Such theories attempt to specify a set of categories of items that may be included in stories and rules that specify their relationships. For example, a story has a setting, and a setting may consist of some combination of characters, location, and time. These part–whole relationships between story elements result in hierarchical representations for stories analyzed according to a story grammar. There is also some serial ordering specified by story grammars. For example, the setting may be required to come before the resolution.

Most of the stories analyzed using story grammars are goal-based. The main character is trying to achieve some result, and the story consists of attempts to reach the goal and reports of the results. In such grammars, a story is typically said to be composed of a setting, a theme, a plot, and a resolution. The setting may contain information about the time, place, or state of the world for a story. This can give the reader some idea of the appropriate knowledge structures to have ready to supply inferences. The theme is a statement of the main character's goal, combined optionally with events that set it up. The plot follows and consists of one or more episodes. Each episode consists of a goal, the plan of actions to attain it, and the result of the effort (Rumelhart, 1977; Thorndyke, 1977). The resolution reveals the success or failure of the main character to reach the main goal. Several experimental results have been adduced in support of story grammar theories. One very basic finding is that if story statements are ordered differently from the order specified by the story grammar, presumably making it more difficult to establish the links suggested by the story grammar, the resulting texts are less comprehensible, according to subject ratings (Thorndyke, 1977).

If the hierarchical structure suggested by the story grammars reflects the way stories are stored in memory, or at least the way they are retrieved, then statements corresponding to structures high in the hierarchy should be remembered better than those corresponding to those lower in the hierarchy. Such effects have, in fact, been observed (Black & Bower, 1980; Graesser, 1981; Rumelhart 1977; Thorndyke, 1977). Again, when subjects summarize a story, they are more likely to include higher-level statements (Rumelhart, 1977).

There is empirical evidence that the episodes defined in story grammars reflect real, psychological divisions in stories. Black and Bower (1979) showed that episodes as defined by story grammars are recalled independently. That is, varying the length of one episode affected recall of sentences in that episode, but not in other episodes. Mandler (1978) found that even when actions from one episode are interleaved with those of another within a story, the episodes are separated at recall. This demonstrates that interconnections exist between parts of an episode, either encoded in memory or formed by the retrieval process. Glenn (1978) found that when subjects elaborate elliptical stories (i.e., stories with much left implicit) at recall, short episodes are elaborated more than long episodes. Haberlandt, Berian, and Sanderson (1980) found that reading time increases for sentences at the beginning and end of episodes. This indicated that episodes are cognitively real units within stories.

The goal structure of a story has been shown to be an important factor contributing to the cohesiveness of the story. If goal information is placed late in a story or misplaced, memory is adversely affected (Thorndyke, 1977). If the goals in a story are obscure, as in a story from a different culture (Bartlett, 1932, Kintsch & Greene, 1978) summaries are inferior in quality. Mandler (1978) has shown that events related to the same subgoal tend to be recalled together, even when this does not reflect the ordering present in the text. Black and Bower (1979) have found evidence that the divisions between subgoals are also cognitively real. They showed that the number of events related to a given subgoal affects the probability of recalling any one of those events, whereas it does not affect the recall of events clustered under another subgoal.

While story grammars have been useful in predicting certain empirical results, it seems that in some cases there are processes at work in story understanding that they are not able to capture. Story structure as embodied in story grammars does not include many important features of stories. For example, the outcome of an episode may be either a success or failure in reaching a goal or subgoal. Story grammars do not distinguish these, since structurally they are equivalent. Nevertheless, there is evidence that people tend to remember the successful path to a main goal and forget attempts that failed (Black & Bower, 1980; Egan & Green, 1974; Reed & Johnson 1977). Or, to take another example, according to story grammars, setting information should be uniformly well remembered. However, there is evidence that this is only true if the setting information is causally linked to the action described in the rest of the story (Black & Bower, 1980).

In sum, while story structure can be captured to some extent by story grammars, the actual analysis of stories in terms of such structures probably takes advantage of some other knowledge of the world that readers have. The contribution that the structure makes beyond such world knowledge is specific to stories and is not generalizable to every day situations.

Motivational Inferences

The important contribution that story grammars have made to the study of understanding of text is to point out the importance of characters' goals and plans in the representation of text. In the same way as causal inferences, motivational inferences can be crucial in forming links between sentences in text. In many, if not most, cases, knowledge of physical causation and scripts is not sufficient to link together the events in a story so that it can be represented as a cohesive whole. A causal relationship may hold between two actions in a story even when the combination of actions is novel and unique. This occurs commonly when a character in the story has an intention and tries to fulfill it. In order to deal with these situations, representations of goals and plans have been developed for story understanding. Knowledge that people are likely to have certain classes of goals (such as preserving their own health, or obtaining the use of objects such as money), and that there are some standard classes of plans that they use to accomplish these goals (such as moving away from dangerous situations, approaching the object they want to use, or requesting the use of the object from another person if it is already being used), is crucial in making inferences which yield a connected text representation in memory.

Knowledge of the motivations, or goals, of characters includes knowledge of themes, goals, and plans, as discussed by Schank and Abelson (1977). One part of the information package associated with goals is the actual item, event, or state desired. If a state is desired, it is likely to be a change from the current state to a desired state. This type of information would be expressed in text by such sentences as "Joey wanted the blue truck," or "Jack thought that all reckless drivers should be in jail."

Another important piece of information associated with a goal is the source of the goal. Goal-source information can be contained in thematic expressions, such as "Jack was a policeman." A change of world state— either natural or due to action by another character—may also motivate a goal, as in "It started to rain." Passage of time can be a source of a goal since it can result in a change in personal state relevant to a homeostatic goal. This type of goal has been discussed by Wilensky (1978a). For example, the longer a character has been awake the more likely he will be to seek sleep. "Mary had been awake for two days," would be considered as a source of the goal "She wanted to go to sleep." One common goal source is a person schema, which might include role, theme, and personality variables discussed below under characters. This constitutes a linkage between goal and character representations, and raises the possibility that they may be parts of the same overriding structure.

The path which a character follows toward a goal in the presented text must also be included in the to-be-stored unit representing a goal. This can be a commonly recognized means for achieving a goal (as in "Joe was thirsty. He got a beer from the refrigerator."), or a plan which must be formulated to deal with a particular goal (for example, "Joan wanted some money. She put a gun in her purse and headed for a liquor store.")

A reason for expecting a prominent role for source–goal–plan units (henceforth SGP units) in the text understanding process is that the general knowledge readers have about goals can help them actively search for the appropriate information in a text to add to a known structure. This knowledge helps link information, which may be found widely separated in the text, and directs inferences to link the information in memory. SGP units also have a general utility in situations other than the understanding of a particular text. Organizational units such as these can facilitate the use of information in a text to understand events in the world. Understanding text in terms of goals can later help in formulating predictions about possible courses of behavior for other people who have the same general goal as the people described in the text. These units also provide information about possible goals of a person who shares a social role with a character in a story. Finally, observation of a person performing an action can permit inference of his or her goals through use of this kind of unit.

Graesser, Robertson, and Anderson (1981) have provided evidence that implicates some of the components of SGP units in people's representations of text. By asking subjects why events and actions in stories took place, they determined that what they termed "physical state nodes" (corresponding to some of the goal sources described above) are frequently stated as reasons for action or goal nodes (which correspond, in our terminology, to a combination of plans and desired objects, states, and events). However, while Graesser, et al., showed that these concepts are inferrable from each other at understanding time, they do not give direct evidence that they form interconnected units in the memory representation for stories. They also do not consider the possibility, raised by Kintsch's theory, that the mere repetition of concepts contributes to the connections people make.

Lichtenstein and Brewer (1980) investigated subjects' memory for common events, such as writing a letter, when the events were presented on videotape or as prose descriptions. By questioning subjects about the reasons for the actions that were included in the events, they were able to construct hierarchies in which the lower actions were performed "in order to" perform higher actions. Thus, tearing a stamp from a stamp booklet would be accomplished in order to put the stamp on an envelope, and so would be lower in the hierarchy. Although the actions themselves are more detailed, the relationship between them is conceptually similar to that between goals and plans as described above. Lichtenstein and Brewer found that items high in their hierarchies were better remembered than those lower in the hierarchies, and that overall, comparing items in the plan hierarchies with those not included, the items in the hierarchies were better recalled. Also, if an item was presented out of order with respect to its usual temporal position in the plan hierarchy, it was nevertheless recalled in its proper place. These results indicate that the presence of goals and plans of characters can be used to predict recall of events, and that the representations people use to recall these goals and plans permit reordering of input events in memory. Lichtenstein and Brewer, however, do not consider the contribution that knowledge of the sources of goals might make to the organization of memory representations, nor do they consider the possible contribution of argument repetition to their results.

More evidence for the use of plan and goal information in understanding can be found in an experiment by Seifert, Robertson, and Black (1982). Sentences of a text were presented one at a time and reading times were measured. When a goal or plan was stated, as opposed to being implicit, in one of the series of sentences, reading times were speeded for the succeeding sentence. It appears, therefore, that motivational inferences must be made, and that this takes time. This was also the finding in an experiment by Smith and Collins (1981). Subjects were given pairs of sentences which varied in the complexity of motivational inferences that would be needed to connect the sentences. Pairs that required complicated series of inferences took longer to read than those in which the connection was straightforward.

Experimental Study of Coherence Relations

There are several ways in which we might experimentally test for particular organizational units in text representation resulting from use of alternative information in understanding the text. The use of an organizational unit implies that inferential links have been formed between parts of the unit. Thus, they are, in some sense stored together. For example, it seems reasonable to expect that if schematic knowledge of the world is used in extracting information from text, pieces of information in the text that are related to the same schematic information should be stored together in memory. If, on the other hand, the text is processed in the way suggested by the argument repetition hypothesis, it should be possible to find links between parts of a text containing repeated concepts. In general, then, the connections between items in a unit should provide a common retrieval route passing through the various parts of the unit.

This general line of reasoning suggests the following specific experimental strategies in studying the memory representation of text:

1. Propositions which are linked into a common unit will tend to be output together in free recall. That is, they will tend to be more tightly clustered at recall than at presentation (Black & Bern, 1981). The conditional probability of recalling one item in the unit, given recall of another, will be greater than the same measure for items not so related (Abbott & Black, 1982).

2. There should be differences in cued recall between items which form a unit in memory and items which do not form such a group. It should be possible to increase probability of recall for a whole group with a common cue when items form a unit in memory. When there is no such unit, a cue will only be effective for one item.

3. Items will prime each other in a timed recognition test when they are parts of the same unit (McKoon & Ratcliff, 1980b). That is, when subjects are asked to say whether a sentence occurred in a paragraph they have read, they should be quicker to confirm a veridical item when the preceding item was from the same unit. This technique will, in addition, allow us to conclude that these connections are not an artifact of strategic processes at retrieval time, but are actually present in the text representation.

4. On a recognition test over a presented narrative, members of a unit not seen by a subject will be falsely recognized when other members of

the group were actually presented (Abbott & Black, 1980; Bower et al., 1979).

In an experiment investigating people's organization of text, we used conditional probability of recall as a means of evaluating the contribution of SGP units to people's organization of text, as compared with mere argument repetition. If SGP units are organizing subjects' memory, then the conditional probability of recalling a part of a SGP unit when another part has been recalled should be higher than a corresponding measure for other pairs of sentences related only by repetition of concepts.

Subjects read six short stories, each of which contained three sentences corresponding to each of two SGP units. The three sentences reflected, respectively, the source of a goal, the goal, and a path to the goal. The stories also included parallel three sentence sets containing repeated concepts. Subjects were then asked to recall, in writing, the stories they had read. We calculated the conditional probability that subjects recalled sentences corresponding to parts of the SGP sets, given that they had recalled at least one other sentence from the same set. The average conditional probability of recall for sentences in SGP sets was .82. The corresponding measure for argument-repetition sets in the same stories was .38, a large advantage for SGP sets.

Another way of determining whether items are linked in memory is to compare the distribution of recall to a binomial distribution. If items from a set are recalled independently, the cases in which a set is represented in recall by zero, one, two, or three of its constituent sentences should be distributed binomially with p equal to the overall probability of recall of sentences in the set. If, however, sentences from the sets are *not* recalled independently, that is, if recall of one tends to increase probability of recall of the others, then the observed frequencies should be higher than expected frequencies for recall of zero and of three items from the set. This tendency was seen in the SGP sets but not for the sets of sentences that simply contained repeated concepts. The distributions of expected and observed frequencies are presented in Table 6.1 below.

We confirmed these results using a *chi*-square test. The observed frequencies for concept repetition sets did not significantly differ from those expected from a binomial distribution, $X^2 = 3.53, p > .05$. The observed frequencies for SGP sets differed reliably ($X^2 = 33.44, p < .001$) from the frequencies expected if recall of separate items is independent.

It thus seems that part the process of recalling text involves the use of goals and plans. That is, upon recalling that a character had (for example) a particular goal, the subject might search memory for any plan that might serve that goal and for a reason the character might have had the goal. Such a strategy would be interesting of itself. However, it is important to

TABLE 6.1
Observed and Expected Frequencies of Recall
of Zero, One, Two, and Three Sentences
From Concept Repetition and SGP Sets

		Number of Sentences Recalled			
		0	1	2	3
Concept Repetition Sets	Expected	32.4	58.1	34.7	6.9
	Observed	27	68	29	7
SGP Sets	Expected	1.9	17.9	55.3	56.8
	Observed	9	15	40	68

investigate whether the results of the above study could be the result of such a strategy alone, or whether the actual structure of the memory representation incorporates information about characters' goals and plans.

In another experiment, therefore, we used a sentence-priming paradigm to assess which parts of the text are connected in subjects' memory representations. The advantages of this method for probing memory representations for text have been extensively reviewed by McKoon and Ratcliff (1980a). This paradigm is less sensitive to subjects' recall strategies than the free recall used above. If sentences constituting SGP units show interdependent recall but do not serve to prime each other in a timed recognition test, this indicates that these units are used in a retrieval plan, but do not directly serve to organize the representation of text (Anderson & Pichert, 1978). If the sentences do prime each other, then SGP units are implicated directly in the organization of these representations.

After reading stories similar to those used in the above experiment, subjects were asked to verify whether selected sentences actually appeared in the stories they read. If a sentence was preceded in the recognition task by another sentence close to it in the memory representation, it would be verified more quickly than if preceded by an unrelated sentence. The hypothesis that people organize representations of text according to conceptual units such as SGP units predicts that sentences from the same goal set should prime each other.

SGP unit sentences primed each other significantly, which indicates that sentences in SGP units are indeed stored together in memory. These results are summarized in Table 6.2 below.

SGP unit sentences primed each other significantly, ($F(1,32)$ = 4.19, p < .05), while concept repetition sentences did not, ($F(1,32)$ = 0.86, ns.), despite the repetition of words in the latter sets.

These results indicate that sentences in SGP units are indeed stored together in memory, and that this is not necessarily the case for sentences related only by concept repetition.

However, there were interesting differences in priming between different types of sentences in SGP sets. The strong priming effects seen for SGP units are localized in two out of the three types of priming pairs investigated. Plan sentences are strongly primed by both source sentences and by goal sentences. These results demonstrate that there are interconnections between the parts of SGP units in story representations, even when the retrieval strategies present in free recall are not relevant. Access to the sources of goals and to goals themselves provides access to the plans that are connected to them.

However, we found that goal sentences are not primed by source sentences. One would think that plans ought to be connected to sources through the relevant goal. It is much easier to understand why a policeman calls a paddywagon instead of just issuing a ticket to a bad driver if you understand that this policeman especially wants to get reckless drivers off the roads. The results of this priming study, though, seem to indicate that recognition of a source statement provides access to the plan statement directly without reference to the intervening goal. We could simply accept this, and conclude that, in subjects' representations of narratives, sources are directly connected to plans, but only indirectly connected to the goals that give rise to such plans.

TABLE 6.2
Recognition Times for Items From Concept Repetition and SGP Sets

Unit Type	Primed	Unprimed	Difference
SGP	1846	1960	114 msec
Concept Repetition	2022	2066	44 msec

Another explanation for these results is possible, however. Subjects may be able to focus on selected parts of the information they have available at any given time. If, when they recognize the source statements, they have access to the part of their memory representation for the story which contains information about the relevant goal and plan, they can choose to focus only on the plan. They might do this because, in narratives, the story line generally refers to a series of events. Plan statements refer to events, while source and goal statements refer more to states. Given a choice of whether to maintain a state or event in memory, it is likely that subjects will regularly choose the event (Seifert, Robertson, & Black, 1985). Much of the processing people do involves understanding and prediction of events. A process that directed attention preferentially to events could be so general in application that its use would be the rule rather than the exception. A strategic process of this sort could be robust enough to appear even in a priming paradigm because of its general usefulness.

Whatever the proper interpretation of this particular aspect of our results, however, these experiments clearly show that connections exist in memory between sentences relating to the same schematic unit based on goals, sources, and plans. Information related to a character's intentions is abstracted from text by readers and forms an organizational unit in the representation of the text in their memory. Furthermore, these experiments provide evidence that the connections between sentences relating to the same SGP unit are not simply a result of retrieval strategies, but actually reflect connections present in the memory representation of the text.

FUTURE DIRECTIONS FOR RESEARCH

Trying to pin down exactly when the inferences are drawn that establish this type of connection between parts of text is difficult. It is unrealistic to expect that knowledge of such things as stereotyped action sequences and goals is applied only after a sentence has been "understood." The words used in a text are often ambiguous when seen in isolation, yet this ambiguity can frequently be resolved by referring to a higher-order knowledge structure. For example, the word "scale" has different meanings in the sentences "Mary choked on a scale as she ate her fish at Antoine's." and "The grocer placed the grapes on the scale." While all possible definitions of a word may be accessed for a brief period, the appropriate definition seems to be selected long before a sentence has been read in its entirety (Swinney, 1979). Moreover, it is not likely that the type of connections seen above are developed only after the whole text has been read. That is, it does not seem that the available memories employed in understanding text are not used in constructing memory representations until sometime after the text has been read. However, the investigations above have only addressed these points indirectly by eliminating the retrieval process as the sole source of linkage among sources, goals, and plans. The actual time course of making the necessary inferences and including them in memory representations has not been explored.

Graesser, Robertson, and Clark (in press) have suggested a method for determining when certain inferences are incorporated in a text representation by asking questions after various parts of a text have been read. McKoon and Ratcliff (1982) have also suggested the method of probing particular words at various points in the reading of a narrative to discover what concepts are active at times when inferences might be made. Either of these methods might be used to good effect with the above materials.

If clusters are formed by the preceding mechanisms in a story representation, these clusters may well be formed into larger clusters by other mechanisms. Schank (1982) proposes such a unit, the Thematic Organization Point (or TOP), for use in understanding stories. TOPs are patterns of goals and plans that remain consistent across contexts, and as such might serve to link parts of SGP units into larger complexes. TOPs are concerned with types of goal relationships (such as being in conflict or being mutually held by two agents), and the opportunities and difficulties often encountered in pursuing goals, given the existence of such relationships, as well as with the plans suggested by the combination of goal relationship and condition of opportunity or difficulty. For example, in pursuing a goal in concert with another person, a common difficulty results from the coplanners being periodically unaware of each other's progress in pursuing the goal. A plan to deal with this problem is to frequently inform the coplanner of one's progress. (See Chapter 8 in this volume for a more extensive treatment of TOPs and a related concept, Thematic Abstraction Units [TAUs].)

Many stories have a goal–subgoal structure in which the successful accomplishment of the top-level goal depends on a successful outcome of the subgoal. Thus, goals can form a hierarchy. This also might be a way of coordinating several SGP units into a larger structure. In stories structured this way, more subordinate goals are not remembered as well as top-level goals (Black & Bower, 1980; Graesser, 1981; Thorndyke, 1977). These structures seem to be psychologically real because subjects seem to be using them in recall. If the same structure is repeated with different content in two stories, subjects' memory for the structure of the stories is enhanced, although they are sometimes confused about the content (Thorndyke & Hayes-Roth, 1979). If the linkages from goal to subgoal help in retrieval, creating these links should increase recall, and this in fact has been found (Owens et al., 1979).

In sum, the study of SGP units has been fruitful in exploring the type of memory structures used in understanding text. Characters' goals, plans to reach the goals, and reasons for goals seem to form linked sets in the memory representations of text. It remains to be seen exactly when the necessary linking inferences are made and whether the SGP units can be combined into still larger units.

OTHER KNOWLEDGE STRUCTURES

In the literature on knowledge structures, there has been a considerable emphasis upon scripts, and to a lesser extent on plans. These structures are relatively easy to articulate, and are readily amenable to experimental exploration. Other structures have received far less attention, because of difficulties of definition and design. In the four chapters of this section, we try to narrow the gap with several forays into relatively unexplored knowledge-structure territory. In the course of the ventures, novel areas of application of knowledge-structure theory are opened.

In chapter 7, Scott Robertson considers the phenomenon of the misleading question, in which memory for events is altered via presuppositions slipped into the question. He analyzes the influence of the content of what is to be altered, and in order to do this, he goes back to the most basic level of mental representations— conceptual dependency. He finds that there are systematic variations in the vulnerability of different conceptual structures to the effects of misleading questions.

Chapter 8, by Colleen Seifert, Robert Abelson, and Gail McKoon, explores a type of higher-level knowledge structure, the TAU, or Thematic Abstraction Unit. These units encode ways in which plans can go wrong, and are often embodied in proverbs. The authors use

TAUs in their experimental materials for testing a hypothesis by Schank (1982) concerning the way in which abstract features of an experience can remind an individual of a related experience. It is found that such abstract remindings do not seem to occur automatically, but can be elicited if they serve special purposes for the individual.

In chapter 9, Dana Kay and John Black review several theories of how people manage to extract the essence of text passages in order to create short summaries. They find that a type of knowledge structure called the "plot unit" is very useful in the summarization process. However, plot units alone do not account for all the experimental findings, and the authors formulate the view that summarization is "explanation driven." That is, summarizations partake of whatever strategies the individual needs to explain the text to self and others. From an analysis of summaries of stories in the *Wall Street Journal,* they conclude that experts and novices differ in the details of their summarization strategies, though both are explanation driven.

The concern of chapter 10 is with the structure of persuasive arguments in social and political contexts. Stuart McGuigan and John Black identify three qualitatively different types of structure: analogical, causal, and categorical. They embody these types in a computer program called MAGAC for understanding persuasive arguments, and they apply the lessons learned from MAGAC to an experiment on the relationships between the convincingness of arguments and their recallability.

7 Conceptual Structure, Question-Answering Processes, and the Effects of Misleading Questions

Scott P. Robertson

INTRODUCTION

Background: Misleading Question Research

An impressive body of research has developed concerning the effect of misleading information on memory. Elizabeth Loftus and her colleagues (Loftus, 1975, 1979, 1981; Loftus & Green, 1980; Loftus, Miller, & Burns, 1978; Loftus & Palmer, 1974) have shown time and again that misleading questions and other types of misleading "postevent" information can alter memory for a prior event.

For example, in one study (Loftus, 1975), subjects viewed a slide sequence depicting a traffic accident. After viewing the slide sequence, subjects were asked one of two questions, "Did another car pass the red car while it was stopped at the stop sign?" or "Did another car pass the red car while it was stopped at the yield sign?". Half of the subjects in each question group saw a slide sequence with a stop sign, and half saw a slide sequence with a yield sign. When the content of the question presupposed false information about the sign (both the stop and yield signs), as many as 80% of subjects "recognized" the wrong sign on a later test. This was far above the error rates for subjects who received a nonmisleading question and for subjects who received no postevent information.

Recently, attention in this area has focused on the question of what exactly is happening to memory when misleading information is introduced.

145

A central question is whether the original memory trace is altered by new information or whether the new information coexists with the old information but is more retrievable (Bekerian & Bowers, 1983; Christiaansen & Ochalek, 1983; Green, Flynn, & Loftus, 1982). Experiments are now appearing which attempt to show no memory impairment for the original information, usually by positing methodological flaws in the original experiments (McCloskey & Zaragoza, 1985).

In all of these studies, the researchers observed the behavior of a single memory or a set of memories taken as a group. The memory event is never considered to be a variable itself, although there is reason to believe that different types of memories may behave differently. Just as language items are now routinely considered to be random variables in well-designed experiments (Clark, 1973), it may be time to consider different types of memories and different kinds of memory-altering information in studies of memory alteration. To do this it will be necessary to describe how postevent information interacts with memory structures and to specify what pre-existing knowledge is relevant to memory alteration and to the question-answering process. In this chapter, several experiments on misleading questions that have been conducted in the Yale Cognitive Science Program will be reexamined in order to suggest some of the relevant conceptual variables.

The experiments concerned how information in questions interacts with knowledge structures in memory. We ask specifically whether the type of knowledge structure in which information is embedded makes a difference in terms of alterability. Our conclusion is that it does. Our hypotheses have been guided by the principles of memory structure and function and the question-answering procedures described by members of the Yale AI project (especially Dyer, 1983; Kolodner, 1983; Lehnert, 1978; Schank, 1972, 1973, 1975c; Schank & Abelson, 1977). In this chapter, an overview of what we have learned from the misleading-questions experiments will be presented and, more importantly, our results will be placed in a broader theoretical framework based upon new analyses of the individual memory items that were used in each experiment. Hopefully, these analyses will inform further research on the topic of misleading postevent information.

As background to discussion of the experiments, it is important to review two areas of theory. The first is a theory about how concepts are represented in memory. The structure of concepts in memory and the processes that operate on them during comprehension are relevant to memory alteration. The second important area of theory is question answering. The procedures for matching concepts in a question to concepts in memory and the heuristics for answering questions are relevant to the kind of memory alteration that results from misleading questions.

Conceptual Structure of Simple Concepts

This book contains descriptions of psychological work related to knowledge structures. Most of the knowledge structures examined in this book are global, such as scripts, plans, and themes. In this chapter we will look at a more basic level of conceptual representation, simple ideas or propositions. This level is appropriate for examining the effects of misleading questions, which involve the alteration of the simple concept contained in a question presupposition.

A simple concept consists of a single predicate, which could be a relation ("the book is green"), a motivated action ("John went outside"), physical event ("the car crashed"), or change of state ("the weather grew cold"). Together with the predicate, a proposition contains arguments which specify related nominal concepts that are associated with the predicate. For example, the sentence "Mary adjusted the lamps" contains a single predicate, *adjusting,* and two arguments: the actor, *Mary,* and the object, *lamps.* The action of adjusting always has an actor argument and an object argument. A more complex predicate, like *give,* has more arguments. In the case of *give,* there is always an actor, an object, and a recipient of the object. Thus, in "Mary gave John a dollar," the actor is *Mary,* the object is *dollar,* and the recipient is *John.*

A sentence may be represented by several connected propositions. For example, "Mary adjusted the hanging lamps" contains two propositions. The first is the adjustment proposition just described. The second is the descriptor *hanging* that specifies how the lamps are related to the ceiling (the fact that the lamps are hanging from the *ceiling* is an inference, a point we will discuss later). We can say that this sentence contains the following two propositions: (ADJUST, MARY, LAMPS) and (HANGING, LAMPS, from CEILING). Kintsch & Keenan (1973) have shown that the number of propositions into which a sentence can be decomposed accurately predicts reading time.

Schank (1972, 1973, 1975c), expanding on the linguistic theory of Fillmore (1968), pointed out that there may be a small number of conceptual frames that accommodate the large number of predicates in a language. It is common for someone to misremember a sentence like "Mary handed John a dollar" as "Mary gave John a dollar." The sentences are "conceptually synonymous," and can be represented by the same conceptual frame. In fact, there is a large class of conceptually synonymous sentences in which only instruments or methods vary (e.g., "Mary mailed John a dollar," "Mary sent John a dollar," "Mary left John a dollar," etc.). To account for this, Schank has proposed "conceptual dependency theory" (CD) as a way of representing basic concepts (Schank, 1973, 1975c). In this chapter, we will use Schank's system because we are more familiar with it than with alternatives; however, our conclusions do not critically hinge on this choice.

Conceptual Dependency Theory

CD theory holds that predicates of a language reduce to a small set of *conceptual primitives.* A conceptual primitive is a generic ACT (that corresponds to the predicate) with a set of arguments, also called *slots.* For example, all verbs of physical movement may be represented by the CD ACT: PTRANS. PTRANS has a conceptual frame with four slots. The CD frame for PTRANS appears at the top of Fig. 7.1. The frame specifies that PTRANS always involves an actor causing the movement, a physical or human object being moved, an original location of the object called the *source,* and a final location of the object called the *destination.* The CD representation for "Mary put the book on the table" is shown in the bottom of Fig. 7.1.

The importance of CD frames is that they specify a set of concepts and relations that must be present when an ACT is specified. This allows for the production of local inferences. In the case above, that the book was originally in Mary's hands (POSS-BY is a relation indicating possession) is an inference made in order to fill the source slot in the case frame. Fig. 7.2 shows eight CD ACTs that will be important when we examine the misleading question data. Along with each ACT are examples of verbs that are represented by the ACT and its CD frame.

In addition to ACTs, conceptual dependency theory provides a representational framework for other types of relations. Changes of state, for example, are relations that may not involve an ACT. As an example, consider the sentence "It got cooler." This refers to a change of state on the dimension of temperature. Other dimensions in which state changes occur

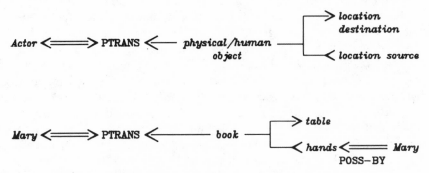

FIG. 7.1. The PTRANS CD frame and a CD representation of the sentence "Mary put the book down."

are loudness, brightness, height, etc. In CD notation, these state changes are indicated by a relation with three slots: the "object" that is affected by the change, the "initial value" of the state, and the "final value" of the state. These relations are shown in the top part of Figure 7.3, and the CD representations of several state changes are shown below it.

There are also relations that link a concept with a modifier. The POSS-BY relation shown in Figure 7.1 is one such modifying relation. Another common modifying relation is physical location, LOC. Modifying relations can be attached to the token in any slot of a CD frame.

Finally, simple concepts are not found in isolation from each other. Concepts are related to each other in regular ways (Graesser, 1981; Graesser & Clark, 1985). The most common relations are those between ACTs, especially cause, enable, reason, and instrument relations. These links between ACTs will become clearer when CD representations are detailed later in this chapter.

Conceptual Structures and Question-answering Processes

A question consists of two parts. One part, the question particle, provides information about *how* to answer a question. This part of a question is typically signaled by words like *why, when, where,* etc. A *why* question requires that a reason or goal be provided as an answer, a *when* question requires that a time be provided as an answer, and so on. The second part of a question provides the conceptual component of the question and identifies the memory *structure* that will be central to the answering process. So, the question "Why did you go to the store?" tells question-answerers that they should check memory for a recent or otherwise significant time that they went to the store, and then search reason links in memory, or create a reason, that can be communicated as an answer to the question.

Question parsing involves decomposition of the question into a CD frame, called the "question concept" by Lehnert (1978). It provides the basis for a search of memory. The question concept (QC) contains the presupposed information that is used to match concepts in memory. In the question "Why did Mary put the book on the table?", for example, the QC is the PTRANS frame shown in the bottom part of Figure 7.1. This frame is used to match the PTRANS in memory that corresponds to the event questioned.

Retrieval of the concept that matches the QC is complex. In initial phases of search, global knowledge structures like scripts, plans, and themes are used to identify the portion of a memory representation that is most likely to contain the concept (Dyer, 1983; Goldman, 1985; Kemper, Estill,

ATTEND: *Use a sense to obtain information.*
Examples: *Look at, listen to, feel.*
CD Frame:

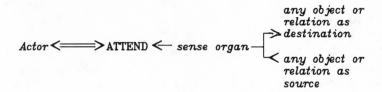

                                        any object or
                                        relation as
                                      ┌─▷ *destination*
  Actor ⟺ ATTEND ⟵ *sense organ* ┤
                                      └─◁ *any object or*
                                        relation as
                                        source

ATRANS: *Transfer of possession.*
Examples: *Give, hand to, leave for.*
CD Frame:

                                            ┌─▷ *human/location*
                                            │   *destination*
  Actor ⟺ ATRANS ⟵ *physical object* ┤
                                            └─◁ *human/location*
                                                source

GRASP: *Hold as an instrumental act of ATRANS or PTRANS.*
Examples: *Hold, grasp, grab.*
CD Frame:

  Actor ⟺ GRASP ⟵ *physical object*

INGEST: *Take into the body.*
Examples: *Eat, swallow, breathe.*
CD Frame:

  Actor ⟺ INGEST ⟵ *food object*

FIG. 7.2. Some conceptual dependency ACTs and CD frames.

Otalvaro, & Schadler, 1985; Kolodner, 1983; Reiser, Black, & Abelson, 1985; Reiser, Chapter 4, this volume). A more local search among connected CD representations is carried out after the relevant global portion of memory has been identified.

After a concept corresponding to the QC is located in memory, question-answering processes begin. The question-answering process is determined by the question type (Galambos & Black, 1985; Graesser & Murachver,

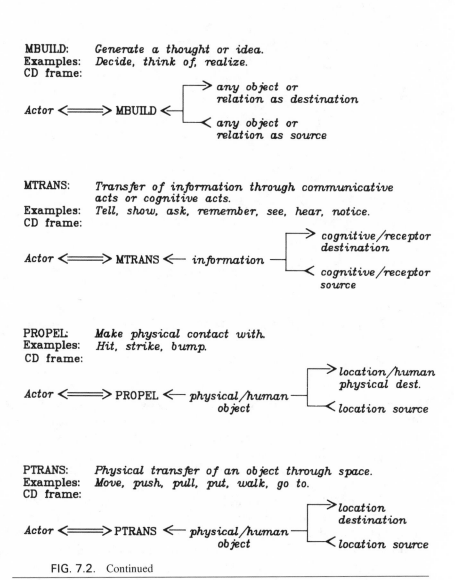

MBUILD: *Generate a thought or idea.*
Examples: *Decide, think of, realize.*
CD frame:

Actor <===> MBUILD <
→ *any object or relation as destination*
< *any object or relation as source*

MTRANS: *Transfer of information through communicative acts or cognitive acts.*
Examples: *Tell, show, ask, remember, see, hear, notice.*
CD frame:

Actor <===> MTRANS <— *information* —
→ *cognitive/receptor destination*
< *cognitive/receptor source*

PROPEL: *Make physical contact with.*
Examples: *Hit, strike, bump.*
CD frame:

Actor <===> PROPEL <— *physical/human object* —
→ *location/human physical dest.*
< *location source*

PTRANS: *Physical transfer of an object through space.*
Examples: *Move, push, pull, put, walk, go to.*
CD frame:

Actor <===> PTRANS <— *physical/human object* —
→ *location destination*
< *location source*

FIG. 7.2. Continued

1985; Lehnert, 1978; Murachver, Murray, & Graesser, 1985; Singer, 1985). A why-question requires traversal of causal or reason links from the question concept. A how-question might require a search for instrument links from the question concept. A where-question might require search of *location* links from the matched QC or inspection of the source and destination slots of an ACT. In all of these cases, it is necessary to locate the ACT and search links from the ACT. For other questions, slots in CD

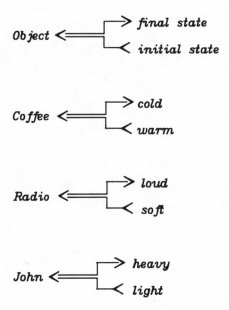

FIG. 7.3.   A CD frame for change of state relations, and examples of the concepts "the coffee got cold," "the radio was turned up," and "John gained weight."

frames must be examined. For example, to answer the question "Was it Mary's book that was set on the table?", the question answerer must first find the correct PTRANS and then search for POSS-BY relations from the "book" token in the object slot.

This view of memory structure and Q/A procedures suggests that question comprehension and answering involve many different kinds of knowledge structures. On this view, widespread effects on memory would be expected from the question-answering process, especially if the question contains misleading information. However, these effects would not be expected to be uniform over all types of questions and in different memory contexts. For example, in our experiments we have shown that memory about static information (physical states, locations, etc.) is easier to alter than memory about action information (*changes* in state). Also, we have found evidence for indirect effects on information that is inferentially linked to directly altered information, especially if it is linked via causal networks. In the next section this work will be reviewed and analyzed in more detail with explicit attention to conceptual processes.

MISLEADING QUESTION EXPERIMENTS

A Study of Importance

In an early study conducted on misleading questions, we attempted to show that the importance of the item being manipulated made a difference in alterability. We designed a simple experiment involving two stories, the "Vacation" story and the "Divorce" story. Within each story was embedded an item to be altered by a misleading question. Each item to be altered had two forms. In one form, the consequences of the alteration were significant, whereas the consequences of the unaltered version were not. In the other form, the altered consequences were less severe than the unaltered ones.

In the less important version of the Vacation story, a character (Brian) stops quickly at a stop sign and skids up to the intersection. In the important version of the Vacation story, the character originally skids *through* the intersection. This item is referred to as the "skid item." Subjects received one of three versions of a question about the skid item after reading the story. The question either confirmed the event as it happened, was neutral, or was misleading. For the skid item the question was "How fast was Brian going when he slid *through/at/up to* the intersection?". The "at" version was neutral. The "through" and "up to" versions were confirming or misleading depending on the version of the Vacation story that a subject read.

In the less-important version of the Divorce story, a character (again Brian) spills water on a friend's (Scott) clothes. In the more-important version of the Divorce story, Brian spills wine on Scott's clothes. This item is referred to as the "spill item." The question presented after the story asked "When did Brian spill his *wine/drink/water* on Scott?". The "drink" version of the question was neutral. The "water" and "wine" versions were confirming or misleading, depending on the version of the Divorce story that a subject read.

Subjects and Design.   Sixty-two subjects participated in the experiment. The subjects read either the Vacation or Divorce story. Half of the subjects read the version of the story with the more significant item and half read the version with the less-significant item. In a set of questions presented after the story, each subject answered either the misleading, neutral, or confirming question about the critical item. Finally, the subjects were given a recognition test which contained (among other things) a version of the critical item that was false with regard to the story (but which was consistent with the misleading question). They rated the item on a 1–7 scale, where 7 meant that the item "definitely was not in the story," 4 meant "unsure," and 1 meant that the item "definitely was in the story."

TABLE 7.1
Mean Recognition Scores for Story Items in the Importance Study Under Different
Question Conditions

Item	Importance	Confirm	Neutral	Mislead	Mean
SKID	Important	6.25	4.33	2.83	4.25
	Not Important	3.33	1.25	1.80	2.27
	Mean	4.50	3.10	2.36	3.29
SPILL	Important	7.00	5.60	4.80	5.71
	Not Important	6.50	4.40	3.40	4.88
	Mean	6.70	5.00	4.10	5.27

Results. The results, shown separately for each story, appear in Table 7.1 (there was some attrition, resulting in unequal n's). Ratings above 4 were always correct rejections since the recognition item was never really in the story. The mean recognition scores were analyzed using an unweighted means analysis of variance on three factors: Question Type (Confirming, Neutral, or Misleading), Importance (Not Important, Important), and Item (Skid, Spill).

There was a strong effect of the misleading question manipulation, $F(2,49) = 8.76$, $p < .01$, with the full effect explained by a linear trend, F.linear$(1,49) = 13.44$, $p < .001$ (nonsignificant residual). The mean recognition score was lowest in the misleading question condition, 3.19, indicating a tendency toward incorrect acceptance of the misleading presupposition; it was highest in the confirming presupposition condition, 5.60, indicating correct rejection; and it was intermediate in the neutral question condition, 4.05.

There was also an effect of importance, with the more important versions of the item leading to higher recognition scores (i.e., correct rejections) than the less important versions, $F(1,49) = 8.76$, $p < .01$. Mean recognition scores were 4.93 and 3.62 for the more and less important versions respectively. Finally, there was a main effect of item, $F(1,49) = 13.44$, $p < .001$, with the skid item showing a lower mean recognition score than the spill item, 3.29 and 5.27 respectively.

Of course, to confirm our hypothesis that importance would affect alterability, we needed to show an interaction between importance and question condition—and we failed on this count. However, examination of the means in Table 7.1 suggests that there were unanticipated effects from other sources, namely the item variable. In fact, the item effect was the strongest effect. While we showed that it was possible to lower subjects' recognition ratings when they received a misleading question, the mean rating in the spill item and the initially important version of the skid item dropped from certain rejection only into the "Unsure" range. In the less-important version of the skid item, subjects were never very sure about the recognition item, even when they answered a confirming question, and the misleading question caused them to accept the incorrect presupposition. How can we account for these item differences?

Conceptual Representation of the Items.   Fig. 7.4 shows a CD representation of the skid item and Fig. 7.5 shows a CD representation of the spill item. The central ACTs for both concepts are indicated by asterisks (both are PTRANS), and connected information from the stories is indicated. (More story information was connected to the spill item than the skid item,

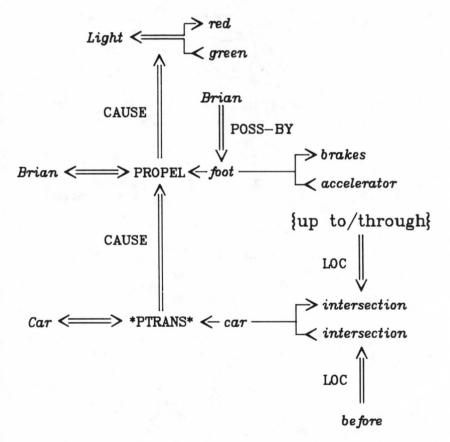

FIG. 7.4.   A CD representation of the "skid item" from the importance experiment.

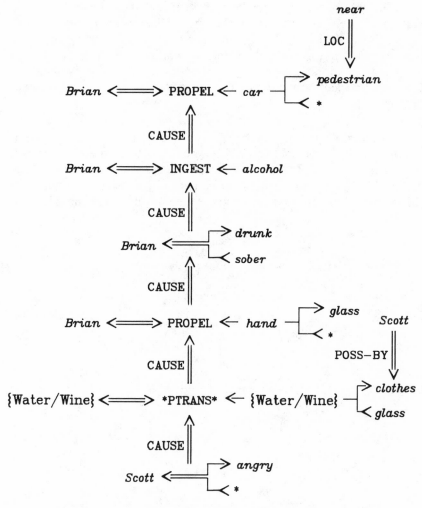

FIG. 7.5.   A CD representation of the "spill item."

as will be explained.) The portions of the CD representations that should have been affected by the misleading questions are indicated in brackets. Fig. 7.4 indicates that the traffic light changed state from green to red, causing Brian to hit the brakes (the PROPEL), causing the car to skid (up to/through) the intersection (the PTRANS). Fig. 7.5 indicates that Brian's near-miss of a pedestrian (the first PROPEL) caused him to drink (the INGEST), causing a change of state from sober to drunk, causing Brian to bump a wine glass (the second PROPEL), causing the wine to spill onto Scott's clothes (the PTRANS).

When answering the misleading questions, subjects must first extract the question concepts. For the skid item, the question "How fast was Brian going when he slid (up to/through) the intersection?" presupposes the *PTRANS* concept shown in Fig. 7.4. Searching for this concept involves, first, a search for the "driving scene." Once the set of ACTs associated with this part of the story is located, each ACT can be compared with the question concept (QC) by traversing causal and other links between ACTs until the specified *PTRANS* is found. A match is found when the QC and CD frames match on the ACT and important slots (i.e., actor and object, sometimes source and destination). At this point procedures for answering "How fast?" are employed. These might involve inspecting the "car" token in the *PTRANS* object slot, or making an inference from the final destination of the car, as specified in the destination slot of the *PTRANS*.

Similar processes occur in response to the question "When did Brian spill the water/wine on Scott?". A drinking scene is located, using knowledge structures that are superordinate to the CD representations. Next, ACTs are searched in this scene until the *PTRANS* shown in Fig. 7.5 is located (by matching the QC with the CD frame). To answer the question, a time marker on the CD might be searched for, or causal links might be used for an answer relative to other ACTs (i.e., "Before Scott got mad," "After Brian almost hit a pedestrian.").

When we look at the conceptual-dependency representations of these items, we see that the parts of the two representations affected by the misleading question manipulation are very different. Both representations involve the physical transfer (PTRANS) of an object from one location to another. In one case (skid), a modifier on the token in the "destination" slot is affected by the misleading question. In the other case (spill), the object slot of the PTRANS is affected. The spill item was more confidently correctly rejected than the skid item. There are several possible explanations for this. One involves the nature of the memory representation. Is it harder to alter the object slot of a conceptualization than it is to alter a slot modifier? Later analyses will suggest that this is so.

A second explanation for the item effect involves the critical ACT's relations with the other ACTs. The skid item was a relatively isolated event in the chain of actions that compose the story. Just before the incident, the traffic light turned red and the brakes were applied quickly. After the event, the story states that "Luckily, everything was OK and Brian drove on. He was more careful the rest of the way." There are no consequences of the critical ACT, and the connected ACTs do not seem anomalous under different alterations of the destination modifier.

Contrast this with the ACT context for the spill item. This item also had a causal antecedent, that the main character had too much to drink. This, in turn, was preceded by a near-accident. After this, the character on whom the wine/water was spilled is described as "annoyed," and the incident leads to a drive home for a change of clothes. The critical item is linked into a larger conceptual chain by several causal links. Also, the change in the object slot of the PTRANS from wine to water might have made the remainder of the conceptualization anomalous. Why would a spilled glass of water lead to such an extreme reaction and require a change of clothes? Indeed, the poor recognition of the (less-important) water version of this item suggests that when water was in the object slot the subjects were unsure about the entire conceptualization. When the misleading question provided "wine" for the object slot, the conceptualization made sense and a strong effect of the misleading question was, indeed, found in this condition.

Conclusions.   There are at least three conclusions to be drawn at this point. First, not all alterations are the same when detailed representations are being considered. While changing *water* to *wine,* or skidding *through* instead of *up to,* may seem like similar types of alterations, they involve very different portions of the isolated CD representations. Second, the conceptual context may play a role. In one case the item was connected in a more complex manner to other conceptualizations. In the other it was fairly isolated. Finally, changes in a conceptualization may render a previously sensible conceptualization anomalous, or an anomalous conceptualization sensible, in its conceptual context. In the next section we will explore these ideas more thoroughly.

A Study of States and Actions

After the importance study, we felt that we should always conduct misleading-question experiments using many different items. These items should differ on some dimension that is relevant to conceptual representation. In the rest of our experiments, we decided that the factor of interest in studying alterability of information in memory is the structure of the information in memory.

The next experiment that we conducted in this area (Lehnert, Robertson, & Black, 1984) focused on two issues. First, is state information more easily altered than action information? And, second, can misleading effects propagate through memory to affect conceptually linked items? Our choice of states versus actions as a criterion for distinguishing types of information in memory was based on several other studies of memory and comprehension. Several studies have demonstrated that actions are remembered better than states in both recall and recognition tasks (Black, 1980; Graesser, Robertson, Lovelace, & Swinehart, 1980), and we had recently demonstrated that actions were inferred during reading while states were not (Seifert, Robertson, & Black, 1985).

In this study, we asked subjects to read a set of five stories and answer questions about them. Later we tested their memory for items in the stories. Each story contained two critical "item pairs." An item pair consisted of two conceptualizations that were connected causally by enablement, or by some other conceptual relation. One of the pairs was a "state-action" pair, specifically, a state that enabled or otherwise led to an action. For example, in one case a character noted that it was a bright day (state) and later got a pair of sunglasses (action). The other item pair in a story was an "action-state" pair, or an action that resulted in or implied a state. For example, in the story just mentioned, a character checked his hair in a car's window (action), which implied that the character was located outside of the car (state).

Subjects and Design. Twenty-four subjects, all Yale undergraduates, participated in this experiment. All subjects read the stories. Half were later asked misleading questions (mixed in with other questions) about the action parts of the action-state item pairs, and half were asked misleading questions about the state parts of the state-action item pairs. For example, the misleading question about the bright day (state) was "Was Jack inside or outside when he noticed it was a cloudy day?". The misleading question about the car window action was "Where was Jack's car when he checked his hair in the rearview mirror?".

After answering the initial questions, we asked subjects a second set of questions. Among these questions were some to test for recall of both parts of each of the item pairs. The state-recall question for our state-action example was "What did Jack notice when he ran out to the car?" (he noticed that it was a bright day), and the action-recall question for the same item was "What did Jack get from the car?" (sunglasses). The action-recall question for the action-state example was "What did Jack do about his hair just before he sprinted across the street . . . ?" (he checked it in the car window), and the state question for the same item was "Where was Jack when he checked his hair, inside or outside the car?" (outside). The answers to these questions were scored by judges as either correct, misled (the answer was wrong, but consistent with the misleading question presupposition), or confused (the answer was altogether wrong, blank, "I don't know," etc.).

Twelve subjects answered misleading questions about the state parts of state-action pairs and neutral (control) questions about the action parts. Twelve subjects answered misleading questions about the action parts of action-state pairs and neutral (control) questions about the state parts. Initially, we calculated two scores for each subject. The first, called a "misleading difference score" (MDS), was the proportion of recalled items scored as misled in the misled condition, minus the proportion of items judged misled in the control condition. A "confusion difference score" (CDS) was calculated in the same way for the items judged confused.

Results. Our findings were that states, as a group, were easier to mislead directly than actions, as a group. The mean MDS for the state part of state–action items was .19, whereas the mean MDS for the action part of action–state items was .05. The corresponding CDSs were .14 and .03. We also found evidence for misleading by inference. For those state–action pairs in which the state part was judged "not misled," the action part was always judged "not misled" also. In contrast, for those state–action pairs in which the state part was judged "misled," 73% of the corresponding action parts were also judged "misled."

A smaller indirect effect was found for action–state pairs. For those action–state pairs in which the action part was judged "not misled," 93% of the corresponding state parts were also judged "not misled." In contrast, for those action–state pairs in which the action part was judged "misled," 50% of the corresponding state parts were also judged "misled."

Our general conclusions were that it is easier to alter states than actions by misleading presupposition. Also, we concluded that conceptually connected information can be altered indirectly, especially connected action information. This latter, somewhat counter-intuitive finding makes sense if we assume that inference processes, consistency checking, and question-concept searching proceeds along conceptual links between ACTs. This would increase the probability that inconsistencies would be encountered indirectly in actions, when compared with states.

Conceptual Analyses of the Items

Large variation among items was again apparent in this study. Those differences will now be explored in the context of conceptual-dependency theory. To facilitate this, new scores were calculated for each item. Tables 7.2 and 7.3 show the proportions of subjects' answers that were judged "misled" or "confused" for each item in the two presupposition conditions. Table 7.2 contains scores for the state–action items and Table 7.3 contains scores for the action–state items. To get these proportions, the number of misled and confused answers were compared with the total number of interpretable answers (some answers did not provide information about the presupposition at all and were not included in the calculations) for each item. The n's from which each proportion is calculated appear in parentheses in the tables.

Also shown in Tables 7.2 and 7.3 are the differences between proportions for each item in the misled and control conditions. A large, positive

TABLE 7.2
Proportions of Answers Judged Misled or Confused for Each State–action Item in
the State-misled and Control Question Presupposition Conditions
(frequencies are shown in parentheses)

Item	State Misled		Control		State Diff.	Action Diff.
State 1	.58	(7/12)	.17	(2/12)	.41	
Action 1	.58	(7/12)	.17	(2/12)		.41
State 2	.58	(7/12)	.11	(1/9)	.47	
Action 2	.33	(4/12)	.17	(2/12)		.16
State 3	.42	(5/12)	.08	(1/12)	.34	
Action 3	.27	(3/11)	.09	(1/11)		.18
State 4	.17	(2/12)	.00	(0/11)	.17	
Action 4	.17	(2/12)	.08	(1/12)		.09
State 5	.25	(3/12)	.08	(1/12)	.17	
Action 5	.50	(2/4)	.80	(4/5)		−.30*
State Mean	.40	(24/60)	.09	(5/56)	.31	
Action Mean	.35	(18/51)	.19	(10/52)		.16

*Fewer than half of the answers were interpretable for this item and the result is not reliable.

difference indicates that the subjects in the misleading-question condition
were misled or confused more often on a particular item than the subjects
in the control condition. (These difference scores are not the same as the
MDSs or CDSs reported above and in Lehnert, Robertson, & Black [1984]
because those scores were calculated for each subject between items in the
two conditions. These are combined across subjects and are calculated
between the same items in both conditions. Also, the current scores combine misled and confused answers. The two sets of scores are related, of
course, and tell the same story.)

The difference scores reiterate the finding that a large number of state
items were misled, whereas few action items were misled. However, we are
now interested in looking at the items one at a time. The primary focus will
be on the types of slots in the CD representation that are most readily
altered.

The State-action Items. The state–action items are arranged ordinally
in Table 7.2, starting with the most alterable (considering both the state and
action parts). It is clear that the items differ considerably. Forty-one percent more of the state answers for state–action item 1 were misled when a
misleading question was asked than when a neutral question was asked.
The same percentage of action answers indicated indirect misleading for

TABLE 7.3
Proportions of Answers Judged Misled or Confused for Each Action-state Item
in the Action-misled and Control Question Presupposition Conditions
(frequencies are shown in parentheses)

Item	Action Misled		Control		Action Diff.	State Diff.
Action 1	.17	(2/12)	.00	(0/12)	.17	
State 1	.08	(1/12)	.00	(0/12)		.08
Action 2	.36	(4/11)	.25	(2/8)	.11	
State 2	.25	(3/12)	.25	(3/12)		.00
Action 3	.00	(0/11)	.00	(0/12)	.00	
State 3	.08	(1/12)	.00	(0/12)		.08
Action 4	.08	(1/12)	.18	(2/11)	−.10	
State 4	.08	(1/12)	.20	(2/10)		−.12
Action 5	.67	(2/3)	1.00	(5/5)	−.33*	
State 5	.58	(7/12)	.75	(6/8)		−.17*
Action Mean	.18	(9/49)	.19	(9/48)	−.01	
State Mean	.22	(13/60)	.20	(11/54)		.02

*Fewer than half of the answers were interpretable for this item and the result is not reliable.

state–action item 1. Compare this with state–action item 4 in which only 17% more answers were misled in the misleading question condition and only 9% more of the action items were indirectly misled. What accounts for these item differences?

One quantitative factor that emerges when the data are examined in this way is the apparent instability of the most alterable items, 1 and 2, in the control condition. When no misleading question was asked, 17% of the state answers for item 1 and 11% of the state answers for item 2 were judged misled or confused. This compares with 8%, 0%, and 8% judged misled in the control condition for items 3, 4, and 5 respectively. The correlation between the proportions misled in the misled and control conditions was .87 (df = 8, $p < .01$) for the state parts of the items and .53 (df = 8, $p < .15$) for the action parts of the items. It may be that items which are less retrievable, or which were not encoded in detail in the first place, are more susceptible to alteration. This would indicate that a misleading question is more likely to add information to a memory representation than to change it. This possibility deserves further consideration.

Can the highly susceptible items be distinguished from the less-susceptible ones by examining the conceptual representations and specifying the question-answering processes that operated on them? Figs. 7.6–7.10 show conceptual-dependency representations of each state–action item, and Table

TABLE 7.4
The Focus of Questions and Location of Misleading Presuppositions
for the State-action Items.

Item	Question Focus	Misleading Presupposition
State 1 (.41)	TIME relation on an ACT	Part of LOC relation in an object slot
State 2 (.47)	LOC relation on an actor slot	Part of a physical state relation in an object slot
State 3 (.34)	Part of a physical state relation in an object slot	Part of a physical state relation to a human in one of the ACT slots or in a relation with an object slot
State 4 (.17)	Actor slot	Source and destination slots on a relation in an object slot
State 5 (.17)	Object slot	Destination slot of an ACT

7.4 summarizes the relevant conceptual components of the CD and QC for the state part of each of these items. These representations ignore surrounding story context (i.e., script, thematic, and other metalevel knowledge) for the most part. They include inferences provided by conceptual dependency structures and some "near" inferences, such as "instruments" and "goals." Below the CD representations for each item are the CD representations of the question concepts, which contain the question presuppositions, for the corresponding misleading questions. Remember that the QC must be matched with the CDs in the memory representation as an important step in the question-answering process.

State-action items 1 and 2 were the most susceptible to alteration, with mean state difference scores of .41 and .47 respectively, and mean action difference scores of .41 and .16 respectively. In both cases the direct state alteration involves *part* of a state relation which is the object of ACTs presupposed by the misleading questions. In state-action item 1 (Fig. 7.6) the relation is a location (LOC) relation specifying where photographic lamps were. This LOC relation is the object of an MTRANS and part of the CD frame for the misleading-question concept. In state–action item 2 (Fig. 7.7) the relation is a specification of the weather. Again, the relation is the object in an MTRANS and part of the CD frame for the misleading-question concept. In both cases, the only part of the question concept that mismatches the memory representation is the descriptor part of state relations in the object slots of the two MTRANS's.

We can speculate that matching the QC with the CD frames in memory involves matching the ACTs and important slots. Certainly, matching the actor and object slots would be important. It might be enough to determine only that the appropriate *relations* were in the object slots, without having

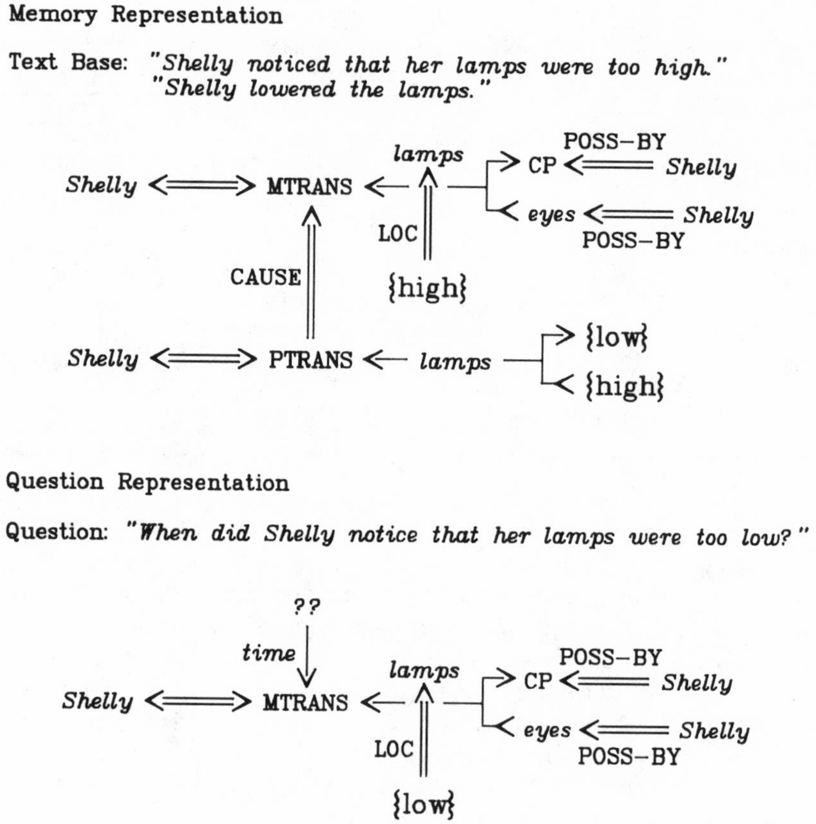

Memory Representation

Text Base: *"Shelly noticed that her lamps were too high."*
"Shelly lowered the lamps."

```
                                      POSS-BY
                            lamps  ┌> CP <═══ Shelly
   Shelly <═══> MTRANS <─ ↑ ─┤
                     ↑      LOC  └< eyes <═══ Shelly
                     ‖               POSS-BY
            CAUSE ‖     {high}
                     ‖
   Shelly <═══> PTRANS <─ lamps ─┌> {low}
                                     └< {high}
```

Question Representation

Question: *"When did Shelly notice that her lamps were too low?"*

```
            ??
        time ↓                       POSS-BY
             ↓        lamps  ┌> CP <═══ Shelly
   Shelly <═══> MTRANS <─ ↑ ─┤
                            └< eyes <═══ Shelly
                     LOC ‖       POSS-BY
                        {low}
```

FIG. 7.6. CD representations of the memory item and the question concept for state-action item 1.

to examine the slots of the relations. This would explain why a contradiction was not noticed and alteration occurred. This predicts that changing the entire relation, for example presupposing that Shelly had noticed that a camera was broken instead of that the lamps were too low, would be less successful than altering only the descriptor part of the same relation.

It is interesting to note that the action part of state–action item 1 was more susceptible to indirect alteration than the action part of state–action item 2 (Table 7.4). Note that the action alteration for item 1 involves switching the source and destination tokens of an ACT (PTRANS) that is directly causally linked to the main concept. In contrast, the action alteration for item 2 involves the object slot of an ACT (GRASP) that is linked to the main concept through intermediary concepts. We saw earlier that it may be harder to alter tokens directly in the main slots of a CD frame and this finding reiterates that observation. Also, since there is a limit to inference generation during comprehension, we might not expect indirect alteration of concepts that are not linked *directly* to the main concept.

The state part of state–action item 3 (Fig. 7.8) was somewhat alterable, mean difference score = .34. The alteration involves a physical-state descriptor of one of the persons involved in the story. The QC is a possession (POSS-BY) relation with a physical state altering the actor slot. It is

Memory Representation

Text Base: *"Jack noticed that it was a cloudy day."*
 "Jack went inside to get an umbrella."

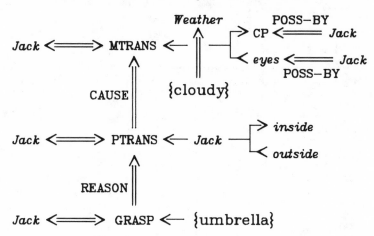

Question Representation

Question: *"Was Jack inside or outside when he noticed it was a bright day?"*

FIG. 7.7.   CD representations of the memory item and the question concept for state-action item 2.

reasonable to assume that search for the QC is driven first by search for ACTs in which the object (pen) would play an important role. Once pen was located and the POSS-BY relation identified, the physical-state descriptor would reasonably *not* play an important role in further matching the concept. If a subject had not encoded the fact that the owner of the pen was portly, he or she would certainly not want to reject a match on the POSS-BY relation.

Again, the successful alteration was a slot in a relation that was, in turn, the filler of a slot in the main ACT. Indirect alteration of the action, who thanked whom for the pen, was not successful. Note that this alteration would involve changing the actor, source, and destination slots of an ACT (MTRANS).

State–action items 4 and 5 (Figs. 7.9 and 7.10) were resistant to alteration. Note that the "state" in item 4 is really a change of state ("losing weight"). In order to alter this concept, two tokens would have to be swapped in the state-change relation. Token swapping is typically a difficult alteration. Note that the QC leaves the actor out of the representation (since the question is about the actor), and hence it may be necessary to use the whole concept in the object slot to identify the conceptualization! This item is a clear indicator that the type of question may affect the misleading effect. For example, a question like "When did John's boss tell John that it seemed John was losing weight?" might cause alteration in this case by providing all relevant slots in the QC for matching the memory representation, and thereby allowing a less-stringent match on the object slot (like state–action items 1 and 2).

State–action item 5 involves alteration of the destination slot of an ACT (PTRANS). Direct alteration of a slot in a CD frame, as we saw in the importance study, is difficult. In this case, the QC again contains an unspecified slot in the CD frame, this time the object slot. As we said when discussing item 4, asking subjects to fill in a slot of a CD frame forces them to look more carefully at the other slots of the CD frame in order to match it in memory. This reduces the probability that a misleading token in the QC will affect the memory representation.

The Action–state Items

As Table 7.3 shows, there was very little, if any, alteration of action–state items. As with the state–action items, there was a tendency for the weaker items to be more alterable. The correlation between answer proportions in the control and misled conditions was .92 (df = 8, $p < .01$) for the action parts of the items and .96 (df = 8, $p < .01$) for the state parts of the items.

Fig. 7.11 through 7.15 show CD representations of the action–state items, and Table 7.5 summarizes the relevant conceptual components of the CD and QC for the action part of each. Again, the memory representa-

Memory Representation

Text base: *"Dr. White was portly."*
             "Dr. White gave back Mr. Haight's pen."
             "Mr. Haight said 'thank you' for the pen."

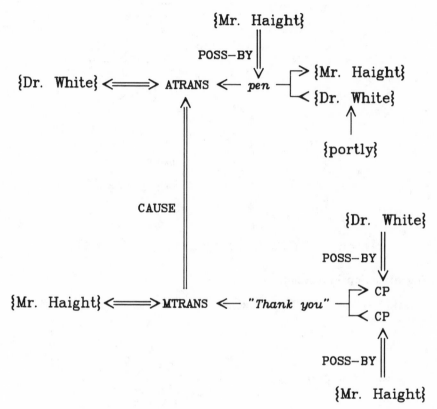

Question Representation

Question: *"What was the name of the portly man who owned the pen?"*

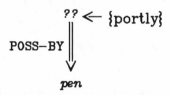

FIG. 7.8.   CD representations of the memory item and the question concept for state-action item 3.

Memory Representation

Text Base: *"John's boss told John that John had gained weight."*
"John decided to lose weight so he didn't
have dessert."

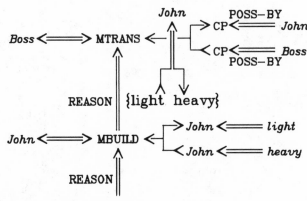

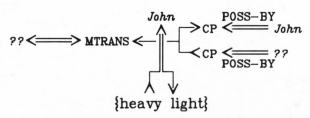

Question Representation

Question: *"Who told John that it seemed he was losing weight ?"*

FIG. 7.9.   CD representations of the memory item and the question concept for state-action item 4.

tion of each item in its local context is shown along with the representation of the misleading question.

Alteration of item 1 of this group (Fig. 7.11) involves swapping tokens on a state change relation. We saw with state-action item 4 that token swapping may be a more difficult alteration and, in fact, the difference scores for these two items are comparable (.17 for the directly misled parts of the items in both cases; .08 and .09 for the indirectly misled parts of the items for action–state and state–action respectively). Again, the QC omits part of the change of state relation that memory matching requires (i.e., the question is about the concept it is designed to alter). This is emerging as an important factor predictive of resistance to alteration.

Action–state items 2 and 4 (Figs. 7.12 and 7.14) are similar in that both of the direct alterations involve swapping the source and destination slots of an ACT (PTRANS in both cases). As we saw with other relations, token swapping is difficult. Even though both items 2 and 4 had low alteration scores, item 4 showed much more resistance than item 2. Again, examination of the QCs for these items reveals that the object slot of the main

Memory Representation

Text Base: *"Cynthia was supposed to leave the instructions in the kitchen."*
"Ed went into the kitchen for the instructions."

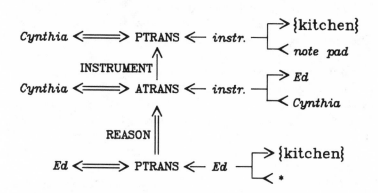

Question Representation

Question: *"What was Cynthia supposed to leave for Ed in the living room ?"*

FIG. 7.10.   CD representations of the memory item and the question concept for state-action item 5.

TABLE 7.5
The Focus of Questions and Location of Misleading Presuppositions
for the Action-state Items

Item	Question Focus	Misleading Presupposition
Action 1 (.17)	Subject slot of a state change	Source and destination slots of a state change
Action 2 (.11)	ACT following the question focus	Source and destination slots of an ACT
Action 3 (0)	Destination slot of a state change	Subject slot of a state change
Action 4 (−.10)	ACT following the question focus	Source and destination slots of an ACT
Action 5 (−.33)	Part of subordinate LOC relation in the object slot of an instrumental ACT	Object slot of an instrumental ACT

conceptualization is being questioned in item 4, whereas in item 2 a subsequent event is being questioned. Again, it appears that questioning a component of the QC in a misleading question leads to resistance of the memory item to alteration.

The misleading question for action–state item 3 (Fig. 7.13) was aimed at alteration of the subject slot of a relation. As we saw before, alteration of a central slot in a CD representation is difficult. Also, for this item the final state slot of the same relation was being questioned. This provides a double explanation for the lack of success.

Finally, the misleading question for action–state item 5 (Fig. 7.15) was aimed at alteration of the object slot of an act (ATTEND). As we saw with the wine/water example from the importance experiment, the object slot is a central slot that is difficult to alter.

Conclusions. While it was a good idea to examine the nature of the information being altered as a factor in alterability, "action" and "state" were categorizations that were too broad. There are many relevant differences between the items in the class of actions and between the items in the class of states. When the structures of detailed representations are studied and the dynamic conceptual processes operating during question answering are specified, the reasons for item differences become apparent. In the future, researchers in this area should specify these details of structure and process.

Although the items differed so dramatically, some suggestions about alterability can be ventured on the basis of this reanalysis. First, an important factor seems to be the location of items to be altered within conceptual

Memory Representation

Text base: *"Gary thought the tape deck was too loud."*
             "Gary asked John to turn the tape deck down."

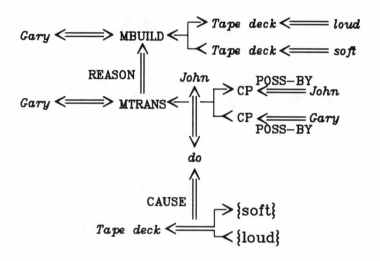

Question Representation

Question: *"What did Gary ask John to turn up..., the radio
            or the tape deck."*

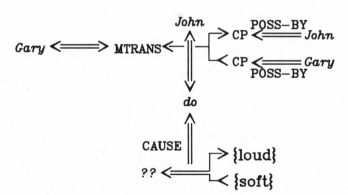

FIG. 7.11.   CD representations of the memory item and the question
concept for action-state item 1.

Memory Representation

Text Base: *"Ed opened the door..."*
"...to let Fritz in."

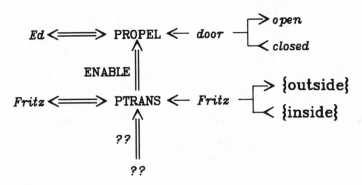

Question Representation

Question: *"What did Ed do after he let Fritz out ?"*

FIG. 7.12.   CD representations of the memory item and the question concept for action-state item 2.

structures. The most alterable items were those in which the alterations were peripheral to the primitive ACT and the slots of its CD frame. Actor and object slots of CDs and simple relations were not alterable, and there was little effect of misleading information on source and destination slots (state 5 in Table 7.4 and actions 3 and 5 in Table 7.5). Token switching, in which both the prior and final state slots of an ACT or relation are changed, was also not observed in response to misleading questions (state 4 in Table 7.4 and actions 1, 2, and 4 in Table 7.5). When successful concept alteration did occur, it involved a single slot that was peripheral to the main ACT or relation, and was usually part of a modifying conceptualization (states 1, 2, and 3 in Table 7.4).

Structure and process cannot be separated cleanly, of course, (Reiser & Black, 1982), and these effects are likely due to matching processes between the QC and concepts in memory. Actor, object, and other slots central to a particular CD ACT must be matched in order to identify the concept uniquely. Peripheral slots or modifiers of slots need not be matched, and hence contradictory information in these parts of a QC have a higher

Memory Representation

Text Base: *"Mascara was smeared on the lens papers."*
            "There was a blue smear on the camera lens."

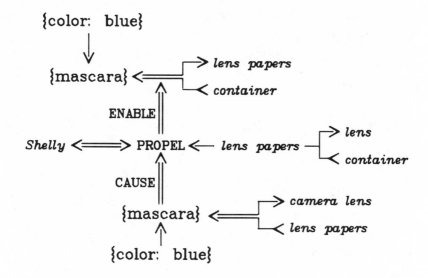

Question Representation

Question: *"What was Shelly's lipstick smeared on ?"*

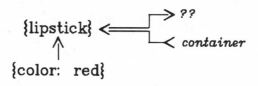

FIG. 7.13. CD representations of the memory item and the question concept for action-state item 3.

Memory Representation

Text Base: *"Mr. Haight opened the window."*
"Susan was too warm."

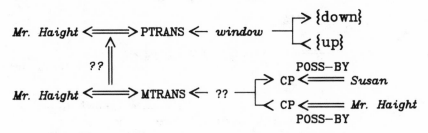

Question Concept

Question: *"What did Mr. Haight ask Susan after he closed the window?"*

FIG. 7.14.   CD representations of the memory item and the question concept for action-state item 4.

likelihood of not being noticed (mismatched during question comprehension). When mismatches are not noticed, alteration is more likely.

Finally, the question concept itself plays a role in predicting alterability. This is again because of matching processes. If a central slot is left out of the QC (because the question is *about* an important part of the concept, e.g., states 4 and 5 in Table 7.4 and actions 1 and 3 in Table 7.5) then more peripheral information must be examined in order to match the concept in memory. This also reduces the chances that a mismatched slot will be overlooked. In the next section these ideas will be further explored.

Item Analysis of a Second State-action Study

A second study, reported in Robertson, Black, and Lehnert (1985), was conducted on states and actions. In order to study alteration by inference

Question Concept

Question: *"Where was Jack's car when he checked his hair in the rearview mirror ?"*

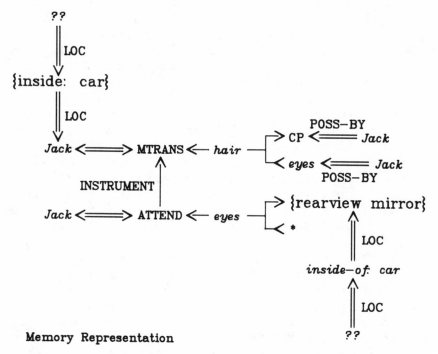

Memory Representation

Text Base: *"Jack checked his hair in the car window."*
Inferred: "Jack was outside the car."

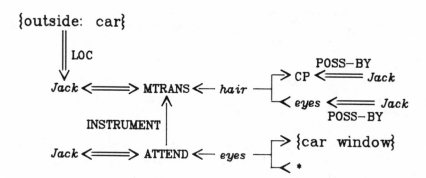

FIG. 7.15.   CD representations of the memory item and the question concept for action-state item 5.

more thoroughly, we generated items that were more conceptually complex. The details of the results of that study will not be covered here. Instead, the alterability of the items will be examined in light of the conclusions drawn above. In the new study, we used 24 items which were embedded in a long narrative. Twelve of the items consisted of an initial *state* and 12 consisted of an initial *action.* After reading the narrative, subjects answered a set of questions which included misleading and neutral questions about the states and actions. Each subject answered both misleading and neutral questions about states and misleading and neutral questions about actions. After answering the questions, the subjects received a recognition test containing items from the story, including the state and action items. Some of the recognition items appeared in the same way that they appeared in the story ("True" items) and some appeared in the way that their misleading questions presupposed ("False" items). The subjects rated each item on a 1-7 recognition confidence scale, with 7 meaning that the item was as it appeared in the story and 1 meaning that the item was not as it appeared in the story.

Twenty-four subjects participated in the study. We calculated mean recognition scores (across subjects) for true and false items in both the misled and not-misled conditions. Ideally, when a misleading question was not asked about a story item, the story item's true recognition item should receive a 7 and its false recognition item should receive a 1. When a misleading question was asked about a story item, the story item's true recognition item should receive a 1 and its false recognition item should receive a 7 (both indicating that the subject was completely misled).

To summarize the data, the mean recognition score for items when misled was subtracted from the same items when not misled in order to yield a "difference score." This difference score should be a high positive value for true items and a high negative value for false items if misleading occurs. These data were reported in Robertson et al. (1985). Here the data will be summarized further by subtracting the difference score for an item in the false condition from the difference score for the same item in the true condition. This "T-F" score will be high and positive when both the true and false recognition scores indicate misleading.

Results. Table 7.6 shows the mean T-F score for each item in this study. The items are arranged ordinally according to the T-F scores, starting with the most alterable. For each item, the original classification of "state" or "action" is shown. Most importantly, the part of the conceptual-dependency representation that should have been affected by a misleading question is indicated for each item, and the type of question that was asked is also listed.

The T-F scores reiterate the finding of Robertson et al. (1985) that the set of states was easier to alter than the set of actions. The mean T-F score for state items was 1.94, while the mean T-F score for action items was .63.

TABLE 7.6
Items from the Second State-action Experiment in Order of Modifiability
as Indicated by True Minus False Scores
(Also shown is the part of the concept to be modified and the question type.)

Item	Misleading Presupposition	Question Type	T-F Score
Item 1 (State)	Part of a LOC relation in the object slot of an ACT	Time of ACT	6.25
Item 2 (State)	Object of an ACT	Time of ACT	5.50
Item 3 (Action)	LOC modifier of the destination slot of an ACT	Reason for ACT	4.50
Item 4 (Action)	LOC modifier of the destination slot of an ACT)	Subsequent ACT	3.75
Item 5 (Action)	LOC modifier of the destination slot of an ACT	Previous ACT	3.25
Item 6 (State)	Quantity modifier of the object of an ACT	Time of ACT	3.00
Item 7 (State)	Physical state descriptor	Consequence	2.75
Item 8 (State)	LOC modifier of the object slot of an ACT	Object of previous ACT	2.25
Item 9 (State)	Previous-final state swap on state change in the object slot of an ACT	Time of ACT	2.25
Item 10 (State)	Physical state descriptor	Previous ACT	2.25
Item 11 (Action)	Source-destination swap of an ACT	Previous ACT	2.00
Item 12 (State)	LOC modifier of the object slot of an ACT	Time of ACT	1.75
Item 13 (State)	Previous-final state swap on stage change	POSS relation	1.50
Item 14 (Action)	Object of an ACT	Previous ACT	1.50
Item 15 (Action)	Actor of an ACT	Time of ACT	1.00
Item 16 (Action)	LOC modifier of the destination slot of an ACT	Reason for ACT	.75
Item 17 (Action)	Destination slot of an ACT	Time of ACT	.50
Item 18 (State)	LOC modifier of the object slot of an ACT	Simultaneous ACT	.00
Item 19 (State)	Part of a physical state relation	Actor	− .75
Item 20 (Action)	LOC modifier of the actor slot of an ACT	Simultaneous ACT	−1.75

(Continued)

TABLE 7.6 (*Continued*)

Item	Misleading Presupposition	Question Type	T-F Score
Item 21 (Action)	Destination slot of an ACT	Reason	−2.50
Item 22 (Action)	Object slot of an ACT	Subsequent ACT	−2.50
Item 23 (Action)	Destination slot of an ACT	Enablement	−3.00
Item 24 (State)	LOC modifier of the object slot of an ACT	Physical state	−3.50

An examination of the distribution of states and actions in Table 7.6, however, reveals that some actions received high T-F scores and some states received low T-F scores. The "misleading presupposition" column shows that many different types of conceptual alteration were attempted.

Following from the prior item analyses, attempts to alter slots that are parts of CD frames (such as actor, object, source, and destination slots of ACTs) would be expected to fail more often than attempts to alter relations (like LOC and POSS-BY) and modifying states (like warm, high, etc.). In Table 7.7 the frequency of items in the top half of the item distribution (the most alterable) are separated from the items in the bottom half (the least alterable), and the frequencies of items of each conceptual alteration type are shown. For the items in this experiment, 8 out of the 24 (33%, items 2, 11, 14, 15, 17, 21, 22, and 23) involved alteration of slots in the CD frame, while the remaining 16 (67%) involved relation- and state-specifier alterations.

TABLE 7.7
Frequency of Items and Mean T-F Scores in the Top and Bottom Halves
of the True-False Score Distribution for Each Type of Modification Attempted

Type of Modification	Top Half	Bottom Half	Total	Mean T-F
LOC modifier on destination slot	3	1	4	3.06
Other modifiers on actor or object slots	1	0	1	3.00
Part of a state relation	4	2	6	2.38
Source-destination swap	1	0	1	2.00
Actor/object slots	1	3	4	1.38
LOC modifier on actor or object slots	2	3	5	− .25
Destination slots	0	3	3	−1.67
Total	12	12	24	
Mean T-F	3.29	− .73	1.28	

The mean T–F score for the eight CD slots was .31 while the mean T–F score for the 16 relations and states was 1.77, t(22) = 1.30, p < .12, a difference that marginally supports the prediction. Sixty-three percent of the relation and state alterations (10 out of 16) fell into the most-alterable category while only 25% (2 out of 8) of the CD slot alterations fell into this category.

The question type should also play a role in the probability of alteration. Table 7.8 shows the frequency of items in the top and bottom halves of the item distribution for each of three types of questions. Time-of-act ("when?") questions, previous-act questions ("what happened before?"), and a grouping of all other question types used in the experiment (because of small n's for each type) are shown. The mean T–F scores for the three question types were 2.89 for time-of-act questions, 2.25 for previous-act questions, and .12 for other question types. An analysis of variance on these data indicates a significant difference among the means F(2,21) = 3.53, p < .05. The conservative Scheffe significant difference test (SSD) for nonorthogonal post-hoc comparisons shows that the effect is due to a difference between the other-questions group and a combination of the time-of-act and previous-act groups, SSD = 6.90 with $F'(2,21)$ = 6.90 as the critical value at p < .05.

Conclusions.   The results suggest again that the memory structure and the type of question being asked have strong mediating effects on misleading questions. Specifically, attempts to alter slots in CD frames directly were not as successful as other types of alterations. Also, time-of-act and previous-act questions with misleading presuppositions were more effective in altering memory than other types of questions. In the final section, these phenomena will be summed up and directions for future research will be presented.

TABLE 7.8
Frequency of Items and Mean T–F Scores in the Top and Bottom Halves
of the True–False Score Distribution for Each Type of Question Asked

Type of Question	Top Half	Bottom Half	Total	Mean T–F
Time of ACT	5	2	7	2.89
Previous ACT	3	1	4	2.25
All others	4	9	13	.12
Total	12	12	24	
Mean T–F	3.29	– .73	1.28	

OVERALL CONCLUSIONS
AND FUTURE DIRECTIONS

In this chapter, items used in several misleading question studies were analyzed at a detailed level of conceptual representation. It was shown that alteration of concepts in memory can have many mediating factors. The important factors to consider in studying memory alteration through postevent information seem to fall into three nonindependent categories: (1) structural properties of the memory representation, (2) structural properties of the question concept and the process of matching the question concept to memory, and (3) question-answering procedures.

Structural Properties of the Memory Representation

Some parts of a conceptual representation are easier to alter than others. In general, slots in CD frames for ACTs are hard to alter whereas modifiers of those slots are easier to alter. Thus, consider the concept "Last Tuesday Mary drove her red car from sunny Mount Kisco to rainy White Plains." The central act is a PTRANS. *Mary* is the concept in the actor slot, *car* is the concept in the object slot, and *Mount Kisco* and *White Plains* are the concepts in the source and destination slots respectively. There are four relations, a POSS–BY relation between the car and Mary, and state modifiers for Mount Kisco (weather), White Plains (weather), and the car (color). Based on hypotheses developed from the above post-hoc analyses, it is predicted that the following misleading questions would be unsuccessful because they mismatch CD slots that are necessary for identifying the question concept:

1. When did John drive the car from Mount Kisco to White Plains? (actor alteration).
2. When did Mary drive the van from Mount Kisco to White Plains? (object alteration).
3. When did Mary drive the car from San Francisco to White Plains? (source alteration).
4. When did Mary drive the car from Mount Kisco to New York? (destination alteration).
5. When did Mary drive the car from White Plains to Mount Kisco? (source-destination swap).

On the other hand, it is predicted that the following alterations would be more successful because they involve modifiers of CD slots that do not have to be matched during question comprehension:

6a. When did Mary drive John's car from Mount Kisco to White Plains? (alteration of part of the POSS-BY relation).

7a. When did Mary drive the blue car from Mount Kisco to White Plains? (alteration of a state modifier).

8a. When did Mary drive the car from rainy Mount Kisco to White Plains? (alteration of a state modifier).

9a. When did Mary drive the car from Mount Kisco to sunny White Plains? (alteration of a state modifier).

The Question Concept

The type of question that is asked has an effect on alteration in two ways. The first is in the structure of the question concept and the second is in the nature of the question answering process. Regarding the question structure, if important slots in the CD frame for the question concept are unidentified, then this will force a closer examination of the memory representation during the matching process. For example, the following questions might reduce the probability that an alteration would occur when compared with question 6a, "When did Mary drive John's car from Mount Kisco to White Plains?":

6b. Who drove John's car from Mount Kisco to White Plains? (alteration of part of the POSS-BY relation, actor slot unavailable for matching).

6c. Where did Mary drive John's car? (alteration of part of the POSS-BY relation, source and destination slots unavailable for matching).

While 6a, 6b, and 6c all contain the same misleading presupposition, less of the CD frame is available for matching in 6b and 6c. In 6c, for example, it is reasonable to assume that the question answerer might adopt a strategy of matching the POSS-BY relation in order to guarantee that the correct PTRANS is located in memory. This would make it likely that the misleading presupposition would be detected, reducing the probability of alteration.

Question-answering Processes

Once a concept is located in memory, question-answering procedures may affect the probability that a concept can be altered. For example, "*when* questions" like 6a involve first locating the ACT and then following a conceptual link from the ACT to a time specifier that will serve as an answer to the question. Consider the following question, however:

6d. What color was John's car that Mary drove to Mount Kisco? (alteration of part of the POSS-BY relation on the object, answer process involves searching a relation on the object).

Once the ACT is located in the case of 6d, modifiers on the object slot must be searched in order to answer the question. Since one of the modifiers corresponds to the misleading presupposition, it is less likely that the misleading presupposition will go unnoticed.

Other Factors

Finally, there are two other factors which we were not able to investigate from our items, but which deserve further study. The first is the role of world knowledge in constraining the effects of misleading questions. In this chapter, analysis has been limited to the level of conceptual dependencies. However, more general knowledge structures would be expected to play a role. Consider the following variation on the example concept: "Mary drove her red car from sunny Phoenix to rainy Seattle," and the following variations on misleading questions:

8b. When did Mary drive the car from rainy Phoenix to Seattle? (alteration of a state modifier, constraints from prior knowledge).

9b. When did Mary drive the car from Phoenix to sunny Seattle? (alteration of a state modifier, constraints from prior knowledge).

Anyone with prior knowledge of weather patterns in Phoenix and Seattle will consider these sentences anomalous. Anomaly is likely to trigger closer scrutiny of the memory representation as an explanatory process, making alteration due to the misleading question presupposition less likely.

Finally, a processing factor that is likely to mediate the effects of misleading questions is interaction among similar concepts in the representation of a connected sequence of events. For example, if the example concept involving driving were embedded in a story in which there were several driving episodes, or several episodes in which Mary traveled from Mount Kisco to White Plains, the process of matching the question concept would be more complex. If several driving episodes were in the representation, then the source and destination slots would have to be specified in a question and matched exactly in order to answer the question. If there were more than one instance of the same CD (i.e., Mary drove the same route many times) more complex configurations of concepts would have to be searched in order to match a question concept (e.g., "the time she was driving and almost had a wreck," "the time she was driving after she met with John," etc.).

In these cases, we would expect close scrutiny of many connected concepts to make a mismatch more noticeable. On the other hand, we might also expect some *very* remote alterations, for example, alteration of a driving episode that is far removed (in a chain of events) from the target driving concept but which is accessed by question-concept retrieval heuristics.

SUMMARY

In this chapter the conceptual representations of several items used in misleading question experiments were examined. Several representational factors became evident that might affect the susceptibility of a concept to alteration by misleading postevent information. In future research, it is suggested that the nature of the knowledge structures and question-answering processes involved be taken into account when predicting alterability.

8 The Role of Thematic Knowledge Structures in Reminding

Colleen M. Seifert
Robert P. Abelson
Gail McKoon

INTRODUCTION

Other chapters in this book have discussed types of knowledge structures such as scripts and MOPs. These structures serve to organize related experiences based upon their similarities; for example, restaurants that share the features of fast-food establishments could be organized under the *fast-food restaurant* script in memory, which would provide the appropriate expectations for that situation. Another kind of similarity between episodes, *themes,* involves a more abstract level of information. For example, consider the many types of knowledge applicable to this story:

> Nixon had struggled hard to beat J. F. Kennedy, but his efforts were not able to win him the election. When his supporters finally accepted the inevitable defeat, there were more than a few tears and hollow hopes for 1968. After successfully challenging Humphrey in 1968, Nixon was finally inaugurated.

In this story, knowledge could be accessed from a variety of concepts, such as Nixon, politics, elections, failed attempts, and optimism. Some of these (e.g., Nixon) are highly specific, while others (optimism) are very general. The most general thematic characterization of Nixon's situation, "if at first you don't succeed, try, try again," is useful information in many settings other than politics. Unlike the *fast-food* information, the theme in this story could serve as a generalized structure in memory that is not dependent on accessing its context, that is, Nixon's election. This abstract thematic information could be organized in memory as more general, high-level schemas so that episodes from a variety of contexts were stored together in memory based on their thematic similarity. Generalized thematic knowledge structures may be needed to understand and encode new episodes, and to recall the thematic information when it is appropriate.

THEMATIC MEMORY STRUCTURES

The Thematic Level of Knowledge

What kind of structures capture the thematic similarity between episodes? Knowledge about the world can be characterized as ranging from completely context-dependent to very abstract. Some of our knowledge of the world can be captured by explicit propositions about the circumstances of an episode; however, other knowledge depends on the relationships between explicit concepts. Typically, *schemas* are proposed to represent knowledge of familiar events as relationships among concepts. The information in a schema is usually assumed to be organized into a structure, reflecting, for example, temporal contiguity, importance, or more abstract relations, such as that between a goal and a plan for its attainment. The content of the schema and its structure define the inferences that can be made when the schema is activated in memory. Some schemas organize information in a very specific context, such as a restaurant, while others represent much more abstract knowledge such as the role of authority or ways to avoid problems in life.

The use of schemas in remembering textual information has been well documented. In early work, Bransford and Johnson (1972, 1973) and Dooling and Lachman (1971; also Dooling & Mullet, 1973) demonstrated that ambiguous stories were easy to understand and recall if they were given a title that referred to appropriate background knowledge but very difficult without the title. Similarly, experts, who can provide extensive background knowledge for themselves, do better at recalling information in their area than nonexperts (Chiesi, Spilich, & Voss, 1979). Schemas have been shown to determine not only how much of a text will be recalled but which parts of a text will be recalled. If a schema is mentioned at the time a text is read, information relevant to the schema is more likely to be recalled (Pichert & Anderson, 1977) and more likely to be recognized (Graesser, Woll, Kowalski, & Smith, 1980; Schallert, 1976). Schema-relevant information is also more likely to appear as intrusions in recall protocols than schema-irrelevant information (Bower, Black, & Turner, 1979). Finally, facts that can be organized by well-known schemas seem to be more tightly connected in memory than facts that cannot be so organized (McKoon & Ratcliff, 1980a).

All of this work (and much more, see Alba & Hasher, 1983, and Taylor & Crocker, 1981, for reviews) provides the necessary background to document the importance of the notion of schemas and to lay the foundation for further research. The particular directions that we investigate in this chapter involve consideration of an abstract type of schema and the kinds of processing in which such schemas might be involved.

Thematic knowledge structures capture this level of similarity by representing the patterns of goals and plans in the episode. The theme, or point, of an episode lies in more abstract relations between concepts. This higher-level, thematic information is often independent of most contextual features. For example, the thematic information involved in the notion of "retaliation" is not dependent on a particular context; one can imagine retaliation occurring in a wide variety of settings. A terrorist group retaliating against a government crackdown with a bombing incident is quite different in context from a child, feeling wronged, tattling on a sibling. The actor information in a representation of the "retaliation" theme has to match both a desert-trained commando and a self-righteous four-year-old; they have little in common on the surface. What they do share is the pattern of the actor being harmed, giving rise to his goal of revenge. So, although quite different in many ways, every episode that embodies the theme of "retaliation" is, at a more abstract level, equivalent.

These patterns could be used to recognize the meaning of an episode, and to organize in memory episodes that share the abstract similarities represented by the pattern. Because the structures are built from experiences, they represent generalizations made across episodes that vary greatly in some respects while sharing more abstract similarities. Schank (1982) outlined a class of thematic structures whose purpose is to characterize complex interactions of goals and plans. "Thematic Organization Points" (*TOPs*) represent the problems occurring during the pursuit of a goal and the issues relating to what happens after a goal succeeds or fails. Because the thematic vocabulary is sufficiently abstract, *TOPs* are useful in recognizing and remembering episodes across domains. TOPs are related to earlier versions of "themes" (Abelson, 1973; Schank & Abelson, 1977), and differ from other structures proposed to capture thematic information (e.g., Lehnert, 1981; Wilensky, 1983) in the emphasis on the overall pattern of goal and plan interaction, the importance of the attached conditions, and their functionality as structures in memory. As a characterization of a particular pattern of goal and plan interactions, *TOPs* as memory structures provide convenient organizations of episodes.

Consider this example from Schank (1982):

X was talking about how there was no marijuana around for a month or two. Then, all of a sudden, everyone was able to get as much as they wanted. But the price had gone up 25 percent. This reminded X of the oil situation the previous year. We were made to wait on lines because of a shortage that cleared up as soon as the price had risen a significant amount.

The *TOP* Schank proposed as the structure of this episode can be labeled "Possession Goal; Commodity Mysteriously Unavailable." This organization point in memory is based upon the significant conditions that affect the planning for the possession goal. Other pieces of information needed in this case would be "becomes available later," "higher price," and perhaps "controlled by unethical people." The conclusion contained in this structure is that unethical people who control a commodity will put it back on the market once the price has risen. The *TOP* also provides planning information, namely that the goods will be available later at a higher price, so one should wait a while and prepare for the future purchase. In this way, matching a new situation to a thematic structure can help in understanding and may suggest a way of solving a problem. In the commodities example, the structure provides the assurance that the commodity will be back on the market soon, but with a higher price.

Schank (1982) uses the functionality of the structure in memory to constrain the representation of the thematic information. *TOP*s as knowledge structures are based on the principle of functional constraints on memory; that is, the form and content of *TOP*s depends on their use. *TOP*s should contain the right information and be organized in a particular way in order to provide appropriate knowledge when needed. Knowledge structures perform several functions: for example, they may aid in recognizing an old story in new trappings, provide expectations about the situation, and predict an outcome for a newly encountered situation. In addition, *TOP*s provide the concise "point" to a story (such as an adage,) and let you guess how something will turn out because you have seen the steps before. The *cross-contextual* nature of *TOP*s makes them of particular interest for learning information in one situation that will apply in another. For example, *TOP*s may bring to mind a story that illustrates a point, thereby providing an explanation of co-occurrences of seemingly unrelated events in order to draw conclusions. One very important function of *TOP*s is to aid in learning about the world from varying contexts.

How can we determine what *TOP*s might exist in memory? It's not as easy as listing the different kinds of common scripts we know about. First of all, since they are based on experiences, the *TOP* structures formed by any individual will be highly idiosyncratic. Second, there exist endless variations of goal and plan interaction patterns: which ones are distinctive and useful in memory organization? Because knowledge structures are based upon common episodes in the world, examining similarities in experiences may uncover some *TOP*s used to organize those experiences. Schank

(1982) has suggested examining the similarities and themes in everyday life that are revealed in common adages and sayings. Adages are patterns of goal and plan interactions that people recognize and share, and that remind people of other experiences. A moral derived from a story is the realization of the point of the story, and so can serve as an effective way of characterizing the theme of an individual episode. It would seem that cultural sayings, based on the commonalities of experiences in a variety of settings, are a good place to begin looking for thematic structures to organize episodes in memory.

Thematic Abstraction Units as Knowledge Structures

Dyer (1983) has used this approach to develop Thematic Abstraction Units (*TAUs*). *TAUs* are based on patterns of goals and plans seen in common adages—in particular, adages that represent expectation failures due to errors in planning. *TAUs* are thus a subclass of *TOPs*. A *TAU* contains an abstracted planning structure that tells where the error in planning occurred, that is, where something that was expected to happen did not. *TAU* structures are important both within a story and as a connection between stories, as they represent the thematic structure of a single episode and serve as episodic memory structures which organize similar episodes. Consider this example story from Dyer (1983):

> In a lengthy interview, Reverend X severely criticized the then President Carter for having "denigrated the office of president" and "legitimized pornography" by agreeing to be interviewed in *Playboy* magazine. The interview with Reverend X appeared in *Penthouse* magazine.

This is a routine news report of a clergyman complaining about pornography. However, because the story demonstrates the minister's involvement in the very activity he condemns, the point or moral of the story is the minister's hypocrisy. A *TAU* captures this point of the story, expressed by the adages *The pot calling the kettle black, Practice what you preach,* and *Don't throw stones when you live in a glass house.* Here is a *TAU* structure for the hypocritical minister's complaint (Dyer, 1983):

TAU HYPOCRISY:

X is counter-planning against Y
X is trying to get a higher authority Z to block or punish Y for using Plan P1 by claiming P1 is unethical
X has also used the unethical plan P1
therefore, X's strategy fails.

In the story, the minister tries to move public opinion against Carter by claiming Carter supports pornography. Since the minister supported it to the same degree, his strategy fails.

In this manner, *TAUs* serve to capture goal and plan interactions involving particular planning failures. These structures explain the pattern of goal and plan elements within the story, and serve as the basis for connections between related episodes. For example, the same *TAU HYPOCRISY* structure captures the minister's complaint story and the following story:

> Karen's swimming coach was a real slave driver. An athlete himself, he had the team working out for many hours every day. Besides their workouts, he insisted that each player be in great shape for the season. During the preseason training sessions, the coach would warn the players that they should avoid drinking, drugs, overeating, and especially smoking. "Everyone knows that athletes should treat their bodies with respect," the coach said as he puffed heavily on his long cigarette.

This *TAU* could have been very useful to the minister: if the minister had remembered and applied the coach story, he might have avoided making the same error of condemning someone when you may be caught doing the same activity. The *TAU* structure stores the planning information that denouncing someone's behavior will lose its effectiveness if you are caught doing the same thing. If the episodes can be organized in memory with the *TAU*, the important information about planning captured by the *TAU* can be available when needed.

Previous research has tested people's sensitivity to these *TAU* patterns (Seifert & Black, 1983). In that study, subjects were given three exemplars of a particular *TAU* pattern such as *TAU HYPOCRISY*, and were asked to write "one new story that has the same type of plot." Asking subjects to write stories based on prototypical stories should indicate whether they are able to abstract the thematic similarities in the prototypes and reproduce that theme in a new context. The three sample stories were "about" very different things, such as jobs or auto mechanics, but shared the same abstract pattern of making a planning error. The 56 subjects were given three sets of example stories and were asked to write three new stories. Eighty-two percent of the stories matched the *TAU*, using other contexts such as school, jobs, and dating to express the *TAU* pattern. In a second study, subjects were given lists of 36 stories, six each of six different *TAU* patterns (written by other subjects), and were asked to group the stories together, using any criteria they wished.

The results were analyzed using Johnson's hierarchical clustering algorithm (Johnson, 1967; Reiser, Black, & Lehnert, 1982), and showed that the stories were reliably sorted into six groups which corresponded to the six

TAUs the stories were based on. These results show that subjects are sensitive to the abstract, thematic structures, and further, that they can use these relationships to perform tasks based on similarities between stories. Subjects were able to preserve the *TAU* pattern in their stories so that it is recognizable to other subjects, and were able to use *TAUs* as the basis for story similarity. These experiments demonstrate subjects' sensitivity to thematic patterns, and indicate the thematic level of information can be used to compare and create stories. It also provides specific suggestions about what knowledge structures contain, for example, the analysis of clustering brought out the importance of *causation* in the thematic pattern. It is clear that the thematic information present in an episode plays a crucial role.

The thematic level of knowledge appears to be captured by structures that contain relatively abstract information about goal and plan relationships. This knowledge is clearly needed to understand the point of episodes based upon themes. Further, these structures may organize episodes that contain similar thematic information. The premise that thematic structures are useful in encoding and organizing related episodes suggests interesting properties of memory. If similar episodes are encoded using thematic structures, these structures may serve as the connection between related episodes. In order to find out more about the connections between episodes, we can look at their function in the phenomenon of *reminding*.

REMINDING BASED ON THEMATIC STRUCTURES

We can learn about *TOPs* by looking at reminding. Schank (1980, 1982) has proposed using reminding as a method to examine the role of knowledge structures and connections between episodes in memory. Reminding occurs when a particular situation causes one to remember another experience that is similar in some way. The relationship between the new input and the old memory retrieved can be at any level of abstraction or similarity. For example, seeing a bearded man in a red suit may remind you of Santa Claus, going into Burger King for the first time may remind you of McDonald's, and seeing "West Side Story" may remind you of "Romeo and Juliet."

The Mechanism of Reminding

Why does one experience remind us of another, especially when the two experiences share little apparent similarity of surface content? Schank (1982) proposes the theory that the second experience—the reminding—is a natural product of the attempt to understand the first. In this view, understanding is a process that involves being reminded of the closest experience in memory to the input experience. Thus, Schank proposes that in understanding the new situation, you are led to structures in memory that categorize the input, and from there retrieve a previous episode which had been stored in the same way. Calling to mind previous episodes is even more likely if an interesting or unusual characteristic is present in the input. Schank's theory, then, is that reminding occurs as a natural part of the process of understanding new situations in terms of previously processed episodes.

Under this theory of memory, understanding an event means finding an appropriate place for a representation of that event in memory. Similar structures and episodes are searched through to find the closest related place in memory to store an input. Therefore, a reminding would indicate that a specific episode in memory has been seen or excited during the natural course of processing the input. To do this we must have been *looking* for the reminding or have *run into it accidently.* In either event, reminding occurs when we have found the most appropriate structure in memory that will help in processing a new input.

Imagine the following situation:

> You've been to McDonald's many, many times, but never to Burger King. The first time you go there, you're not sure what to expect. You walk in, stand in line, read the menu off the wall, order hamburgers and fries, put them on your tray, pay the cashier, and sit down to eat. Finally, you think, "You know, this place reminds me of McDonald's."

From your reminding, it is clear that you have understood Burger King in a sufficiently deep way. You understand Burger King in terms of McDonald's because they share many features. You go into Burger King, and you have to stand in line (just like in McDonald's). Then, you tell the cashier your order (again just like McDonald's). Then, you pay for your food before you sit down and eat it (McDonald's again!). Schank (1982) suggests that these two experiences share so many features that you cannot help remembering one when you first experience the other. Under Schank's theory, experiences that share so many features will also share a representational structure in memory. These shared features form the basis of a mental framework or knowledge structure in memory, and because the two restaurants share these features, both restaurants would be stored under the same structure in memory. If memory is indeed functioning based on the principle that the understanding process will involve accessing the closest related experience, understanding one restaurant experience will mean accessing the same structure in memory that the other shares. As a result of this process, people would be unable to avoid thinking about related memories as they try to understand their experiences.

The Role of Cases in Understanding

Because we believe that it is not accidental that reminding occurs, it is important to consider the functionality of reminding. What is the function of retrieving another episode given a new one? Why would it be advantageous to be able to access a particular case in addition to the generalized structure? We have already seen that the *TOP* structure itself provides a lot of information such as expectations, explanations, categorization, and planning advice. From the structure alone, there is knowledge about making predictions for what is likely to happen, expectations about the problems one might encounter, and tips on the prevention of the same planning errors. While the structure serves many functions as outlined above, remindings must also serve important functions in understanding.

First, remindings may serve to evaluate the categorization of an episode by a *TOP.* When the *TOP* structure provides the generalization, the reminding can serve to evaluate how well the structure characterizes the new situation. With another case from the same memory structure, you can ask, "Are these two episodes really similar?" This can aid in recognizing when you've miscategorized an episode.

Second, because *TOP* structures are built from cases, the cases stored under a *TOP* serve as evidence for the generalizations it contains. At times, it may be useful to question the generalizations the *TOP* embodies: a frequent pattern may or may not be a good rule about the world. Being reminded of previous cases gives you an opportunity to say, "I've seen this pattern a lot—do I believe it?" Because you may discover correlations about the world without a full explanation of its causes, a mechanism to reevaluate the generalizations you form is very useful.

Third, specific cases are useful precisely because structures are generalizations. While the structure can provide general information, episodes can provide specific knowledge about contextual constraints. Some information, such as specific constraints on planning, is important only in some contexts. For example, a generalized rule such as *inform your coplanner of your plan* might be accessible from a *TOP,* but more specific advice to inform them in secrecy would come from a case that requires the same secrecy constraint on the planning. For a couple planning to run off to Las Vegas and marry, coordinating plans is very important. However, if they are facing the opposition of their parents, a specific reminding such as the story of "Romeo and Juliet" would provide the knowledge that they must let each other know about the plans and that they must keep the plans a secret from their opponents. In this way, an old episode may provide additional information comparable with the new situation; for example, actions from the old situation that might be possible in the new, problems to watch for, and specific expectations about what will happen. The information at the *TOP* level is kept general in order to apply to all cases; therefore, remindings of particular cases could provide additional information.

Fourth, reminding plays a role in forming new generalizations. A reminding may provide some information not captured by the *TOP*. Because the *TOP* is built from previous cases, the generalizations it contains are those which proved useful at the present time. Other features may become important, and the generalizations of the *TOP* can be changed as new cases are added which highlight specific features. Thus, in a new episode, some feature may become more important, although it was left out of previous generalizations. The reminding then adds to understanding by pointing out similarities in the two experiences that had not been noticed. In this manner, the information in the *TOP* can be changed to reflect new features.

Without the benefit of case information, drawing appropriate generalizations and determining the limits of their application would be impossible. Cases are needed to form appropriate generalizations; therefore, the crucial role of reminding is to guide the process of learning. Consider this example (Schank & Seifert, 1985):

> X was walking along a beach in Puerto Rico at dusk when he noticed a sign on the beach saying, "No swimming at this point." Yet everyone was swimming happily and it was clearly safe. X walked along further and came upon a new sign saying, *Don't go beyond this point. Dangerous!* X explained this to himself by assuming that the hotel had put up the signs to try to cover itself legally in case of an accident. At this point X was reminded of the signs in Connecticut that say, *Road legally closed, pass at your own risk,* when the road is in full use. X had previously explained these signs to himself by saying that the state of Connecticut, in the event of an accident, wanted to be able to say the road was legally closed, and that they therefore were not responsible.

Once X had explained the hotel signs as an attempt to cover any legal liabilities, the previous experience with the same explanation came to mind. From the two examples, X could make the generalization that institutions, such as states and hotels, are likely to take such steps to protect their liability. However, from only one experience it would be difficult to tell how far to generalize the expectation—to all states? to governments? to road owners? The role of the reminding is to help make the appropriate generalizations, and the second experience is quite functional in constraining and guiding the generalization. Of the many features available, it is important to establish which ones are most relevant. What X had to do with the hotel example is decide that the most relevant feature is protection of one's legal liability through signs.

Thus, the information from a particular episode is very important for the purposes of generalizing across contexts. In order to learn what goal and plan information is important in a particular situation, a related episode can be contrasted to determine what the similarities are. With another episode to serve as a guide, the appropriate generalization can be formed. It is this mechanism of reminding that serves as the basis for learning. However, remindings can serve an important function even after particular *TOPs* are well learned—namely, filling in specific knowledge from very similar cases.

Thus, we constantly receive new inputs and evaluate and understand them in terms of previously processed experiences. Why have these prior experiences been labeled in such a way that they show up at the right times? Consider the similarities between the Minister story and the Karen's Coach story about hypocrisy, discussed in the last section. How must they be organized in memory in order to have one remind you of the other? These two stories have a lot of features—smoking, pornography, publicity, even warnings—that will not be very useful in finding one memory based on the other. However, at the thematic level, the *TAU HYPOCRISY* structure outlined above captures the crucial similarity via the relationships between the goals in the episodes and the interesting deviations in the situation. Features of that goal pattern in one story can activate the *TAU* structure, and may activate the other story stored with the *TAU*. When an episode involves a complex goal pattern, similar episodes that had been understood using that goal pattern may be brought to mind. One is reminded of a particular experience because the structures one is using to process the new experience are the same structures one is using to organize memory. Thus, Schank (1982) proposes, while processing a new input one cannot help but pass through the related previous experiences in memory.

A Process Model of Reminding

How is it that we bump into episodes as we process new experiences? We would like a process model of how episodes are activated through structures. What is the nature of the connections between the structures and the episodes that build them? One possibility is that episodes are immediately activated as a consequence of the activation of a knowledge structure. This view is similar to a model of semantic memory, where related concepts are activated by accessing a node in memory. It appears that the activation of an episode will directly affect the structure that stores it; however, the connections between episodes may be of a different quality. When is a structure accessed and when is a case activated or retrieved? Under what processing conditions is information from episodes likely to be useful; that is, when is reminding most likely to occur?

Let's examine a proposal for how episodes may be stored under thematic knowledge structures. Consider these two episodes from Dyer (1983), both based upon the thematic pattern in the adage "Closing the barn door after the horse has gone."

Academia:

Dr. Popoff knew that his graduate student Mike was unhappy with the research facilities available in his department. Mike had requested new equipment on several occasions, but Dr. Popoff always denied Mike's requests. One day, Dr. Popoff found out that Mike had been accepted to study at a rival university. Not wanting to lose a good student, Dr. Popoff hurriedly offered Mike lots of new research equipment. But by then, Mike had already decided to transfer.

Hired Hand:

The hired hand wanted a raise, but the farmer would not grant it. Finally, the hired hand got an offer to work at a neighbor's farm. When the farmer found out, he offered the hired hand a raise, but it was too late.

The similarity in the two stories involves some general planning information about a common error: waiting too long to act. The general information in the *TAU* structure proposed by Dyer (1983) to capture these two episodes is represented as:

TAU-POST-HOC:

1. X has a problem situation active;
2. X knows a plan that will solve the problem and prevent a negative event;
3. X does not execute the plan and the negative event occurs;
   X attempts to recover from the failure by executing the plan now;
   The plan fails, because it is effective in *avoiding* negative events, but not in *recovering* from the negative event;
4. In the future, X must execute the plan *before* the negative event occurs.

Given the two episodes, and a general structure to encode them, the resulting organization in memory is suggested to be similar to the following pattern (Dyer, 1983):

Recalling an episode involves activating the associated structure, with

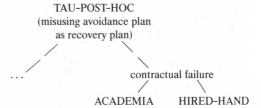

FIG. 8.1.   The memory organization of a TAU structure and related
episodes.

its related inferences and information. This is due to the encoding of each episode in terms of its organizing structure (Bartlett, 1932; Alba & Hasher, 1983). This schema-activation hypothesis suggests that accessing an episode stored under an organizing schema also activates the schema itself. However, the question of when an episode is accessed, given an activated schema, remains unclear. Similarity between episodes serves as the basis for structures; yet, episodes that share structures may or may not activate each other. The conditions under which an episode may remind one of another may depend on more than the thematic structure they share.

We considered four possibilities based upon the model of memory we have discussed above:

1. The current story may activate the abstract *TOP* structure, and through it the previous story; reading the Academia story will activate the Hired Hand story.
2. The current story may activate the previous story either as a whole or by parts as the episodes are matched, and through them the *TOP* may be activated.
3. The current story may activate the *TOP*, but no other episodes.
4. The current story may activate neither the *TOP* nor the other episodes.

In the first two cases, activation might lead to connections in memory between current and previous stories. In the third, in order to traverse the connections between structures and episodes, either more information or different processing demands may be necessary.

Fairly strong claims have been made about the circumstances of reminding and understanding. One theory of memory suggests that "we cannot help but pass through the old memories while processing a new input" (Schank, 1982). This approach implies that related episodes must be activated when a structure is accessed. Whether or not a conscious reminding occurs, the connections between episodes through their shared knowledge structure may result in activation. In a series of experiments, we set out to test the hypothesis that thematic knowledge structures determine the organization of episodes in memory. Specifically, we would like to determine whether related episodes are automatically activated when the structure is utilized. If not automatically activated, under what circumstances do episodes that share a structure activate each other? This question called for a novel approach to investigating reminding.

EXPERIMENTAL REMINDING

An important initial task was to create an experimental methodology that could provide some answers to these and other questions about memory. How can we move the phenomenon of reminding into the lab? Examining reminding empirically depends on developing both a naturalistic task that is analogous to reminding in the real world and a successful measure of the activation of episodes. Success in experimentally demonstrating whether and when a previous episode is called to mind depends on a naturalistic task. How can we manipulate when and how people are reminded so that it will occur during the experiment? What are the appropriate control conditions? How can we accurately measure what people are thinking about?

A novel approach was required to provide a convincing display of reminding. Tight controls are probably impossible when testing the kinds of questions that we are interested in. We cannot control a person's whole set of life experiences for the purpose of a psychological experiment. This concern has led psychologists to develop laboratory experiments to test natural task performance. Another concern is the variety of memory structures that each individual will have formed, as they are based on the individual's experiences.

Our goal was to attempt to get subjects to pass through old memories while processing a new input. We decided to present episodes that were verifiably "thematically similar," and measure whether subjects made connections between the episodes. If two similar episodes were presented to subjects, one after the other, would they encode them using the same thematic knowledge structure? And, if they did so, would they be "reminded" of the first episode when encoding the second? For example, if subjects first read the Academia story, and then read the Hired Hand story, would the two stories be connected in memory? Would reading the Hired Hand story activate (cause a reminding of) the Academia story? This method should determine the degree to which reminding is spontaneous during reading.

Methodology

In our experimental paradigm, subjects were asked to read a series of stories that were based upon thematic structures. The question addressed was whether the stories are connected in memory based upon their thematic similarity. In a series of experiments, we examined the circumstances under which previous story episodes were activated. In each of the experiments, subjects read stories based upon *TOP* structures. We examined what happens when the story that is currently being read has the same *TOP* structure as a previously read story.

We needed a way to measure accurately the reminding, or the activation, of the previous episode. Priming in item recognition has been shown to be a successful methodology for determining if concepts are active in memory (McKoon & Ratcliff, 1980a). In the experiments presented here, priming is used as a measure of the activation of target episodes in memory. The degree of relationship between the two concepts in memory is measured by the response time for one when preceded by the other. If two items are connected in memory, answering a question about one will prime the process of answering a question about the second. So, using our previous example, a question about the Hired Hand story may be asked, and immediately followed by a question about the Academia story. If the two stories are connected in memory, responding to the first question should facilitate responding to the second. Response time to verify an item (answer "true" or "false") should reflect the item's relation to the just-preceding item. If the two test items come from thematically similar stories, and are therefore connected in memory, the response time should be shorter compared with the case where the two items are from unrelated stories.

We also needed materials that were close to naturalistic episodes while being manipulable for our purposes. As discussed above, the *TAU* structures defined by Dyer (1983) seemed to fit our requirements. Because *TAU*s are based upon common adages, their content reflects cultural knowledge that could be familiar to our subjects. The set of *TAU*s we employed involved planning errors captured by familiar adages such as "counting your chickens before they hatch," "closing the barn door after the horse is gone," and "the pot calling the kettle black." While the *TAU*s captured similar themes, they were also distinct from each other. In order to have pairs of stories with similar themes and pairs with dissimilar themes, the themes had to be discriminable. Thus, we selected a set of *TAU*s which seemed to involve the same kind of planning knowledge while being discriminable from each other. This was supported by the experiments discussed earlier, where subjects were able to sort the stories sharing a *TAU* into the same group, and did not group stories across *TAU*s (Seifert and Black, 1983).

In Experiments 1 and 2, priming was used to test for memory connections between elements of two stories. The two stories were read one after another, and then a test list of items was presented. In the comparison of interest, two items, one from each story, were presented one after another in the test list. If the two stories are based on the same thematic structure, verification of an item from one story might speed verification of a similar element from the other related story.

In Experiments 3 through 6, we tested for activation by presenting a single test sentence immediately after a story was read. If the test sentence is from a previously read story with the same *TAU* structure as the story just read, response time might be speeded because the previous story had been activated. The following is an informal description of the experiments; a complete explication is available in Seifert, McKoon, Abelson, and Ratcliff (1986).

Experiment 1. The question we investigated is whether information in a text is encoded with respect to previously read episodes that have the same structure. Is a previously read episode activated and is information from a previously read episode connected in memory to the new episode? In our first experiment, subjects read lists of story pairs based on *TAU* structures. We hypothesized that if two stories based on the same *TAU* were connected in memory, then a sentence from one of the stories should speed response time for an immediately following sentence from the other story.

Twenty subjects were asked to read a series of story pairs presented one at a time on a computer screen. Stories in the Same-Theme condition were paired with a story based upon the same *TAU* pattern, and stories in the Different-Theme condition with stories based upon a different *TAU* pattern. On each of the 44 trials, they read two stories and then responded to eight test sentences about those two stories. The task was to respond, by pressing a key, whether each test sentence was "true" or "false" according to the story it was from. For each of the stories, there were four test sentences: the "conclusion" sentence of the story, a true filler and two false fillers. For example, the conclusion or outcome for the story about the graduate student in Table 8.1 was "by then, Mike had already decided to transfer." The critical priming pair was the conclusion sentence from the first story immediately followed by the conclusion from the second. If the two stories share the same *TAU,* verifying the conclusion sentence from the first story should speed the verification of the conclusion from the second story, compared with the response times when the stories do not share the same *TAU.*

A control condition showed that two items from the same story *did activate* each other relative to items in the same presentation pair but not the same story. Thus we have an indication that our methodology is sensitive enough to register connections in memory, replicating previous work

TABLE 8.1
Sample Stories

Dr. Popoff knew that his graduate student Mike was unhappy with the research facilities available in his department. Mike had requested new equipment on several occasions, but Dr. Popoff always denied Mike's requests. One day, Dr. Popoff found out that Mike had been accepted to study at a rival university. Not wanting to lose a good student, Dr. Popoff hurriedly offered Mike lots of new research equipment. But by then, Mike had already decided to transfer.

True filler: Popoff always denied the requests for equipment.
Conclusion: By then, Mike had already decided to transfer.
False filler: The doctor was known as a terrible researcher.
False filler: Mike decided to buy his own research equipment.

Phil was in love with his secretary and was well aware that she wanted to marry him. However, Phil was afraid of responsibility, so he kept dating others and made up excuses to postpone the wedding. Finally, his secretary got fed up, began dating and fell in love with an accountant. When Phil found out, he went to her and proposed marriage, showing her the ring he had bought. But by that time, his secretary was already planning her honeymoon with the accountant.

True filler: Phil made up excuses to postpone the wedding.
Conclusion: His secretary honeymooned with an accountant.
False filler: Phil didn't even know she wanted to get married.
False filler: Phil proposed marriage with no ring to offer.

(McKoon & Ratcliff, 1980a) that showed that the elements of an individual story are connected to each other. However, when verifying the conclusion of a story, preceded by the conclusion of another story, it made no difference whether the stories expressed the same theme or a different theme, F's < 1 for both response times and error rates. Mean response time was 1538 ms (3 % errors) in the Same-Theme condition, and 1516 ms (5 % errors) in the Different-Theme condition.

Experiment 1 thus failed to demonstrate an effect of thematic similarity upon verification time. While the similarities in the stories appear quite salient, especially when presented in pairs, this manipulation did not affect the time to verify the conclusion of one story when preceded by the conclusion of the other. Apparently, either subjects did not recognize the intended similarities, or if they did, elements of similar stories were not connected to each other. In order to determine if subjects were at all able to make use of the thematic similarity in the story pairs, a second experiment was designed to stress the use of the themes in understanding the stories.

Experiment 2.   In this experiment, we attempted to encourage subjects to recognize and use the thematic similarities in the story pairs by providing explicit instructions about thematic similarity.

Twenty subjects participated in an experiment identical to Experiment 1, but with two additions. First, they were given specific instructions about the themes in the stories. While in Experiment 1, no mention of themes was made to subjects, in Experiment 2 they were given a description of the type of themes used in the experiment and an explicit example of theme in a story, and were told to think about the theme of each story. Second, the subjects rated the similarities of the stories after each test list on a seven-point scale, 1 meaning very different and 7 meaning very similar.

In contrast to Experiment 1, response time for a conclusion was faster if it was primed by another story conclusion with the same theme rather than with a different theme. Mean response time was 1567 ms (10 % errors) in the Same-Theme condition and 1649 ms (14 % errors) in the Different-Theme condition. This difference was significant with subjects as a random factor $F(1,19) = 4.7, p < .05$, and marginally significant with test sentences as a random factor, $F(1,46) = 3.2, p = .10$. The difference in error rates was not significant. The similarity ratings from Experiment 2 show that the subjects were reliably able to detect the intended thematic similarity in the story pairs. For the Same-Theme pairs, the mean rating was 6.19; for the Different-Theme, the mean was 2.97. In Experiment 2, subjects did make use of the thematic similarity in the story pairs, resulting in a marginally significant effect of the thematic connections between the stories. This effect was found when subjects were instructed to consider thematic similarity while they read (in Experiment 2), but not in Experiment 1 when they were not so instructed.

Experiment 2 shows that subjects are sensitive to the thematic structures of these stories. Intuitively, the thematic structures must be accessed to understand the story, because to the extent that the thematic structure captures the point of a story, failing to recognize the thematic structure is failing to understand the story completely. In addition, our measure of activation was sufficiently sensitive, as shown by a control condition. Therefore, we argue that subjects do understand the themes in the stories even without specific instructions, but that this understanding does not automatically provide connections between elements in two instances of the same theme. Instead, it suggests that the connections between episodes require some strategic processing during reading (as in Experiment 2).

Experiments 3 and 4.   Experiments 1 and 2 are subject to the criticism that the testing occurs *after* both stories have been encoded into memory; the testing is separate from the reading process. Because of the need to test for activation of the previous episode *during encoding,* two more experiments were designed to test for priming immediately after reading the second story. In this design, the second story itself functions as a priming item for the test sentence from the first story in the pair. In an attempt to pace the comprehension process so that all subjects were encoding the last line of the story just prior to testing, the stories were presented word by word at a natural reading rate.

In these two experiments, each subject read a series of stories on a computer screen, some of which were followed by a single test sentence from the immediately preceding story, to which the subject responded "true" or "false" as in Experiment 1. Two stories presented one immediately after the other could have either the same or different thematic structures. In Experiment 3, as in Experiment 1, subjects were given no specific instructions about the themes of the stories. In Experiment 4, as in Experiment 2, subjects were given instructions about the themes in the stories, a rating task, and a few extra seconds of reading time for each story.

The hypothesis, as in Experiments 1 and 2, was that subjects would be faster to verify the conclusion of a story when it was presented immediately following a story with a similar theme (Same-Theme condition). However, in neither experiment was there a significant effect. The respective means for the Same- and Different-Theme conditions were 1659 ms (8 % errors) and 1659 ms (8 % errors) in Experiment 3 and 1698 ms (6 % errors) and 1752 ms (8 % errors) in Experiment 4. While the difference in Experiment 4 was 54 ms, it was not significant ($F(1,19)$ = 2.4 with subjects as the random variable) and for only 11 of the 20 subjects was the difference in the right direction. Subjects in Experiment 4 were reliably able to detect the intended thematic similarity in story pairs: for Same-Theme pairs, the mean rating was 5.85; for the Different-Theme pairs, the mean rating was 2.90.

When test sentences were presented immediately after a story was encoded, there was little evidence of the activation of thematically similar information. Even in Experiment 4, where specific instructions were given and ratings indicated that subjects did recognize the intended thematic similarities, they were simply unable to make use of the similarities they saw. When a story is presented word by word, as in Experiments 3 and 4, it may be much more difficult for subjects to invoke either the encoding processes needed to set up the memory representation for later retrieval by a thematically similar story or the retrieval processes necessary to find such stories. In Experiments 5 and 6, we attempted to make these processes easier by giving subjects extensive study on the stories that would later need to be retrieved by thematic similarity.

Experiments 5 and 6.   In these experiments, subjects prestudied a set of stories. This set was intended to be the experimental analogue to a set of previous experiences in memory. Each prestudied story was paired with two test stories: one based on the same *TAU* as the prestudied story, and one based on a different *TAU.* For both stories, the test sentence was the conclusion of the prestudied story, as shown in the examples in Table 8.1. We hypothesized that, in the Same-Theme condition, reading a test story with the same thematic structure as the prestudied story may remind subjects of the old story, leading to faster response times for the test sentence.

There were three phases to Experiments 5 and 6, a prestudy phase, a study-test phase, and a final free-recall phase. In the prestudy phase, subjects were asked to read and summarize eight target stories, each of a different *TAU* pattern. In the study-test phase, new stories were presented word by word and were followed by a test sentence which always referred to one of the prestudied stories. Eight of the new stories were paired with the eight prestudied stories so as to have the same thematic pattern (Same-Theme condition), and another eight were paired with the prestudied stories so as to have a different thematic pattern (Different-Theme condition). Thus, each conclusion sentence from a prestudied story was presented for testing twice, once in the Same-Theme condition and once in the Different-Theme condition, counterbalanced for order of presentation.

Two different tasks were used as reaction-time measures. In Experiment 5, subjects made a true/false decision as in the other experiments. In Experiment 6, an identification task was used; subjects pressed a response key as soon as they could remember which story the test sentence referred to. After responding, they wrote a one-sentence description of the story referred to by the test sentence. In the final, free-recall phase of each of the two experiments, subjects were asked to recall the prestudied stories. Eighteen subjects participated in Experiment 5 and eight in Experiment 6.

In both experiments, responses in the Same-Theme condition were faster than responses in the Different-Theme condition. In Experiment 5 (verification), the mean response time in the Same-Theme condition was 2376 ms (3 % errors), and in the Different-Theme condition, 2554 ms (1 % errors). This difference was marginally significant, *min* $F(1,15) = 3.8$, $p < .08$. The difference in error rates was not significant. In Experiment 6 (identification), mean response time in the Same-Theme condition was 1253 ms, and in the Different-Theme condition, 1474 ms. These means were significantly different, *min* $F(1,14) = 5.4$, $p < .05$. All subjects had completed the accuracy check of writing an identifying phrase from the story after hitting the response key. In the final free recall phase, subjects were able to generate 75% of the prestudied stories in both experiments.

These experiments provide strong evidence for the effect of thematic similarity in activating previous episodes. In both the verification task and the simpler identification task, response times for a test sentence from a prestudied story were faster when the story preceding the test sentence matched the test sentence's story in thematic structure. New stories appeared to activate stories already encoded in memory on the basis of their thematic similarity.

Conclusions from the Experiments

In our experiments, we sought to determine some of the circumstances under which reminding occurs during reading. We wanted to know whether activation and connection processes during reading were automatic or strategic encoding processes. Schank (1982) has claimed that schematic information like that represented by *TAU*s is automatically activated and automatically connected to other schematically similar information in memory.

Our conclusion was that a story currently being read does not automatically activate a thematically similar (previously read) story, nor are elements of the two stories automatically connected to each other. However, when subjects were encouraged with instructions, then there was weak evidence that the connections were made. Further, when instructions were combined with extensive prestudy, strong evidence for the activation of thematically similar episodes was observed. These experiments show that thematic similarities can serve as the basis for reminding when there is a functional purpose of reminding in the task. The conditions under which activation and connection occur appear to depend on the strategies in which subjects engage during reading, and the ease of remembering old episodes. When subjects are not encouraged to remember previous episodes, there is no evidence for activation or connection. However, when subjects are encouraged with instructions, then there is weak evidence that the connections are made. Finally, when there is a built-in purpose for reminding in the task, as in Experiments 5 and 6, activation of episodes is functional to the task and subjects have no trouble activating the episodes in memory.

THE FUNCTIONALITY OF REMINDING

We propose that the significance of these results lies in the demonstration of the functionality of abstract memory structures. It appears that one thematic episode does not automatically activate or become connected to another similar episode. Rather, strategic processing seems to be involved. When subjects in Experiment 1 were not given instructions to rate the thematic similarity of the stories, there was no reason for one story to bring to mind a similar story. But such reminding became functional when the rating task was introduced (Experiment 2). Similarly, in Experiments 5 and 6, remembering the prestudied stories was functional because all of the test sentences came from those stories. Thus when recalling previous episodes serves a function, this type of strategic processing may be observed.

Do our experimental results alter the conception of reminding expressed by Schank (1982)? Schank focused on the role of reminding in *understanding* new episodes. In that view, understanding meant "being reminded of the closest concept in memory to the one being processed." It was not clear whether episodes that share structures activate each other or under what conditions the activation of the episode was likely. We have seen that while two episodes can activate the same structure during encoding, they do so only under certain circumstances. That is, when there is a built-in functionality or processing goal to consider case information, reminding will occur.

Intentional Reminding

Schank (1982) proposed three conditions in which remindings occur:

1. Current structures can't handle the case, and you are forced to learn a new structure;
2. An episode serves as the structure due to its prototypical nature;
3. Under some circumstances you can be intentionally reminded.

Our results suggest that, at the least, intentional reminding plays a much bigger role than previously indicated and seems to be the best prospect for further experimentation. In this type of reminding, processing is directed by a desire to call a relevant past experience to mind. It is an attempt to come up with a relevant experience that will help to understand the current situation. "Intentional" is not meant too literally; that is, it is not always consciously intended, but can come from just thinking about a situation in a particular way. For example, consider conversation: an understander seeks, in the processing of new input, to be reminded of a memory that relates to what he or she heard and provides substance for a reply. In intentional reminding, whether a conscious search process or not, accessing a previous episode is fostered by implicit goals in processing. These goals, part of particular tasks, make the recall of episode information more likely. Rather than relying on the structural generalizations needed for simple expectations, some tasks require more specific case information. Therefore, the goals in processing are more likely to lead to recalling previous episodes.

The issue of the functionality of reminding suggested by these experiments is reminiscent of previous work with analogies. For example, Gentner and Tenney (1984) have found little evidence for the spontaneous use of analogies such as water for electricity where neither domain is well understood. Schustack and Anderson (1979) found that recognition of facts about fictional persons was not helped by analogies with famous people unless the analogy was pointed out, both at the time the facts were studied and were tested. Likewise, Gick and Holyoak (1980, 1983) have found that subjects are not likely to be able to use the analogy between a story they study that contains a solution and a problem that needs a similar solution, unless they are instructed or given more than one story to study. We think that the similarities between two thematically similar stories in our experiments are much more obvious than the similarities in either Schustack and Anderson's or Gick and Holyoak's experiments. Yet, subjects were not able to use them without aid (instructions and/or prestudy). Thus, the present experimental results suggest that the functional purpose of reminding and analogy must play a role in determining when it occurs.

What functions do remindings serve? What kind of processing goals are implicit in these tasks that would foster reminding? If you look closely at the remindings people offer, you can see how they are used to augment general principles. Consider this example reminding:

> X was analyzing the problem of how they got Mr. Ed to speak on the old TV show. She contended that it was easier to train a horse to talk like a person than to take a person and teach them to be a horse. She was then reminded of a situation that occurred in Paris where training was required. An opera company there was putting on a Russian production and needed singers who knew Russian. Because the singers had such difficulty with the Russian, they rounded up all the Russian cab drivers in Paris and taught them to sing. X then said, "training a horse to talk is no worse than training Russian cab drivers to sing when opera singers couldn't learn Russian."

In this case, the general principle of "reversing the training because it is a simpler proposition" is evident in the horse example. However, the reminding of the Russian singers serves the function of buttressing the argument and adds a claim about its feasibility ("it's not worse than . . . "). Thus, in this example, being reminded made the argument stronger by providing an actual experience where X's claim is supported. In a second example, the reminding plays the role of supporting a proposed plan by providing an example of its successful previous application:

> Y was lamenting that it was awful to be at Teletrack, the local indoor betting arena, due to the smokers who were impossible to avoid. Smoking is, in fact, prohibited at Teletrack, but everyone ignores that and consequently smokers are spread all over the arena. The authorities try to ban all smoking and are unable to control it. Y proposed that he should ask that smoking be allowed at Teletrack; if smoking were allowed, smoking and nonsmoking sections would have to be designated and Y would have a section where he wouldn't have to sit next to smokers. Z was then reminded of the action England took to control the use of heroin in the country: under a complete ban, the use was

not controllable. Once it was legalized, the government had control over those who needed to buy the drug.

Z's reminding serves the function of supporting the proposed plan with an example of its success. The claim that restricting smoking produces the end result of a smokeless section better than prohibiting it is supported by the heroin control in England. Without the reminding, it might be hard to reason out the possible effects of the plan.

Remindings can serve a variety of functions in particular tasks. For example, in conversation, a response is formulated that puts forward a point of view. In order to express the view without totally disregarding the question asked, relevant information from memory must be found that relates the topic asked about to the point of view. *TOPs* are needed so that specific inputs can be processed by general structures containing memories that relate to those inputs in an interesting way. Formulating a good response often requires one to draw analogies from other contexts. The rules the speaker has for responding require relevant memories upon which to operate. The understander seeks, in processing of new input in conversation, to be reminded of a memory that relates to what was heard and provides evidence for the point of view to be defended.

Remindings can serve to verify your analysis of an episode, illustrate why your reasoning is valid, justify or support a claim, give specific solution information, and perhaps provide an analogy that may be revealing. Thus, finding a reminding can be a much more active process than accidental fallout from understanding, and may be required by rules and strategies in the reasoning process.

Goals Foster Reminding

Some tasks being modeled in computer programs may assume reminding occurs with every input. For example, in the *CYRUS* program (Kolodner, 1984), the goal was to retrieve a particular episode in memory given a set of features. Reconstructive strategies were applied to the memory network of episodes and structures to retrieve an episode whenever enough features distinguished an episode from its organizing structure. Clearly, retrieval of episodes through *TOP* structures alone will not occur very frequently. As discussed earlier, experiences will not serve as great a function, and therefore be recalled less frequently, when the *TOP* structure is well learned. Therefore, while activating a *TOP* in memory will not frequently be likely to cause a reminding, some types of processing goals may be more likely to produce remindings. If we look carefully at the tasks chosen to study reminding through computer simulation, we can discover the kinds of strategies in reasoning that make use of remindings, and are therefore more likely to produce them. Implicit goals in reasoning processes that make use of remindings may foster the retrieval of experiences from memory.

The kinds of tasks which utilize case-based information have implicit goals to guide processing. For example, the *JUDGE* program (Bain, 1984) attempts to determine a fair sentence for an offender by evaluating all possible information. Both thematic structures, such as justification strategies (i.e., *Parity Retaliation,* where a victim strikes back to an equal degree of harm to offender and victim), and previous instances play a role in the reasoning process. In this task, previous experiences are very useful in evaluating possible outcomes of a sentencing. In fact, the judge's responsibility is to try to find the best sentence to make certain outcomes more likely; therefore, remembering past cases where particular sentences had particular results would be very useful. In addition, remembering cases is important in trying to maintain some consistency in sentencing across individuals.

In the *WOK* program (Hammond, 1983), the goal of creating a new recipe guides the search in memory for useful information. Comparing past recipes based on a new dimension is an important part of being creative, and, therefore, the need to examine past cases is an important part of the process. For example, a failure situation will be analyzed to help search memory for a solution. In the *beef and broccoli* example from this program, cooking the items together fails because the meat produces too much water for the broccoli to handle. This problem of a side-effect of one goal interacting with the carrying out of another goal is captured by a *TOP* structure. Using the structure as a starting point, memory is searched for other plans that would prevent this side-effect. Through some search strategies, the program comes up with a plan used before to cook two things that have different cooking times, such as pork and snow peas: cook the two ingredients separately. In this type of task, where the creation of new plans occurs by comparing past successes and failures, reminding as a strategy is very important.

What types of tasks will include processing goals that promote remindings? Clearly, any type of problem-solving task will tend to require the kinds of processing demands we have been discussing. In situations where complex situations are represented by prototypes, recall of episodes will be important. For example, in the legal domain, cases often stand as prototypes for decisions, and lawyers need to recall cases as exemplars to formulate arguments. Reminding is the basis for analogical thinking, and in situations where there is a lack of domain knowledge, drawing upon past experiences that share some similarities will be necessary.

In complex problem-solving tasks, where detailed reasoning is required, remindings can aid in thinking through the factors involved in the problem. For example, in the domain of psychiatric diagnosis, where complex information is available to be considered, recall of previous cases may suggest correlations not previously observed (Kolodner & Simpson, 1984). Finally, in examining alternative conceptualizations or scenarios, possible solutions can be used as memory indices to find past instances where the solutions were tried, and the resulting episodes can be compared to the current instance.

Modeling these types of tasks will likely give us better access to the reminding process. Because of their intentional nature, they are likely to provide more instances of reminding across contexts. If we look for the kinds of processing goals that foster reminding, we are likely to find rich problems that will involve interesting knowledge structures and strategies for finding cases. Further, these kinds of tasks are likely to be more amenable to psychological experimentation in the laboratory. "Strategies" in experimental settings have been viewed as negative factors that impede the measurement of some more interesting process. However, some strategies are very interesting and integral parts of the reasoning processes we are interested in studying. By focusing on a naturalistic task, and devising news ways to test hypotheses in the laboratory, these strategies can be investigated as they function in reasoning.

9

Explanation-Driven Processing in Summarization: The Interaction of Content and Process

Dana S. Kay
John B. Black

Summaries can help individuals grasp the most important facts about events without being distracted by peripheral information. A good summary not only includes central ideas, but presents these ideas in a succinctly organized manner that results in a coherent representation of an event. If given this smaller, general representation, readers can begin to create a knowledge structure for the summarized event, this structure can later guide the reader in understanding the event's details. We would like to understand how "good" summaries can be generated and how these summaries can be used to aid comprehension. Initially, however, we need to investigate the more general aspects of summarization.

The goal of our research was to investigate the generation of summaries. To understand what people do when they are asked to give a summary of an event described in a text, we posed two questions: (1) What is the memory representation of the text that will be used to generate the summary? and (2) What is the process that acts upon this representation to condense the structure? From these two questions, we identified three aspects of the problem to consider: (a) the content of the presented event (e.g., goals, plans or actions), (b) the structure of the representation of the event (e.g., hierarchical or heterarchical), and (c) the process that is used to transform this information into a more concise and coherent representation (e.g., choose the top-most node of the hierarchical representation). Thus far, summarization research has focused primarily on the structure of the representation of the event. Investigators who have proposed models of story comprehension have also shown that their models can be applied to summarization and used to predict the information that will be present in summaries (Rumelhart, 1975a, 1975b; van Dijk & Kintsch, 1977).

However, when these models are examined closely, it appears that they are unable to predict the summaries of text that do not themselves conform to text structures licensed by the models of story comprehension. Furthermore, they present a sketchy account of the process involved in summarization. We agree with past investigators that text structure is an important aspect of summarization. However, our research has led us to believe that a purely structural account of summarization is doomed to failure. Readers' summaries reflect both the content of the texts and the use of various summarization procedures.

Before presenting our approach to summarization, we would like to give a brief account of what we believe to be taking place during summarization. When we ask someone to summarize a text, we are asking them to use all the information that they have about a story or event and simplify this information so that only the most important issues are discussed. This simplification process entails two subprocesses—selection and abstraction.

The selection subprocess requires that whoever is giving the summary choose the most central features of the story or event without being sidetracked by the peripheral features. For example, if a story about a man going on a trip includes the fact that the man was wearing black shoes, it is more important to state in the summary that the man went on the trip than that he was wearing black shoes. This subprocess has been addressed by a number of people, and in general, it has been found that the structural representation of the text (whether it is schematic or propositional) directs selection to the most important information. That is, within the representation of the text, there is a global, or "macro," structure that is necessary in linking the entire memory representation together and this high-level structure corresponds to the central information in the text.

In the abstraction subprocess, generalizations are drawn from more specific information present in memory (e.g., if a person in a story buys oranges, apples, and pears from a market, we can generalize in the summary and state that the person bought fruit). In previous summarization research, abstraction has not been investigated as completely as selection. Kintsch and van Dijk (1978) discussed generalization as part of their story comprehension model. Generalization is proposed as a rule that allows people to condense microstructure representations of a text into smaller more abstract macrostructure representations. This generalization is presented in conjunction with other rules that aid in this same condensation process. However, most of the research addressing generalization and abstraction is found in the learning and memory literature (Anderson, 1982) and has not been applied to summarization.

As in other chapters in this book, our investigation of summarization presents a combination of psychological experimentation and psychological and artificial intelligence theories. We will present a model of summarization from artificial intelligence and illustrate how through experimentation and the addition of a new component to this model, we can propose a model that provides a more complete account of the summarization process.

PLOT UNITS

Lehnert proposed that "to summarize a story, it is necessary to access a high level analysis of the story that highlights its central concepts" (1981, p. 293). To this end, she presented the application of her *plot unit* model to the process of summarization. In this model, conceptual structures—plot units—are used to represent the behavioral patterns of the character(s) in a narrative. Lehnert proposed that during summarization, *patterns* of goals, events, and outcomes are more important than the individual goals, events, and outcomes. For example, competition between two characters is represented by a pattern in which two people have the same goal but only one character achieves this goal, resulting in a positive outcome for the successful character and a negative outcome for the unsuccessful character. When a story is analyzed using plot units, it is broken down into overlapping conceptual structures that represent patterns of behaviors for the characters in the narrative. Once the story is mapped onto these individual structures, these structures are linked to form a complete representation of the plot of the story.

In our discussion of Lehnert's plot unit model, we will describe the mechanisms of the model, describe how these mechanisms apply to the generation of summaries, and then compare the plot unit model of summarization with previous models of summarization.

The Model

Plot units are causally linked "affect" states distinguishing between "positive" events, "negative" events and mental states of the characters in the narrative. In the competition example previously mentioned, competition between two persons is represented by mental states for each person that are causally linked to a positive event for the winner of the competition and a negative event for the loser. Fig. 9.1 gives a graphic representation of the competition plot unit.

The first step in recognizing a plot unit depends on the recognition of the "affect" states that are interacting. Lehnert proposed taxonomies for each type of "affect" state, using the knowledge structures presented by Schank and Abelson (1977). For example, if there is an intended plan, then this plan is represented with a "mental state," M. The failure of this plan

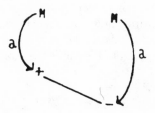

FIG. 9.1.   Competition plot unit.

would be represented by a "negative event" (−) and the success of the plan would be represented by a "positive event" (+). For each state, Lehnert proposes the existence of a system of demons for building specific plot units. These demons can be activated by the existence of various other plot units to which they have been previously linked. If there is a relationship between the target demons and the newly activated demons, then the related states are linked and a "primitive" plot unit is built. For example, the primitive plot unit for "success" is represented by a mental state and a positive event that are connected by a link representing the actualization (a) of the plan. An example of the success plot unit as part of a more complex unit is found in the left-hand portion of the competition plot unit in Fig. 9.1. Primitive plot units are the building blocks for the more complex plot unit configurations that are needed to form a complete representation of the narrative.

Once primitive plot units are formed, there is demon activation across the primitive plot units that directs the linking of these units to form high-level, cross-character, plot unit configurations. Speech acts (such as promise and threat) are examples of structures that must be represented using these complex configurations. Fig. 9.2 presents a story and its complete plot unit representations, including primitive and complex plot units (adapted from Lehnert, 1981).

Plot Units in Summarization

By following this process and recognizing the various plot units present in a narrative, we can obtain a high-level analysis of the narrative that includes information about the activities and interactions in the narrative. Lehnert proposes that it is the interactions represented in the high-level analysis that should also be present in "good" summaries. She argued intuitively that those summaries which appear to be the best are the summaries that contain more plot units, especially those important in the story.

Evidence for this proposal is presented in a rough comparison of summaries with and without the high-level information. According to Lehnert's analysis, the plot units embedded in the complex diagram of Figure 9.2 are:

Problem resolution, in which John handles the crook discovery problem by arresting Alice's father; *retaliation,* in which Alice produces a negative outcome for John because he produced one for her; *loss,* in which Alice's action terminates the positive engagement state of John; and *tradeoff,* in which Alice's action terminates her own positive state. Table 9.1 presents a series of summaries for this story. Although she provided no "goodness" ratings for the summaries, Lehnert argued that the fifth summary was the most accurate because it included all four plot units in the configuration (tradeoff, retaliation, problem resolution, and loss).

Thus, Lehnert proposed that from the narrative information represented by the plot unit structures, she can predict the quality of the summaries. In addition, she presented a process model for the generation of summaries for simple plot unit clusters. In this model, the first step is the identification of all the top-level plot units of the narrative. From these plot units a plot unit graph structure is built to represent the text. Given this structure, the pivotal plot unit (i.e., the plot unit that is most highly connected to the

John was thrilled when Alice accepted his engagement ring. But when he found out about her father's illegal mail-order business, he felt torn between his love for Alice and his responsibility as a policeman. When John finally arrested the old man, Alice called off the engagement.

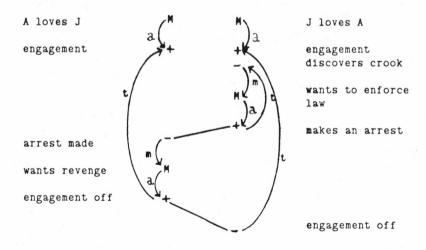

The notations beside the links are these: "a" for *actualization*; "m" for *motivation*; "t" for *termination*.

FIG. 9.2.   Plot unit representation for John and Alice story.

TABLE 9.1
Example Summaries for John and Alice Story

1.	When John arrested Alice's father, she interfered with his wedding. (no tradeoff for Alice)
2.	When John arrested an old crook, Alice called off their engagement. (no retaliation for Alice)
3.	When Alice's father was arrested, she called off her engagement. (no problem resolution for John)
4.	When John arrested Alice's father, she called off her engagement. (no loss for John)
5.	When John arrested Alice's father, she called off their engagement. (all units present)

other plot units) is identified. Each plot unit is associated with a "generational frame" which allows for the expression of the plot unit information in natural language. The "generational frame" for the pivotal plot unit is used to form a base-line summary of the text and it is this base-line summary to which additional narrative information (from the plot units linked to the pivotal plot unit) is added to complete the summary.

Since the plot unit model is based on the creation of connections between various plot units to form a graph representation of the narrative, the most important step in the generation of summaries is the identification of the most highly connected plot unit in the representation of the narrative. Lehnert named this unit the "pivotal" plot unit. In the Alice and John story, the pivotal plot unit is Alice's retaliation (i.e., her decision to break the engagement). This unit links all the main events in the plot of the story. The retaliation results in John's loss of Alice and is caused by John's decision to arrest Alice's father and Alice's decision that her father is more important than John.

Once the readers recognize the central plot of the story, they must then express the plot unit structure in natural language. To explain the transition from "affect" states and links to sentences, Lehnert posited generational frames associated with the individual plot units. She described two types of generational frames—weak and strong. Weak generational frames represent the generic way of expressing the plot unit information, and strong frames present more domain-specific information.

Lehnert (1981) used the competition plot unit to illustrate the difference between these generational frames. If we assume that there is a competition plot unit in a story in which X and Y are competing for a job in their company and X gets the job, then the weak generational frame for this unit is "X and Y wanted the same thing, but X got it." However, if we also assume that the person conveying this message has domain-specific information about competition for a job, then the strong generational frame will override the weak generational frame and the event could be stated "X got promoted over Y." These statements convey similar ideas; however, the weak generational frame could be used to represent any competition and the strong generational frame is only for competition for a job.

Lehnert acknowledged that there are problems with the implementation of this process model. The algorithm proposed is general and there are various special cases that the model is not be able to account for. For example, plot unit representations cannot be created for text that does not contain goals, plans, etc. However, these representations do provide an additional method for examining most narrative summaries and the processes involved in their generation.

The Plot Unit Model
and Other Models of Summarization

Lehnert's plot unit model provides an alternative to the previous models of summarization. Rumelhart (1975a, 1975b), building upon a story grammar approach, presented a structural hierarchy model. In this model, structural rewrite rules are applied recursively to the text to form a hierarchical representation of the text. For example, the top level of a story might consist of a goal, an attempt, and an outcome. To construct a summary using this representation, the top-most nodes of the hierarchy are chosen and reported. If a more expanded summary is needed, nodes from the next level down in the hierarchy are included. A hierarchical model was also presented by van Dijk and Kintsch (1977; Kintsch & van Dijk, 1978). In this model, the text is represented by a set of propositions that can be reduced and reorganized into a global representation (or macrostructure) of the text. The macrostructure contains the central information from the text that is necessary in a summary.

Before we present an empirical comparison of the plot unit model of summarization to these other summarization models, we will note certain general differences among the models. The first difference is the structure of the representations used to generate the summaries. The other models rely on a hierarchical representation of the information in the narrative. Proponents of these models argue that the most important information is represented at the top of the hierarchy. Using rules for trimming the hierarchical representation, this information is chosen for the summary. Plot unit representations, however, are heterarchical. That is, the overall configuration of the plot units is dependent on the interactions within the narrative. In these representations, the most important information is the most highly connected information. Thus, inclusion of information in a summary generated from a plot unit graph structure is dependent on connectivity in the structure as defined by the interactions in the text rather than the systematic application of all relevant transformation rules.

In these hierarchical models, the focus is on the use of episodes or microstructures to represent the text. Therefore, it is only important to note that these structures are used to represent the text and not that there are different types of structures within the representations. In the plot unit model, however, the focus is not only on goals and plans, but also on the types of goals and plans that are used together to form patterns such as the competition plot unit. Thus, the plot unit model presents an attempt to incorporate content as well as structural aspects of the text into the representation.

A third difference among these models addresses the process aspect of summarization and the direction of the processing. Hierarchical models use primarily a top-down process. In this approach, there are a number of expectations that must be met during the processing of the text. Therefore, summaries of narratives that do not conform to the general narrative schemas present in these models cannot be generated. The plot unit model uses what might be called an "inside–outside" process. That is, the process recognizes the central, most connected plot unit (i.e., the pivotal unit) and works out to the peripheral, least-connected plot unit.

Experimental Evidence
for Plot Units in Summarization

When the plot unit model was proposed, Lehnert, Black, and Reiser (1981) experimentally investigated the predictions of the model. The main hypothesis in this study was that summaries should contain information that refers to the most highly connected units in the narrative. This prediction was contrasted with the hierarchical prediction that the higher the information was located in the hierarchical representation of the narrative, the more likely it was to be present in the summary.

In this experiment, three versions (S1, S2, S3) of a single story were used. These story versions were similar in content and involved deeply nested sets of subgoals that the main character devises and achieves. There were four main goals that could be present in the stories, but one or more were omitted in each version. Appendix A illustrates these goals within the text by presenting story version 1.

The hierarchical and plot unit models made a number of similar predictions about what information from the stories would be found in the summaries. However, to tease apart the models, Lehnert, et al., examined four instances where the two models differed in their predictions. For each instance, predictions were made about the presence/absence of a target proposition(s) in the summaries of the three story versions. For the hierarchical models, the predictions were based upon where the target proposition was located in the hierarchical representation of the text. For example, in the hierarchical representation for the story in Appendix A, the proposition, "Mike builds a patio," is at the top level of the hierarchy and the proposition, "Mike gets accountant to trick boss," is at the sixth level of the hierarchy. Therefore, the prediction from this representation is that building the patio is more likely to be present in the summary than getting the accountant to trick the boss. In the actual experiment, the predictions are made across story versions, rather than within stories. Our example uses a within story comparison for clarity.

The plot unit model predictions were based upon whether or not the proposition was part of a highly connected plot unit for which a strong generational frame would be used to express the plot unit. For example, in the plot unit representation for the story presented in Appendix A, the proposition, "Mike builds a patio," is part of the plot unit "Mike gets Paul away to build patio." This plot unit is weakly linked to the other plot units in the story (e.g., "Mike obtains boss's agency to get Paul away"). As a result, the plot unit model predicts that a weak generational frame (Mike wanted to get Paul out of town), rather than a strong generational frame (Mike wanted to get Paul out of town because he wanted to build a patio for his birthday) will be instantiated to express this plot unit. Therefore, the proposition is not likely to appear in the summary of the story.

The first proposition, when analyzed using the hierarchical model, appeared at the sixth hierarchical level for story versions S1 and S2 and at the fifth level for story version S3. The hierarchical model predicts that the target statement will appear more often in a summary for the S3 version of the story than in the summaries of the other two versions. However, because the target statement is at the same level in the hierarchy for the S1 and S2 versions, the model cannot make separate predictions for these two versions. From the plot unit representation of the story, the proposition is part of a weak generational frame (i.e., a plot unit that is weakly linked to the overall representation) for S1, a moderate generational frame (i.e., a plot unit that is moderately linked to the overall representation) for S2 and a strong generational frame (i.e., a plot unit that is strongly linked to the overall representation) for S3. Therefore, the prediction was that the proposition would be present most often in S3, moderately often in S2 and least often in S1. Lehnert, et al., examined the summaries for the three story versions and recorded the frequency with which the target statement appeared in the summaries. The proposition appeared most often for S3, moderately often for S2 and least often for S1, these differences being statistically significant. Although both models predicted that the proposition would be present most frequently mentioned for S3, the plot unit model was also able to distinguish between S2 and S1 and correctly predict that the proposition would be present more often for S2.

For the second target proposition, again the hierarchical model was only able to predict which of the three summaries was most likely to contain the target sentence because the proposition was at level 3 for S1 and S2 and at level 2 for S3. The plot unit model was able to make separate predictions about the likelihood of the target proposition for each story version summary based on the generational frames associated with the proposition. Again, the results supported the plot unit predictions.

The third analysis looked at the predictions for two target propositions. In this analysis, the hierarchical model predicted that since the first proposition was higher in the hierarchical representation for each version of the story, it would be more likely to appear in the summaries than the second proposition. Since both propositions were part of the weak generational frame for S1, moderate generational frame for S2, and strong generational frame for S3, the plot unit model predicted that the two propositions were equally likely to appear in all three summaries. In the results, the second proposition appeared significantly more often for the S1 and S2 versions of the story and the two statements appeared equally often in the S3 version. Therefore, both models were incorrect for the S1 and S2 versions, but the plot unit model made the correct prediction for the S3 version.

The final target proposition was present in only two of the three story versions. In both of the hierarchical representations, the target proposition was at the top level of the representation. Therefore, the hierarchical model strongly predicted that this proposition would be mentioned in the summaries of these two versions. However, the plot unit model did not predict the presence of this proposition because it was only weakly linked to the pivotal unit. The results for this statement supported the hierarchical prediction. Lehnert, et al., propose a self-containment explanation to account for this result. This explanation is discussed in the next section.

From the results of this study in which three of the four target areas were better predicted by the plot unit model, Lehnert, et al., argued that the plot unit model is better able to account for summarization behavior. They also argued that the one instance where the model failed in its predictions could be accounted for by nonstructural factors. Therefore, they proposed that summarization is a function of both internal memory structures and other nonstructural factors.

SELF–CONTAINMENT

As previously mentioned, the plot unit model was not able to account for the fourth target area of the Lehnert et al., (1981) study. They proposed that the target sentence predicted to be absent from the summary (Mike wanted to build a patio) was present because the subgoal of the story was not self-contained. That is, the goal was "instrumental" to another part of the story (getting a friend out of town). The goal, when presented by itself, begged for an explanation that was only provided by a related goal present in the story. This account is an *ad-hoc* addition to the plot unit model. Later we will propose a principled account of containment effects.

To examine this idea further, Lehnert, et al., (1981) performed a post-hoc analysis using two structurally identical stories which differed only in whether or not the subgoal of the story was self-contained. In one story (from Rumelhart, 1975b), a farmer wanted to go to a square dance, but before he could go, he had to get his donkey in the shed. In the other story (taken from the original plot unit experiment and adapted from the farmer/donkey story), a man wants to build a patio for his friend as a birthday surprise, but before he can do this, he has to get the friend out of town (see Appendix A). Lehnert, et al., proposed that in the summaries of these stories the high-level goal of building a patio would be mentioned more often than the high-level goal of going to the square dance. This differential prediction was made because in the patio-friend story, the subgoal of getting a friend out of town needs further explanation that is provided by the high-level goal of building a patio and therefore, the subgoal is instrumental to the high-level goal. However, in the dance-donkey case, a farmer putting a donkey in a shed needs no explanation and is therefore self-contained.

The results of this analysis were in agreement with this prediction. The high-level goal was mentioned significantly less often in the dance/donkey case. This result contradicts the predictions of the hierarchical and plot unit models in that the hierarchical models predict that the high-level goals will be mentioned in the summaries for both of the stories and the plot unit model predicts that the subgoals will be mentioned in the summaries because they are highly connected within the representation of the story.

We decided to further explore this self-containment factor, using several stories rather than one story, and extend the results to cover cued recall as well as summarization (Kay & Black, 1984a). Our hypothesis was that if self-containment does affect text processing, then when a subgoal is self-contained, it is less likely that the high-level goal associated with that goal will be mentioned in summarization and recall. It is important to note that our use of a recall task in addition to summarization assumes that the same representations and processes are used in these two tasks. It becomes evident later in this discussion that our assumption is not necessarily true. We performed two experiments to test the self-containment hypothesis.

Self-containment Experiment

We used eight different high-level goals. These goals constituted the first sentence of each story and conveyed an initial motivation for the protagonist's actions. In the stories each of these goals was paired with two subgoals to create two structurally identical versions of the story. One of the subgoals was "self-contained" (i.e., it was considered to be a fully explained episode) and the other subgoal was "instrumental" to another event in the text (i.e., it needed further explanation). The majority of the story was devoted to the subgoal, which was expanded into a couple of paragraphs. An example of the goal pairings used is:

High-level goal: Graduate student wants to go to a rock concert.
Self-contained: Graduate student must get data analysis done for adviser.
Instrumental: Graduate student needs to find a car to borrow.

The prediction is that the graduate student going to the rock concert will be mentioned more often when paired with finding a car to borrow because the student finding a car to borrow needs an explanation that is provided by the goal of going to the concert. After reading each story subjects wrote a one- or two-sentence summary of the story. Then, after a short intervening task, subjects were given the story titles as cues and asked to recall all the stories.

Collapsing the results across tasks, we found support for the original prediction that the high-level goal would be mentioned more often in recall and summarization when paired with an instrumental goal. When the summary and recall data were separated, we found that the high-level goals were mentioned in approximately one-fourth as many summaries when paired with the self-contained goals as when paired with the instrumental goals. This difference in the summarization results is reliable and supports the original self-containment prediction. For the recall data, again, the high-level goals for the self-contained stories were mentioned significantly less frequently. Table 9.2 presents the percentage of the high-level goals and the subgoals mentioned in each story type for the summarization and recall tasks.

From these results, there is evidence that self-containment of a goal influences summarization and recall behavior. High-level goals related to self-contained subgoals are infrequently mentioned in summarization, and are not uniformly recalled. However, an alternative explanation for these results may be that because of the nature of the self-contained subgoals, the subjects were not able to see the connection between the high-level goal and the subgoal. To investigate this explanation, Experiment 2 was performed. This experiment was identical to Experiment 1 except that new stories were added in which the connection between the subgoal and the high-level goal was made explicit.

TABLE 9.2
Percentage of Goals Mentioned in Summarization and Recall

	Summarization		Recall	
Goal Type	Self-Contained	Instrumental	Self-Contained	Instrumental
High-level	27	91	73	95
Subgoal	100	100	96	96

Explicit Connections and Self-containment

In this experiment there were 32 different stories that were divided into two groups. One group of stories was designed in the same manner as the stories in Experiment 1, that is, there were eight high-level goals that were paired with a "self-contained" subgoal and a "instrumental" subgoal. The second group of stories used those stories from the first group, but added a phrase or sentence to the stories that explicitly tied together the high-level goal and the subgoal. This manipulation was performed to facilitate the subject's ability to connect the actions in the story. Using the self-contained subgoal from the graduate student example that was mentioned in Experiment 1 (the graduate student must get data analysis done for his adviser before going to a rock concert), the implicit/explicit difference is as follows:

IMPLICIT: Bill became frantic because he would have to do some fancy juggling to satisfy his academic and social desires.

EXPLICIT: Bill became frantic because he would have to do some fancy juggling to satisfy his academic and social desires. He decided that if he worked quickly he could get the data done just in time for the concert.

The procedure for this experiment was the same as that of Experiment 1 except that in this experiment there were two groups of subjects. One group received stories with the explicit connecting phrases and the other group received the same stories without the connecting phrases. Subjects in both groups were given eight stories (four self-contained and four instrumental).

Collapsing across task and story type we again found results that supported our original hypothesis. However, when we considered each story type and each task within story type, we found that there was no significant difference between the story types and that the significance of the overall results stemmed from the summarization task only. That is, for both the implicit and explicit stories, when the subgoal was self-contained the high-level goal was mentioned significantly less often in the summaries of the stories. For the recall of both types of stories there was no significant difference between goal types. Therefore, it appears that our previous assumption that recall and summarization would be influenced equally by the self-containment of goals may not be true.

One possible explanation for the difference between summarization and recall is related to the demands of each of the tasks. A recall task asks for all the information in the text and, therefore, both the high-level goals and the subgoals are mentioned regardless of the type of subgoal. However, summarization asks for only the most important information from the text. Since the high-level goal is more important for the instrumental subgoals than for the self-contained goals, it is mentioned more often in the summaries of the stories containing instrumental subgoals. Table 9.3 presents the percentage of goals mentioned in the summaries for the explicit and implicit stories.

Explanation-driven Processing: Supplementing the Plot Unit Model

We have seen that the plot unit model, while generally successful, fails to account for self-containment effects. We performed two experiments to pursue these effects, and now propose that an explanation-driven processing model should be added to the plot unit model, if we are going to be able to account for the summarization results of our studies. Explanation-driven processing (Dyer, 1983; Wilensky, 1983), proposes that in processing the text, the reader searches for explanations for the events in the text. Previous research has investigated explanation-driven processing during comprehension (Seifert, Robertson, & Black, 1985), but we have also found it operating in summarization.

Our experiments suggest that there are certain content-oriented factors that influence the relative importance of the events to the text and thus, the

TABLE 9.3
Percentage of Goals Mentioned in Summaries

Goal Type	Explicit		Implicit	
	Self-Contained	Instrumental	Self-Contained	Instrumental
High-level	74	99	50	96
Subgoal	100	99	98	100

likelihood of the events being reported in a summary of the text. One content-oriented factor is self-containment. Fig. 9.3 presents a flow-chart representation of explanation-driven processing as it pertains to self-contained subgoals. The first step in the process is choosing the most highly connected event in the text, presumably the central event of the most pivotal plot unit. If there is an already existing knowledge structure for this event, then there exists a "canned" explanation for the event. Therefore, the event is fully explained and the summarization process ends with the report of the main event and the high-level structure that explains the event. This was the case with the self-contained goals in our stories. However, when the event is instrumental, there is no previously existing knowledge structure to generate a canned explanation. To find the necessary explanation, inferences are generated to link the event with other information found in the text. Once an explanation is found, then a summary is generated that contains the main event and the event(s) that are necessary to explain the main event.

Implicit in this process is that when summarizing a text, the goal is to present a coherent representation of the main event in the text. The plot unit model specifies how to locate the main event, but not how to make it coherent. To produce this coherent representation, the event must be fully explained. This explanation process usually entails connecting the event with other events in the story. However, the current experiments suggest that in summarizing text, the process of explaining new information using previous information from the text can be "short-circuited" in the presence of a normal event, goal, or plan that provides a canned explanation (Wilensky, 1983). Thus, in the presence of standardized information, not all possible explanations for a situation are needed for a coherent account of an event.

The structural hierarchy model (Rumelhart, 1975a, 1975b), the propositional hierarchy model (van Dijk & Kintsch, 1977) and the plot unit model (Lehnert, 1981) focus on the structural representation of the narratives and propose that the process of summarization entails choosing the top-most levels of a representation. In contrast, we elaborate this process and propose that explanation-driven processing (Dyer, 1983; Wilensky, 1983) can be used to predict summarization results. In all three of these models of summarization, the proposals have been based upon analyses of goal-based, fictional narratives that discuss characters participating in an environment similar to the real world. Therefore, the readers are familiar with the types of events that take place in this environment. However, if a model of summarization is to present a complete account of summarization, then it should be able to predict summaries for goal-based texts in which the domain is not as familiar.

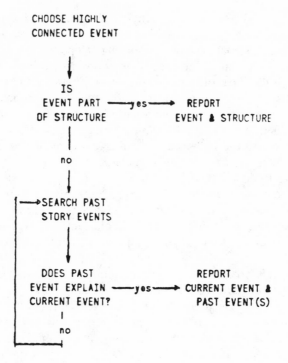

FIG. 9.3. Explanation-based processing for stories with self-contained subgoals.

EXPERT AND NOVICE SUMMARIZATION

Recently, we began to extend our explanation-driven processing approach to less familiar goal-based texts (Kay & Black, 1984b). We chose articles from the *Wall Street Journal* as our first extension of the model. We chose this newspaper because although the text is goal-based, the goals pertain to the business domain (and were not familiar to our Yale undergraduates). Thus the goals in these articles would have a structure similar to those of the fictional texts, but differ in content. For example, one goal that is prominent in these articles is AVOID-BANKRUPTCY. This goal is structurally similar to the goal PRESERVE-HEALTH that is familiar to most people, but the plans and actions associated with the goal are quite different. If our explanation-driven model can account for summaries of this type of text, then we can be more confident that the model is not tied to a specific context.

Another reason for our choice is that there are "expert" summaries of some of the more important articles on the front page of each newspaper. The label expert can be applied to these summaries from two perspectives. From a summarization perspective, these summaries are written by people who have been hired by the *Wall Street Journal* to write summaries of articles in the paper. Therefore, one can assume that these people have mastered the art of summarization through all the experience they have in the task. The other interpretation of experts is that these people were hired for their expertise in the business domain. That is, they are familiar with the normal course of goals, plans, and actions which are present for business transactions and therefore, they are better equipped to write summaries of articles about this domain.

The expert/novice distinction that we made for these summaries has a direct relation to the self-contained/instrumental distinction of the previous experiments. If one assumes that the experts in our experiment are experts because they have had experience with the individual events presented in the articles, then we can propose that they have built up knowledge representations for the events in the text and therefore, the events are fully explained or self-contained. On the other hand, the novices have not been previously exposed to these events and therefore, there is a need to explain why the situations exist as they do. As a result, the two types of subjects should differ in the amount of explanation that they feel is important to the summary.

We used six articles. These articles were chosen because (a) they were summarized on the front page of the paper and (b) they were written in a narrative style rather than the style of a stock report (we wanted to be sure that the articles could be read by someone who is not a stockbroker). The stories were about economic concerns such as bankruptcies and marketing changes. Appendix B presents a sample story. Subjects, who served as the novices in our experiment, were asked to give the story a title and write a one- to two-sentence summary of the story. The expert summaries were taken directly from the *Wall Street Journal* and were roughly the same length. In addition to testing the ability of the explanation-driven model to account for the expert and novice summaries, we also wanted to explore the differences (if any) that exist between the two types of summaries and give some insight as to why these differences occur.

The titles generated by the novices were used to assure us that the subjects understood the main topic of the article. For all the stories, the titles were similar to the actual article titles. In some cases, the titles stated the main topic, while in other cases, the novices sensationalized the titles to sound like a newspaper article. The latter finding suggests that the subjects were using their knowledge of typical newspaper articles, though the articles were referred to as "stories" in the experiment.

To exemplify the novice/expert differences that were observed, Table

9.4 presents a sample expert summary along with a two novice summaries. These summaries are for the article in Appendix B.

Before comparing the novice and expert summaries, we analyzed the content of each type of summary and considered possible strategies that could account for the information that was selected from the article. It should be noted that each story generally presented a main event and several subevents that either elaborated upon the main event or described past events relevant to the main event. For example, the Osborne story discussed the possible failure of the company, how the company is dealing with this possibility, how the company hopes to avoid the failure, and possible causes for the failure.

There are three types of information reported in the expert summaries. The first information type is a concise statement of the main event. This statement is usually a condensed version of the first paragraph of the article (e.g., Osborne Computer faces failure). The second type is an elaboration of the event, using other information present in the article. In the second sentence of the example above, Osborne's failure is defined by its debt, furlough of employees and halting of computer production. The final type of information present in the data refers to implications of the current situation. In the example above, this information is the denial of involvement by ITT.

TABLE 9.4
Expert and Novice Summaries of Osborne Story

Expert Summary

Osborne Computer faces possible failure, unless it finds a purchaser. The company is deeply in debt to suppliers, just furloughed nearly 80% of its employees and has halted computer production. One possible buyer, ITT, denies any involvement.

Novice Summaries

Osborne Computer Corp., a portable computer industry, is failing and looking for someone to acquire it and lend it money for debts. The company began as a prosperous, fast-growing company which was ruined when it tried to change the computer market and tangled with the jumbo companies such as IBM.

Osborne Computer Corp., being deeply in debt, faces failure unless it is acquired by a larger company, possibly ITT. Its downfall can be attributed to too rapid a climb, trying too much, and pressure from a much larger competitor, IBM.

For the novice summaries, only one of the experts' three types of information is present. Novices present the main topic of the story, but do not elaborate the event or note the implications of the event. Instead, they include information about the causes of the situation. Examples of this information can be seen in the second sentences of the novice summaries previously presented. This type of information was found in more than half of the novice summaries for each article, suggesting that novices see causes of an event as more important than elaborations or implications of an event. (Further details are given in Kay and Black, 1984b.)

Experts, it would appear, decide on the main event of the article and then infer a possible goal that is active for this event. Using this goal, the expert follows the events associated with the goal and notes the success or failure of these events. The novice summarization process begins in the same manner as the expert process in that the current goal is inferred. However, rather than carrying the goal through to the possible implications, novices attempt to explain the goal by reporting other events that are causally linked to the active goal and present these events.

From these algorithms, it appears that the novices and experts are using different selection and abstraction strategies. When selecting what to report in a summary, novices focus on the causes of the main topic, whereas experts focus their attention on the possible outcomes of the event. In addition, experts present a more detailed representation of the event, rather than presenting a number of causally related events at less-detailed levels.

Why Does This Difference Occur?

There are various explanations for our results, depending on the perspective that one wishes to take with respect to the "expert" summaries. If the experts are expert summarizers then the differences result from differences in summarization ability, that is, differences in the use of the selection and abstraction subprocesses. We propose that novices are viewing summarization as a process by which one attempts to put as much information as possible from the article into the constraints of the summary (e.g., constraints on the number of sentences used in a standard summary). Thus, they are doing more selecting than abstracting from the text. As a result, they present less-detailed versions of as many events as possible. On the other hand, experts see summaries as brief, coherent presentations of the most important event in the passage. They seem to be better able to abstract the central event that ties together the series of important events selected from the text. Thus, experts can present a more detailed account of the event and the implications of that event that might later be of importance. This explanation illustrates that summarization is indeed a skill to be acquired. A future step in pursuing this proposal is to attempt to teach novices to summarize stories and track their progress and examine whether or not the summaries that are generated after training are more similar to the expert summaries.

Recent work in the artificial intelligence has become more focused on explanation and its role in learning. Schank (1984) made a distinction between what he termed "making sense" and "cognitive understanding." Making sense means merely putting the events that took place into some relationship that is based upon one's own perception of the world, regardless of the perception of the world possessed by the actor in the events. Cognitive understanding represents one comprehension level above this in that there is some understanding of the actor's perception of the world, but it is not as though the understander and actor are the same person.

We used this distinction to elaborate our results. It is possible that the novices were merely making sense of the article since they did not have the background information necessary to understand the article fully. Therefore, their summaries reflect this making sense by presenting the main event and those events that the novices felt helped to make sense of the event. On the other hand, the experts were able to understand the events in the articles cognitively and this allowed them to be able to draw inferences about the implications of the event.

An Explanation-driven Processing Account of the Expert/Novice Differences

The results of the content analysis confirmed our previous hypothesis that the events in the articles would differ in how self-contained they were, depending on who was writing the summary. For the novices, the events in the articles are perceived as instrumental to other parts of a larger event. To understand why the event occurred, they must search through the other events in the text for an explanation. Once they find the necessary information, the novices generate a summary using the main event and the explanatory (causal) links associated with the event.

For the experts, the events in the articles are self-contained. That is, they have previously existing knowledge structures for the events that present explanations, and furthermore, they know that the typical reader of the *Wall Street Journal* shares most of these knowledge structures. In addition, these knowledge structures allow the experts to generate inferences about the implications of the events. Fig. 9.4 shows the explanation-driven processing model of the self-containment studies and applies it to the current results. The only additional process is the generation of implications from the "event" knowledge structure. For the experts, as for the self-contained goals, the explanation process is "short-circuited" because there is an already existing knowledge structure to explain the event. For the novices (and the instrumental goals), the text must be searched to find other events that will explain the occurrence of the main event.

Although we would like to propose that the differences observed between the novice and expert summaries result from the development of knowledge structures for specific events, there is an alternative explanation for these results. It is possible that writing summaries for the *Wall Street Journal* forces the experts to focus on the implications of the events so that the readers of the paper will be able to make decisions about their investments. We are currently testing our explanation-driven processing against this alternative account. We are presenting novices (college undergraduates) with a series of *Wall Street Journal* articles on a specific topic (e.g., the bankruptcy of the Osborne Computer Corp.) and asking the subjects to write short summaries after reading each story. Our proposal is that as the subjects read more about a given topic, they will build on-line knowledge structures for the main event. Thus, when the subjects get to the last article of the series, the event will be more self-contained than it was

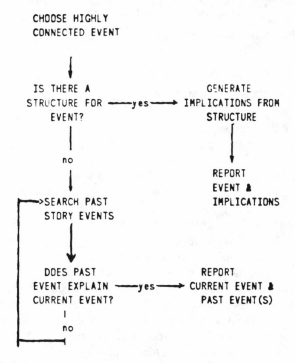

FIG. 9.4. Explanation-based processing for Wall Street Journal stories.

initially. We are measuring this change by noting: (1) a decrease in the number of causal statements about the main event, (2) an increase in the number of implication-based statements and, (3) an increase in similarity to the summaries generated by the experts employed by the newspaper. At this point, the preliminary data seem to support our explanation-driven processing hypothesis.

Because of the complexity of this task, there are many other future directions to be taken. Presently, we are considering three other directions. The first direction is to replicate our study, using summaries from the *New York Times* or *Newsweek,* and examine whether or not the same differences occur between the summaries in the paper or magazine and the summaries generated by the novices (undergraduates). The second direction that we plan to take is to ask business-school students to write summaries of the *Wall Street Journal* articles. If we assume that these students are familiar with the business domain, but not with summarization, then we can assume that any observed differences result from the summarization process, rather than familiarity with the domain. Finally, we are planning to instruct both undergraduate students and business-school students to pretend that they are working for the *Wall Street Journal* and to write summaries that would be relevant to the readers of the newspaper. This study investigates the possibility that the experts and novices have different goals directing the summarization process and leading to summarization differences.

EXPLANATION–DRIVEN PROCESSING

Past models of summarization have focused primarily on the structure of the knowledge that is used to generate the summary of the text. Many of these models proposed a hierarchical representation of the information in the text. This representation results from a top-down process that uses pre-existing knowledge structures to direct comprehension. Once this hierarchical representation is created, summarization entails choosing the top-most node in the hierarchy and reporting the information represented by this node. Although these models were able to predict summarization for a number of stories, all the stories used to support these models were similar in the knowledge structures that were used to represent the text. The types of knowledge structures presented were general categories of actions that failed to take into account the content of the actions and how the actions were related. These models focused more on the individual knowledge structures than on the patterns of structures.

Lehnert's plot unit model illustrates an attempt to account for these higher-level relationships. This model is consistent with the previous models in that there are knowledge structures that are used to organize the material in the text. However, the knowledge structures ("affect" states) that she proposes start at a lower level of detail than those of the previous models. This increase in detail, combined with the bottom-up process necessary to recognize the low-level structures, increased the ability of the model to account for the role of content in the organization of the information.

Although this model does account for the structural and content aspects of summarization, the process proposed still uses a single "global" structure, the pivotal unit, to direct summarization. Therefore, although the plot unit model shows a first step in integrating relationships across structures into a summarization model, a model such as the explanation-driven processing model is still needed.

Wilensky (1983) proposed that understanding can occur without rigid, pre-existing knowledge structures (e.g., scripts) by generating explanations on a lower level and using the relationships that exist between goals, plans, and actions. We have shown that summaries can be generated without pre-existing schemas for narratives by generating explanations for the main events in the text. We propose that during summarization, when people are confronted with an event that they do not completely understand, they generate a series of explanatory inferences to explain the event. We found that the type of explanations generated are a function of the structure of the event. This was illustrated in that the explanations for the instrumental goals were goals or plans, while the explanations for the *Wall Street Journal* events were plans or actions.

We also found that Wilensky's "shortest path" algorithm that proposes that readers find the shortest possible link between new input and a part of the text already represented in memory can be applied to summarization. However, it was noted that the three-step algorithm could be "short-circuited" in the presence of canned information in them. As previously stated, this proposal reveals why summaries with self-contained goals have little explanatory information. For these goals, there is a previously existing knowledge structure that provides the explanation for the goals and, therefore, the person writing the summary does not have to complete the explanation algorithm (i.e., search through the other information in the text) to explain the goal.

In generating summaries, we propose that one must present both necessary and sufficient information from the text. Past models have only addressed the sufficient information. The necessary aspects of a text are those pieces of information that allow the events presented in the summary to be fully explained. In texts where the event or knowledge structures are self-explanatory (e.g., self-contained goals or *Wall Street Journal* events when read by an expert), the necessary and sufficient information is present in the event or knowledge structure. However, if the event or knowledge structure needs further explanation for the person comprehending the story, then further explanation is also needed for the person who will be comprehending the summary. In this case, additional explanatory information will be present in the summary.

The implication of this is that the function of summarization is to present a concise and coherent representation of the text. Conciseness of summaries is satisfied with simple processes in which the information in the summary is selected based upon either its level in a hierarchy or its connectedness in a plot unit graph structure. However, coherence of the summary requires a more complex process. A coherent summary must present a complete thought, just as a coherent text must present a complete story. If the reported information is not complete, then explanatory inferences are generated. Schank (1984) gave a name to explanations that are generated to fill in missing pieces: "coherency explanations." These are the types of explanations generated by the subjects to create coherent summaries. We propose that "good" summaries must present not only a concise statement of the main point of the text, but also a coherent representation of that point. If we want to model these summaries, then we need a process that addresses coherence as well as conciseness.

In the beginning of this chapter, we posed two questions that we felt were important to consider in modeling summarization. Our first question concerned the memory representation that would be used to generate a summary. This question has been addressed by both the hierarchical models and the plot unit model. We prefer the plot unit model, because the structures that it uses are less constrained and attempt to consider the content of the information present in the text. In this model, a representation is built "inside–outside" and therefore, the interactions of the behavioral patterns of the characters in the text can influence the formation of the representation. The second question that we posed concerned the process by which information is selected and abstracted from the memory representation and put in the summary. We proposed explanation-driven processing as an answer to this question. However, this type of processing does not address the first question. Therefore, we would like to propose the use of the plot unit model to structure the text and explanation-driven processing to guide the selection and abstraction processes that will be used to generate the summaries from the plot unit structures. This combination of models represents an attempt to account for summaries generated across a greater range of types of text than has previously been used. In the future, we plan to extend this model and perhaps, to use the complete model in teaching summarization techniques.

APPENDIX A
VERSION OF STORY FROM LEHNERT ET AL. (1981)

Mike and Paul had been close friends ever since their high school days. But now Mike wanted Paul out of town for a few days so that he could build a patio in Paul's backyard as a surprise birthday present. He suggested to Paul that he get away for a weekend, but Paul said he wasn't interested. On another occasion, Mike casually spoke about the joys of fishing or camping trips. But Paul told him he enjoyed puttering around in the house much more. Paul was getting very settled in his old age.

Finally, Mike went to Paul's boss and asked him to send Paul on a business trip. But Paul's boss had had a bad day and he wouldn't hear of it. Mike thought awhile about what to do next. Then he had an idea.

Mike went to a friend of his who handles the accounting records for Paul's company. He explained the situation to the accountant and told him, "If you tell Paul's boss that there are irregularities in Paul's records and that you would like to examine them for a few days, then Paul will be sent away on some pretense." The accountant replied, "I'd be happy to pull the scam, but I expect a little favor in return. How about an ounce of grass?" Mike felt this was not unreasonable.

So Mike called his connection, Joe, and asked him for an emergency ounce. But Joe answered, "Sure thing, as soon as you pay up your tab with me." Mike personally delivered a cash payment immediately. When Joe got his money, he handed Mike an ounce. As soon as the accountant got the grass, he picked up the phone and called Paul's boss. And within an hour of the phone call, Paul's boss was telling Paul about an emergency situation in Peoria that needed supervision. Paul was on a bus for Peoria that evening.

APPENDIX B
EXAMPLE OF *WALL STREET JOURNAL* STORY

Unless help arrives soon, the company that created the portable-computer industry may become its first major casualty.

Osborne Computer Corp. now faces possible failure, unless it can quickly find someone to acquire it. The company is deeply in debt to major suppliers. It has just furloughed nearly 80% of its remaining 350 employees and ceased all manufacturing of computers. "The question of payroll (this week) is up in the air," says an employee. "Osborne won't exist unless it gets a lot of money."

That money could come from an unexpected source—ITT Corp. of New York or a subsidiary. "It is true that the furloughing is often an indication of imminent acquisition," says Jeffrey Boynton, Osborne's director of human resources. "It is also true that ITT and several other companies have been actively looking at us." ITT, however, denies any involvement with Osborne.

Osborne, once a red-hot computer-maker with more than 1,000 employees, now is practically broke; as of today, it has only 80 employees. The story of how Osborne arrived at this point is a uniquely high-tech parable about life in the world of fast circuits, fast successes and fast failures. Osborne suffered all the maladies. It grew too fast. It tried to do too much. And it was severely shaken by the biggest tremor to roll through the computer industry yet—the introduction of International Business Machines Corp.'s Personal Computer. The aftershocks of that event helped kill a new Osborne machine even before it was introduced.

10 Creation and Comprehension of Arguments

Stuart McGuigan
John B. Black

Most literate people, certainly those reading this, come into contact with myriad written messages every day. The bulk of this reading material is not composed of interesting stories but of bits of nonnarrative text. News articles, advertisements, bulletins, and pamphlets rarely exceed a few hundred words, yet these comprise an important part of our total reading. Much of this text is written to influence our beliefs and behaviors. Advertisements, editorials, and political statements are blatant attempts to affect our choice in what we buy and how we vote. Newspaper and magazine articles are usually more subtle in tone; the opinion being expressed is often presented as description.

Most nonnarrative writing, whether scientific or popular, is intended to serve two purposes: to communicate ideas and to convince others of the validity of those ideas. These two goals give structure to the text and determine the style used by the writer. If the content is controversial or the audience is hostile, for example, the author will pay particular attention to the argument structure. He or she must prove every point. If a government source were to compose a text for the scientific community, he or she would need to write more if arguing that scientific funding should be decreased than if arguing for an increase. When we know our work will be opposed, we need to support every assumption and conclusion. Much of the text itself has to be devoted to the argument and proportionally less to the content. If the material is generally accepted or the audience is receptive, less attention need be given to the argument structure and more to description. Authors can take assumptions for granted and be confident of their conclusions. Similarly, the argument structure and the views of readers determine how the material will be processed. If readers are suspicious, they will pay attention to the argument. When a passage is consonant with readers' beliefs, the conclusion is already accepted and fine-grained analysis is not needed. When the passage is in conflict, the validity of the argument, for the reader, is part of what will determine attitude change. Judgments of validity are based on the content and the form of the argument. This chapter presents a model of argument generation and comprehension that simulates how people create and evaluate arguments.

PERSUASION AND RHETORIC

Rhetoricians have been prescribing methods for creating convincing arguments for more than two thousand years. Aristotle's rhetoric consisted of various "modes of persuasion" that all people participated in to a greater or lesser degree. According to Aristotle, emotions, such as pity or anger, bear no relation to the "facts," which exist independently of men's attitudes toward them. Aristotle believed that all convincing arguments are either self-evident or appear to derive from statements that are self-evident. Some a priori basis for agreement must be established for an argument to be effective. An arguer finds a starting point in the line of argument which both the receiver and arguer share as prior knowledge. The simplest form of argument consists of three parts: An introduction of the topic or domain of discussion, presentation of evidence, and a conclusion following from the evidence. Aristotle also identified two lines of argument. First, there are facts of the "necessary type" used to form syllogisms. In this type of deductive argument, acceptance of the premises requires acceptance of the conclusion. If Plato is a man, and all men are fallible, then Plato must be fallible. This type of surety is relatively rare, thus persuasion relies on induction, which uses instances to form more general categories. Socrates is mortal; Socrates is a man; therefore all men may be mortal.

According to contemporary rhetoricians (e.g., Brooks & Warren, 1972; Fogelin, 1978; Wilson, 1980) the best method for a receiver in evaluating the merit of an argument is to examine the kind of evidence used to support the conclusion. These philosophers indicate the ways by which premises may be identified and separated from the rest of the argument, so that each point can be evaluated and attacked individually. Usually, this entails the search for key words or phrases, such as "thus," "therefore," and "in view of which." The statement previous to these is often a premise important to the argument. Once the premises are identified they can be evaluated for relevance and accuracy. Though this advice may be useful in the practice of creating and refuting arguments, it is not informative for those interested in processing details of language comprehension. Cognitive scientists must go further and ask how the premises are understood once identified, how they are integrated into the argument once understood, and what the effect of all this processing is on the apparent strength of the argument from the point of view of the reader.

THE PSYCHOLOGICAL STUDY OF PERSUASION

Social psychologists have long been interested in the mechanisms of attitude change. Hovland, Janis, and Kelley (1953) developed an experimental paradigm to uncover the variables and conditions that affect attitude and resulting behaviors. They manipulated sender (the source of the argument), message (the medium and topic of the argument), and receiver (the reader or auditor) variables and then assessed attitude changes. Hovland et al., (1953) found it necessary to use noncontroversial materials to produce a measurable change. Highly charged issues are more resistant to persuasive change than areas of less emotional interest. Because of the then-current ascendancy of learning theory, changes in behavior were considered the essential measure of psychological change. Social psychologists have since shifted their interests to more cognitive measures and interpretations, but many of the issues remain the same. What causes and maintains attitude change?

Psychologists have believed that memory bears an important relationship to attitude change (Levine & Murphy, 1943). Arguments available to the receiver at a later assessment of attitude should have a more lasting effect than arguments that are forgotten. What is the evidence for a relationship between memory and persuasion? Thus far it has been inconsistent; some studies have found a positive one (Johnson & Watkins, 1971; Rosnow, 1966; Wilson & Miller, 1968), others have found no relationship (Greenwald, 1968), and there is even evidence for a negative relationship between recall and persistence of attitude change after a period of six weeks (Watts & McGuire, 1964).

Papageorgis (1963) hypothesized that memory for the theme or conclusion of a message must affect the durability of a change in attitude. The memorability of an argument, according to his theory, is a function of the compatibility of that argument with the conclusion. His data supported his ideas, but methodological problems prevented any strong conclusions and subsequent studies failed to find the same effects. Understanding of text processing at the time was limited; most of the principles known were developed in a verbal learning paradigm and are not easily generalized to more complex materials. Extrapolations from list-learning research led some researchers to look for and find primacy and recency effects in argument presentation order, recall of the arguments and persistence of attitude change (Beigel, 1973; Richey, McClelland, & Shimkunas, 1967). With few exceptions, however, these researchers did not concern themselves with the content variables of the materials they used.

Attempts at replication of other memory effects have often failed. Waly and Cook (1966) tested Levine and Murphy's (1943) finding that positions consonant with a reader's beliefs were remembered better than those inconsistent. They also attempted to replicate Jones and Kohler's (1958) finding that material consistent with a subject's beliefs is learned more quickly than text that is inconsistent. Neither of these relationships held. Waly and Cook examined and dismissed several alternative explanations for the failure to replicate prior results but did acknowledge that the topic used, that of segregation and racial prejudice, had become more controversial in the 1960s. As Hovland, et al. (1953) had earlier pointed out, memory effects may be lost in the variability of emotional reaction. Thus, while it has been acknowledged that memory for content must play an important role in persistence of attitude change, reliable effects have yet to be demonstrated (Cook & Flay, 1978).

An exception to the early limitations in text analysis can be found in a series of experiments performed by Kanouse and Abelson (1967). Their interest was not in the relationship of some general "memory" measure to attitude change but in comprehension and understanding. The basic methodology was the same for both studies. Subjects were given short paragraphs and were asked a question requiring an inductive or deductive inference. Several conclusions were drawn from this research. With induction, there was greater generalization across objects than subjects and for concrete verbs over abstract. With inferences requiring deduction, there was more agreement with subject generalizations and for verbs with negative affect (such as "hate") than those with positive affect (such as "like" or "want").

Cognitive scientists have been investigating how people understand a persuasive message, how it is represented, and how it is retrieved. Schmidt and Sherman (1984) have approached the problem of representation and memory for persuasive messages using script-research methodology. They were interested in testing the schema-pointer + tag model (Graesser, Woll, Kowalski, & Smith, 1980) for comprehension of nonnarrative texts. Subjects were presented with passages on a variety of topics that had been rated as typical or atypical for each issue. They were later asked to recall the arguments they had read. Schmidt and Sherman (1984) found that atypical arguments for well-known issues were better recalled than typical ones and that typical arguments showed more memory intrusions. As predicted by the theory, unusual arguments are "tagged" to the schema of an issue and automatically accessed when the schema is retrieved from memory. Typical arguments only access a general schema, making retrieval of specific instances more difficult. These results replicate the findings of Bower, Black, & Turner (1979) for narrative scripts. The elusive relation between memory and persuasion in previous research (Cook & Flay, 1978) is attributed to lack of knowledge of the effect of typicality. Schmidt and Sherman did not manipulate convincingness; all the materials were equally persuasive. The relationship between different *levels* of persuasion and memory for the text was not studied.

Other researchers have studied reasoning without regard to persuasion. Johnson-Laird (1980) put forward his theory of "mental models" for how people understand the world in general, and syllogisms in particular. A mental model is an internal representation of the world that can be manipulated in a "thought experiment" to see what will happen. To process a syllogism, the reader assembles specific entities for each premise and checks to see if the conclusion can be true for any arrangement of entities in this model world. This can explain the content bias in syllogistic reasoning. Investigating the effect of the content of the argument on people's evaluation of syllogisms, Kneale and Kneale (1962) found subjects judged syllogistically invalid conclusions to be valid (following necessarily from the premises) when they knew them to be true, independent of the syllogism. Subjects judged:

Every man is an animal.
No stone is a man.
Therefore, no stone is an animal.

to be valid but accepted the invalidity of the syllogism:

Every man is an animal.
No horse is a man.
Therefore no horse is an animal.

The information bias is predictable if subjects are comparing new information with prior knowledge, rather than manipulating an abstract representation of the argument by syntactical inference rules. People bring much more knowledge to bear on a problem than is represented by the premises of a syllogism. Therefore, what they know to be true can override what is supported by the bare bones of the text in front of them. Revlin and Leirer (1978) argue that people convert the premises of a syllogism to a basic form when processing the argument. When given "Some A's are not B," they also infer "Some B's are not A," except when the result is obviously factually false. Evans, Barston, and Pollard (1983) tested this idea directly by having subjects read believable or unbelievable conclusions that either followed or did not follow logically from the premises given. They found a strong effect for believability; the validity of the argument did not affect judgments for believable conclusions, but had a strong effect for unbelievable conclusions. Where prior knowledge can enter into the evaluation of an argument, it seems to overwhelm the formal processing otherwise possible. These studies all indicate that the type of support used in an argument is more important than the context-free aspects of its form.

The Structure of Arguments

Upon examination of a large number of arguments, we found that argument structures can be divided into three basic types: argument by analogy, categorical argument, and causal argument. An argument by analogy compares two instances or tokens. "I think your dog will get fleas because my dog got fleas" is an analogy-based argument. The assertion about your dog is supported by the instance of my dog and both assertions are at the same level of generality. "Your dog will get fleas because all dogs get fleas" is a categorical or deductive argument. I am asserting membership in the category "dog" for your dog, and members of that category have the feature "has fleas." The argument can be expressed as a syllogism:

> All dogs get fleas.
> Your dog is a dog.
> Therefore, your dog will get fleas.

A second kind of categorical argument involves induction, using purported members as support for the existence of the category or the addition of a new feature to an old category. If your dog, the neighbor's dog, and my dog all have fleas, this is evidence that all dogs possess this feature.

A causal argument could go as follows: dogs like to run in the woods, making them accessible to fleas that jump at the opportunity to find a new home, and as a result of this your dog will get fleas. The argument rests on an explanation of the ineluctable *process* whereby dogs get fleas. The three argument types are complementary. Analogies can be used to develop new categories or add new features to old ones. Causal knowledge can also be (and is ultimately always) derived from analogies and can be used to construct or alter categories.

We believe that the representations and processes used for argument also serve for understanding the world in general. The three types outlined above were selected to be both general and distinct. The use of categories in organizing knowledge has been well recognized (Rosch & Lloyd, 1978; Smith & Medin, 1981). Categories allow us to slice up the world into useful pieces. The structure of categories depends on the use for which they are developed and the structure of the world they represent. Most of the work has been concerned with well-learned natural-kind or taxonomic categories. Though certainly useful in day to day identification of animals or office furniture, these unchanging structures do not represent the only kind of categorical knowledge. Barsalou (1983) investigated the formation of what he termed ad-hoc categories, categories used for a specific function or for the first time. These included "things you find at a garage sale," "things that smell," and "ways to make friends." Ad-hoc categories showed the same graduated structure that common categories have, in which members have different degrees of similarity to the best exemplar of that category.

Ad-hoc category formation is essential for handling new situations or information from unfamiliar domains. When people are faced with any substantial amount of new information, it must be organized quickly and flexibly: quickly to handle new items and flexibly if the category needs adjustment. To use a familiar analogy in an unfamiliar way, when man first came upon the animal he now calls "bat," he probably noticed a salient feature, the power of flight. Based on this feature, bats become a member of the category "bird." This allows attribution of other features from "bird" to "bat," such as having warm blood and eating insects. A counter-arguer could point out that bats do not lay eggs or have feathers. Therefore, bats are not birds, but must be assigned to a new category, which may have to be modified to accommodate it. The category "mammal" can no longer have the feature not-fly. Similarly, when President Reagan's and other supply-siders' economic theories were branded "voodoo economics," a category was being formed: economics theories that rest on superstitious beliefs. It was part of Reagan's success that this categorization failed and the coiner of the term became his vice-president. Dynamic use of categories reflects an active understanding process and is central to creating and comprehending arguments. Arguers create, modify, and destroy categories in many active on-going arguments.

The search for causal knowledge is common to all people, especially scientists. It would be unproductive to enter into the metaphysical debate concerning the true nature of causality, but it is important to clarify our use of the term. Research in Artificial Intelligence (Schank, 1975c; Schank & Abelson, 1977) has shown that the processing of narrative text requires an understanding of the causal relationships between events. If one event causes another, the two become linked. When all the connections are made the result is a causal chain. Causal chaining of actions and states determines the cohesion of narrative text. "Cause," as used here, is a broad concept and involves the presence of conditions sufficient for an event to occur. In the sentence "the recent snowfall resulted in an avalanche," the weight of the new snow *caused* the avalanche. A cause can also be the *absence* of conditions, which then prevent an expected event from occurring. "Bill didn't have coffee this morning because he was out of cream." In this example, Bill's coffee drinking was prevented by the lack of cream, without which, presumably, he will not have coffee.

Good arguments frequently contain compelling or memorable analogies. An analogy, as used here, is a comparison made at the same level of generality as the conclusion. If we were trying to determine whether, in fact, dogs have fleas, then an appropriate analogy would be that cats have fleas. If we were interested in golden retrievers, then an Irish setter becomes an appropriate same-level analogy. When evidence of a different level of generality is used for support at the level of the conclusion, a hierarchical category structure is necessary. In discussing dogs in general, we would be using the category *dogs* to deduce a feature for a type of dog. To use experience with a specific golden retriever as support is to use induction. Information from the one retriever changes the structure of the category of all golden retrievers. Analogies are useful for understanding new instances when only one prior case is known. If only one dog has ever been encountered, then the knowledge of that one dog is used to deal with a new (second) dog. If an initial experience is traumatic enough, it may form the basis for all subsequent encounters.

Counterargument

The model handles counterargument with the same processes used for constructing arguments. Perhaps the most ubiquitous counterargument is the counterexample. To your assertion that my golden retriever will bark all night because your setter does, I can reply that the neighbor's Labrador is very quiet. Your reply to this can take two forms. You can come up with another analogy to counter my counter, but this leaves the possibility of another counteranalogy. Instead, you can attack my counteranalogy and defend your initial analogy by examining the relevant features and showing that an Irish setter is more like a golden retriever than is a Labrador retriever, based on the feature "highly excitable," which is more related to the "barking at night" than is being a retriever or having the same hair color. A good analogy, therefore, is one which shares *relevant* features with the original instance. This process is similar to Tversky's (1977) model for calculating similarity. In his model, a function of the number of distinguishing features is subtracted from a function of the number of shared features to produce an index of similarity. Relevance is determined by the feature under debate or the current needs of the understander. Knowing what features discriminate barking and biting dogs from just barking ones could be useful.

For answering categorical arguments, two strategies are available. Initial category membership can be shown to be inappropriate by a feature conflict, or another category can be shown to be more appropriate because of greater relevant feature overlap. The argument:

All dogs get fleas.
Wylbur is a dog.
Therefore, Wylbur will get fleas.

can be countered by showing that, in fact, Wylbur the four-legged, furry animal is not a dog because it eats plants instead of meat. The conclusion from the argument does not follow from the new premises. Alternatively, the animal in question could roam the mountains of Colorado hunting sheep. Although it possesses many of the features found in "dog," it shares even more of the features of the category "wolf." Now the argument from the dog evidence is demoted to the status of argument by analogy and is subject to counterexample.

Causal arguments are vulnerable along any step of the causal chain beyond that which is known explicitly. The chain:

> dogs like to run in the woods, making them accessible to fleas who jump at the opportunity to find a new home, and as a result of this your dog will get fleas

is vulnerable at a number of points without contradicting any of the facts in the series. Fleas may be notoriously poor jumpers who almost never reach their target. The dog may swim in a mountain stream before coming home, drowning or freezing whatever fleas may have landed. Although causal knowledge may be the most desirable, it is also the most fragile.

The Memory Representation of Arguments

We have developed a model of argument generation and comprehension (MAGAC) that simulates how people create and evaluate arguments. We use a frame architecture (Minsky, 1975) to represent the knowledge and procedures for filling slots and linking frames. To work through an example, suppose the reader is confronted with the following argument:

> The introduction of computers into society is a great technological innovation. The introduction of new technologies, over a short period of time, causes a disruption of the current, established culture. Therefore, the spread of computers will result in great unhappiness for many people.

The first sentence introduces the domain, the recent inroads of computers into everyday life. This has been a fairly controversial topic and has received some play in the press. To begin comprehension, the reader needs to create a structure to process the argument. When the text is fully processed, the representation will be organized around the conclusion in a conclusion organization frame (COF). After the first sentence, the representation looks like COF1.

COF1: INTRODUCTION OF Computers
AKO: New Technology
TIME: Current
TIME COURSE: Short
RESULT: ?

The heading slot for COF1 is the "introduction of computers" (into society). The *A Kind Of* (AKO) slot tells of what more general class of things this specific knowledge is a member. The TIME slot indicates the time frame to which the knowledge or event being represented belongs. As the INTRODUCTION of an object is a process, it must take place over a period of time. The slot TIME COURSE is filled with information concerning how long an event took or will take in the future. In this case, "short" is a term relative to the introduction time of other technologies, such as the manufacturing of steel or the production of clocks, both of which took hundreds of years. The presence of a RESULT slot bespeaks the causal underpinnings of the representation. The effects of the process represented or procedures for determining the effects are stored under the RESULT slot. Goals and plans of entities, such as the U.S. government, are stored under GOALS and PLANS slots. The actual representation of the goals and plans would be stored elsewhere.

COF1 contains the information that was actually in the sentence and some that the reader already had and knew was appropriate. The second sentence gives the reader general information which is represented in SOF1, an instantiation of a "support organization frame."

SOF1: New Technology
AKO: Social Change
PROPERTY: Origins in science
GOALS: Achieve new goals, previously blocked
           or
         Achieve old goals more efficiently
RESULT: (Change in work force)
          (Less resources needed to accomplish goal)
           ((If TIME course is short
              then cultural disruption)
           (If TIME course is long
              then no disruption))

Even if the receiver has not heard this argument before, it will not conflict with related knowledge. New objects or processes cause change and change can be disruptive. From this knowledge, SOF1 could be constructed for the purpose of understanding and remembering the argument should it be encountered again. The knowledge of goals is also very general. Technology is meant to achieve new goals, such as rapid communication by satellite, or improvement of the efficiency of achieving old goals, such as generating nuclear power. Such improvements are accompanied by problems and dissent. The third sentence forms the conclusion. The reader already knows from experience that people often find change upsetting, especially swift and pervasive changes in existing culture. SOF2 is constructed or instantiated to handle this information.

    SOF2: Social Change
    AKO: Cultural Process
    PROPERTIES: Disruptive
                 Creates opportunity
                 Creates unhappiness

Several general procedures are necessary for connecting the three frames. The first procedure is that which connects the topic to the evidence. For this example, a straightforward inheritance from the AKO (a kind of) slot is used to fill empty slots. We know that if an X is a kind of mammal but something else about it is not explicitly known, the most appropriate thing to do is to assume default characteristics of a general "mammal" which would be stored in that higher level frame. In this case, "computers" are a kind of new technology. The result slot of "computers" is open and thus can be filled with the result slot of "new technology." In this causal argument, the process is applied and the result is calculated from SOF1.

Procedure 1

If RESULT *SLOT* is empty then fill with corresponding RESULT *SLOT* from AKO *FRAME*.

Next, the connection between "new technology" and "social change" must be found. In this case, *Procedure 1* again provides the link. New technologies are one kind of social change. It is important that it be a kind of social (rather than personal) change so that the generalization in the conclusion is warranted. The result is not given but requires calculation because it is dependent on the time course of events. Gradual social change is not disruptive, but sudden change is. Thus, the RESULT slot of COF1 is filled in with "cultural disruption."

The same conclusion could have been supported in a different way. Other evidence could be brought to bear and other arguments formed. Instead of referring to a general causal principle, the writer could have made an analogy to when something similar had happened in the past. In the absence of more definite knowledge, a similar instance can be used to understand a new one. This process of understanding is often used in argument. The analogy shows that X *can* have quality Y, that this is (at least) a possibility. In our example, the first and third sentences of the paragraph remain the same but the body of the argument is changed to: "Automatic looms were also considered a great innovation in their day and resulted in a redistribution of the workforce."

The comparison of computers and the automatic loom is based on their both being an example of a new technology that radically affected the surrounding community. Nineteenth-century Britain's labor force was profoundly upset by the new mills and the resulting loss of jobs. The implication is that use of computers will also cause loss of jobs. From there, it is a fairly straightforward inference that people will be unhappy. The representation for "Automatic Loom" looks like SOF3.

SOF3: INTRODUCTION OF Automatic Loom
AKO: New Technology
TIME: Past
TIME COURSE: Short
RESULT: Unhappiness
       Opportunity

Both the AKO and TIME COURSE slots match those for COMPUTERS frame. If two frames have the same AKO slots, then they are both members of the same general category and may be compared. No alteration of the category structure will occur, nor is any feature from the category frame being used to make the argument. The more slots two frames share, the stronger the comparison. If one frame has a slot filled that the other has blank, an IF–NEEDED connection is made from one slot to the other. In this case, the result slot from COMPUTERS can be filled with that from AUTO LOOM, if the information is desired. The slot filling is not a logical necessity and this is reflected in the IF–NEEDED connection. The result here, redistribution of the workforce, is AKO social change. The conclusion derives from the SOCIAL CHANGE frame's RESULT slot. The procedure for connecting the frames is:

Procedure 2

If AKO *SLOT* of X matches AKO *SLOT* of Y then create pointer from X to Y.

The connections in this argument are not as direct as in the previous one, though the conclusion is the same.

The third argument type is the deductive or categorical argument, which has the traditional, syllogistic structure underlying it. First, category membership is asserted for the object or idea being debated. Then, by virtue of membership, other features from the category are attributed to it. Using the same example, a categorical argument would be: "New technologies are a feature of social change. Social change is always disruptive for those living in the current established culture."

On the surface, this support is similar to the causal argument and a similar causal structure underlies this category. The representation and procedures of this argument, however, are different. Unlike analogy-based arguments, the AKO slot is used to proceed to a higher level, in this case to the frame SOCIAL CHANGE. As a member of the category SOCIAL CHANGE, the frame COMPUTERS inherits any slots that do not contradict existing ones. The relationship is a necessary one. If something is a member of a category, then it must possess features *stored* at the category level. This type of argument bypasses the causality inherent in the frames, making use of the existing static knowledge in categories. The only counterarguments possible are denial of the category or the categorization. If both are accepted, than the conclusion must also be accepted. This is the general form of deductive arguments. The slot is filled with procedure 3.

Procedure 3

Fill empty SLOT from COF* with PROPERTY SLOT(S) from SOF* indicated in AKO slot.

There are two sides to every issue and the same facts can be used to support different conclusions. The conclusion of the example paragraph can be changed without loss of coherence to: "Therefore, the spread of computers will result in great opportunities for many people."

Those held in check by an existing social system would have the opportunity to change their status when the system were disrupted. This information can be added to the frame SOCIAL CHANGE in the RESULT slot. The writer had the option to select the conclusion he desired. A reader has the option of accepting the writer's reasoning or of forming a counterargument. Which conclusion stands will depend on further reasoning, but both are acceptable.

An Empirical Study

What are the predictions made by MAGAC? When COFs are created for causal and categorical arguments, and the new knowledge corresponds with existing knowledge, then the argument will be convincing and easily recalled. The COF provides a retrieval structure for accessing the support and the conclusion as required. The argument by analogy SOF is connected to the COF by an IF–NEEDED link. This maintains two separate structures and thus will be a less-integrated argument, which would be less likely to be recalled all at once. However, unlike causal rules and categories, examples used for analogies have independent worth as new knowledge about the world. Therefore, when higher-level arguments fail, it is likely that little will be recalled, but the support from an analogy argument could be recalled independently.

The paragraph analyzed in the previous section was taken from the set of materials used in a study designed to evaluate the effect of argument source on memory and persuasiveness of short messages. Three types of arguments were used: analogical, causal, and categorical as described above. Furthermore, the conclusions were varied to include assertions favorable and hostile to the topic introduced in the first sentence. The bias of the experimenter/author is thus controlled and ratings of convincingness are not a function of the author's eloquence. The topics of the paragraphs were taken from everyday sources: magazine articles, newspaper articles, and editorial columns. The issues ranged in topic from military intervention by superpowers to the high salaries of athletes.

The paragraphs were three or four lines and 30 to 40 words each. They consisted of an introductory sentence that set the domain, an argument section, and a conclusion. Each subject saw each paragraph once, but across all the paragraphs saw all combinations of argument type and conclusion. The subjects were asked to rate each paragraph on a scale of -10 to $+10$ on how convincing it was. A negative score corresponded to a lack of convincingness, a zero indicated that the argument had no bearing on the conclusion, and a positive score indicated that the argument supported the conclusion. After reading the 12 paragraphs, the subjects were given a surprise recall test, with the story titles as cues.

A look at the results showed two different patterns, indicating that two sets of paragraphs existed in our materials. Five paragraphs received consistently negative ratings, two were close to or at the zero mark, and the remaining five received positive ratings. The negatively rated paragraphs seemed to deal with more controversial subjects (such as military intervention or Reagan's policies) than the positively rated (e.g., sports, course requirements). Controversy most likely involves strong emotion mechanisms which probably have little to do with comprehension. The "zero" paragraphs were assigned to the group they most closely matched and the two sets of six paragraphs were analyzed separately. Table 10.1 shows the paragraphs separated into the two groups. The overall positively rated paragraphs were analyzed separately as shown in Table 10.2.

The percentage of recall of each argument section was broken down by support type and convincingness rating (low = 1-4, medium = 5-6, high = 7-10). Recall of analogy-based arguments was fairly even across convincingness judgments and paragraph section. Data for cause and category based arguments show a stronger pattern. Recall for the introduction was flat across all variables. Recall for the support and conclusion, however, increased with judgments of convincingness. The support and conclusion

TABLE 10.1
Convincingness Ratings (– 10 to + 10)
for Positively and Negatively Rated Paragraphs by Support Type

	Analogy	Cause	Category
Negative	– 1.4	– 3.2	– 4.1
Positive	3.1	6.2	5.8

TABLE 10.2
Percentage of Recall of Argument Section
by Level of Rating and Support Type
for Positively Rated Paragraphs

	Low	Medium	High
ANALOGY			
Introduction	61	57	68
Support	57	69	75
Conclusion	71	76	72
CAUSE			
Introduction	62	61	67
Support	60	79	94
Conclusion	59	84	98
CATEGORY			
Introduction	52	61	60
Support	63	77	96
Conclusion	64	78	92

from paragraphs judged most persuasive were recalled at near-ceiling levels.

Ratings of convincingness predicted recall of the conclusion of positively rated paragraphs. The higher the rating, the more likely it was that subjects would recall the conclusion. These ratings, however, were unrelated to recall of the introduction or argument of the paragraph. Once a conclusion is accepted, the argument is needed only to defend it. The argument is not accessed with the conclusion but this does not mean that it cannot be re-created when necessary. It would be unwieldy to recall all the justifications every time we recalled an opinion. The relation between rating and recall is not the result of materials bias as there was no for/against main effect or interaction. In addition, recall of the argument predicted recall of the conclusion, independent of rating and recall of the introduction sentence. The connection between argument and conclusion must be unidirectional. The argument directly accesses the conclusion and indeed the argument is not of much use without the conclusion. This effect would be expected for causal arguments where temporal ordering is fixed, but it also held for categorical arguments.

It would seem that learning new categories and causal rules requires effort. People need to be convinced that the new knowledge is necessary or useful before they will update their knowledge. When the argument is not convincing, readers do not bother to learn it. Analogies are stored because their use is independent of the conclusion and the conclusion does not of necessity follow from the use of an analogy. Examples are pieces of data to be used later for other reasons. Many questions now arise from these observations. Under what conditions are new, high-level structures learned and integrated into memory? What degree of level-of-generalization separation can be tolerated between support and conclusion? What are the consequences for writers, politicians, and presenters of papers? The answers to these questions bear not only on how people create and understand arguments but on how all new information is received, processed, and represented by an active understander.

References

Abbott, V., & Black, J. B. (1980). The representation of scripts in memory. *Technical Report No. 5.* Cognitive Science Program, Yale University.

Abbott, V., & Black, J. B. (1982). *A comparison of the memory strength of alternative text relations.* Paper presented at the Annual Meeting of the American Education Research Association, New York.

Abbott, V., Black, J. B., & Smith, E. E. (1985). The representation of scripts in memory. *Journal of Memory and Language, 24,* 179-199.

Abelson, R. P. (1973). The structure of belief systems. In R. C. Schank & K. M. Colby (Eds.), *Computer models of thought and language.* San Francisco, CA: W. H. Freeman.

Abelson, R. P. (1976). Script processing in attitude formation and decision making. In J. S. Carroll & J. W. Payne (Eds.), *Cognition and social behavior.* Hillsdale, NJ: Lawrence Erlbaum Associates.

Abelson, R. P. (1981a). Psychological status of the script concept. *American Psychologist, 36,* 715-729.

Abelson, R. P. (1981b). Constraint, construal, and cognitive science. *Proceedings of the Third Annual Conference of the Cognitive Science Society.* Berkeley, CA.

Alba, J. W., & Hasher, L. (1983). Is memory schematic? *Psychological Bulletin, 93,* 203-231.

Anderson, J. R. (1974). Retrieval of propositional information from long-term memory. *Cognitive Psychology, 6,* 451-474.

Anderson, J. R. (1976). *Language, memory, and thought.* Hillsdale, NJ: Lawrence Erlbaum Associates.

Anderson, J. R. (1980). Concepts, propositions, and schemata: What are the cognitive units? In J. H. Flowers (Ed.), *The Nebraska symposium on motivation.* Lincoln, NE: University of Nebraska Press.

Anderson, J. R. (1982). Acquisition of cognitive skill. *Psychological Review, 89,* 369-405.

Anderson, J. R. (1983). *The architecture of cognition.* Cambridge, MA: Harvard University Press.

Anderson, J. R. (1984). Spreading activation. In J. R. Anderson & S. M. Kosslyn (Eds.), *Tutorial essays in learning and memory.* San Francisco: W. H. Freeman.

Anderson, J. R., & Bower, G. H. (1973). *Human associative memory*. Hillsdale, NJ: Lawrence Erlbaum Associates.

Anderson, J. R., Kline, P. J., & Beasley, C. M. (1979). A general learning theory and its application to schema abstraction. In G. Bower (Ed.), *The psychology of learning and motivation*. New York: Academic Press.

Anderson, R. C., & Pichert, J. W. (1978). Recall of previously unrecallable information following a shift in perspective. *Journal of Verbal Learning and Verbal Behavior, 17*, 1-12.

Bain, W. M. (1984). Toward a model of subjective understanding. *Technical Report No. 324*. Computer Science Program, Yale University.

Banks, W. P. (1977). Encoding and processing of symbolic information in comparative judgments. In G. H. Bower (Ed.), *The psychology of learning and motivation, 11*. New York: Academic Press.

Barr, A., & Feigenbaum, E. A. (1981). *The handbook of artificial intelligence*. Stanford, CA: Heuris Tech Press.

Barsalou, L. W. (1983). Ad hoc categories. *Memory and Cognition, 11*, 211-227.

Barsalou, L. W. (1985). The content and organization of autobiographical memory. *Proceedings of the Second Annual Workshop on Conceptual Information Processing*, Yale University, New Haven, CT.

Bartlett, F. C. (1932). *Remembering: A study in experimental and social psychology*. London: Cambridge University Press.

Becker, C. A. (1979). Semantic context and word frequency effects in visual word recognition. *Journal of Experimental Psychology: Human Perception and Performance, 5*, 252-259.

Becker, C. A. (1981). Semantic context effects in visual word recognition: An analysis of semantic strategies. *Memory and Cognition, 8*, 493-512.

Becker, C. A., & Killion, T. M. (1977). Interaction of visual and cognitive effects in word recognition. *Journal of Experimental Psychology: Human Perception and Performance, 3*, 389-401.

Beigel, A. (1973). Resistance to change in differential effects of favorable and unfavorable communicators. *British Journal of Clinical and Social Psychology, 12*, 153-158.

Bekerian, D. A., & Bowers, J. M. (1983). Eyewitness testimony: Were we misled? *Journal of Experimental Psychology: Learning, Memory and Cognition, 9*, 139-145.

Black, J. B. (1980). *Memory for state and action information in narratives*. Twenty-first Annual Meeting of the Psychonomic Society, St. Louis, MO.

Black, J. B. (1982). Psycholinguistic processes in writing. In S. Rosenberg (Ed.), *Handbook of applied psycholinguistics*. Hillsdale, NJ: Lawrence Erlbaum Associates.

Black, J. B. (1984). Understanding and remembering stories. In J. R. Anderson, & S. M. Kosslyn (Eds.), *Essays on learning and memory*. San Francisco, CA: Freeman.

Black, J. B., & Bern, H. (1981). Causal coherence and memory for events in narratives. *Journal of Verbal Learning and Verbal Behavior, 20*, 267-275.

Black, J. B., & Bower, G. H. (1979). Episodes as chunks in narrative memory. *Journal of Verbal Learning and Verbal Behavior, 18*, 309-318.

Black, J. B., & Bower, G. H. (1980). Story understanding as problem-solving. *Poetics, 9*, 223-250.

Black, J. B., & McGuigan, S. M. (1983). *The memory strength of inferences in text understanding*. Paper presented at the Twenty-fourth Annual Meeting of the Psychonomic Society, San Diego, CA.

Black, J. B., Wilkes-Gibbs, D., & Gibbs, R. W. (1981). What writers need to know that they don't need to know. In M. Nystrand (Ed.), *What writers know: Studies in the psychology of writing*. New York: Academic Press.

Bobrow, D. G., & Norman, D. A. (1975). Some principles of memory schemata. In D. G. Bobrow, & A. Collins (Eds.), *Representation and understanding*. New York: Academic Press.

Bobrow, D. G., & Winograd, T. (1977) An overview of KRL, a knowledge representation language. *Cognitive Science, 1,* 3-46.

Bower, G. H. (1978). Experiments in story comprehension and recall. *Discourse Processes, 1,* 211-232.

Bower, G. H., Black, J. B., & Turner, T. J. (1979). Scripts in memory for text. *Cognitive Psychology, 11,* 177-220.

Bransford, J. D., Barclay, J. R., & Franks, J. J. (1972). Sentence memory: A constructive vs. interpretive approach. *Cognitive Psychology, 3,* 193-209.

Bransford, J. D., & Johnson, M. K. (1972). Contextual prerequisites for understanding: Some investigations of comprehension and recall. *Journal of Verbal Learning and Verbal Behavior, 11,* 717-726.

Bransford, J. D., & Johnson, M. K. (1973). Considerations of some problems of comprehension. In W. G. Chase (Ed.), *Visual information processing.* New York: Academic Press.

Brewer, W. F., & Dupree, D. A. (1983). Use of plan schemata in the recall and recognition of goal-directed actions. *Journal of Experimental Psychology: Learning, Memory, and Cognition, 9,* 117-129.

Brewer, W. F., & Nakamura, G. V. (1984). The nature and function of schemas. In R. S. Wyer, Jr., & T. K. Srull (Eds.), *Handbook of social cognition.* Hillsdale, NJ: Lawrence Erlbaum Associates.

Britton, B. K., Graesser, A. C., Glynn, S. M., Hamilton, T., & Penland, M. Use of cognitive capacity in reading—effects of some content features of text. *Discourse Processes, 6,* 39-57.

Brooks, C., & Warren, R. P. (1972). *Modern rhetoric.* New York: Harcourt, Brace Jovanovich.

Brown, J. S., & van Lehn, K. (1980). Repair theory: A generative theory of bugs in procedural skills. *Cognitive Science, 4,* 379-426.

Cantor, N., & Mischel, W. (1977). Traits as prototypes: Effects on recognition memory. *Journal of Personality and Social Psychology, 35,* 38-48.

Cantor, N., & Mischel, W. (1979). Prototypes in person perception. In L. Berkowitz (Ed.), *Advances in experimental social psychology, 12.* New York: Academic Press.

Cantor, N., Mischel, W., & Schwartz, J. C. (1982). A prototype analysis of psychological situations. *Cognitive Psychology, 14,* 45-77.

Charniak, E. (1978). On the use of framed knowledge in language comprehension. *Artificial Intelligence, 11,* 225-265.

Chiesi, H. L., Spilich, G. J., & Voss, J. F. (1979). Acquisition of domain related information in relation to high and low domain knowledge. *Journal of Verbal Learning and Verbal Behavior, 18,* 257-274.

Chomsky, N. (1968). *Language and mind.* New York: Harcourt, Brace & World.

Christiaansen, R. E., & Ochalek, K. (1983). Editing misleading information from memory: Evidence for the coexistence of original and postevent information. *Memory and Cognition, 11,* 467-475.

Clark, H. H. (1973). The language-as-fixed-effect fallacy: A critique of language statistics in psychological research. *Journal of Verbal Learning and Verbal Behavior, 12,* 355-359.

Collins, A. M., & Loftus, E. F. (1975). A spreading activation theory of semantic processing. *Psychological Review, 82,* 407-428.

Collins, A. M., & Quillian, M. R. (1970). Facilitating retrieval from semantic memory: The effect of repeating part of an inference. *Acta Psychologica, 33,* 304-314.

Cook, T. D., & Flay, B. R. (1978). Experimentally induced attitude change. In Berkowitz, L. (Ed.), *Advances in experimental social psychology, 11,* New York: Academic Press.

Craik, F. I. M., & Tulving, E. (1975). Depth of processing and retention of words in episodic memory. *Journal of Experimental Psychology: General, 104.*

Cullingford, R. E. (1978). Script application: Computer understanding of newspaper stories. *Technical Report No. 16.* Computer Science Program, Yale University.

DeJong, G. F. (1979). Skimming stories in real time: An experiment in integrated understanding. *Technical Report No. 158,* Computer Science Program, Yale University.

den Uyl, M., & Van Oostendorp, N. (1980). The use of scripts in text comprehension. *Poetics, 9,* 275-294.

deVilliers, P. A. (1974). Imagery and theme in recall of connected discourse. *Journal of Experimental Psychology, 103,* 263-268.

Dooling, D. J., & Lachman, R. (1971). Effects of comprehension on retention of prose. *Journal of Experimental Psychology, 88,* 216-222.

Dooling, D. J., & Mullet, R. L. (1973). Locus of thematic effects in retention of prose. *Journal of Experimental Psychology, 97,* 404-406.

Dresher, B. E., & Hornstein, N. (1976). On some supposed contributions of artificial intelligence to the scientific study of language. *Cognition, 4,* 321-398.

Dreyfus, H. (1979). *What computers can't do.* New York: Harper & Row.

Druian, P., & Omessi, E. (1982). *A knowledge structure theory of attribution.* Unpublished manuscript. Grinnell College, IA.

Dyer, M. G. (1983). *In-depth understanding: A computer model of integrated processing for narrative comprehension.* Cambridge, MA: MIT Press.

Egan, D. E., & Green, J. G. (1974). Theory of rule induction: Knowledge acquired in concept learning, serial pattern learning, and problem solving. In L. Gregg (Ed.), *Knowledge and cognition.* Potomac, MD: Lawrence Erlbaum Associates.

Einhorn, H. J., & Hogarth, R. M. (1983). Diagnostic inference and causal judgment: A decision making framework. *Center for Decision Research Memorandum,* University of Chicago.

Evans, J. St. B. T., Barston, J. L., & Pollard, P. (1983). On the conflict between logic and belief in syllogistic reasoning. *Memory and Cognition, 11,* 295-306.

Feldman, J. (1975). Bad-mouthing frames. In R. C. Schank & B. Nash-Webber (Eds.), *Theoretical issues in natural language processing.* Cambridge, MA: Bolt, Beranek, & Newman.

Fillmore, C. (1968). The case for case. In E. Bach & R. Harms (Eds.), *Universals in linguistic theory.* New York: Holt, Rinehart, & Winston.

Fillmore, C. (1975). An alternative to checklist theories of meaning. *Proceedings of the First Annual Meeting of the Berkeley Linguistics Society.*

Fillmore, C. (1982). Approaches to the study of the psychology of language. In T. Bever, J. M. Carroll, & L. A. Miller (Eds.), *Talking minds: The study of language in cognitive sciences.* Cambridge, MA: MIT Press.

Fischler, I. (1977). Associative facilitation without expectancy in a lexical decision task. *Journal of Experimental Psychology: Human Perception and Performance, 3,* 18-26.

Fischler, I., & Bloom, P. A. (1979). Automatic and attention processes in the effects of sentence contexts on word recognition. *Journal of Verbal Learning and Verbal Behavior, 18,* 1-20.

Fischler, I., & Goodman, G. O. (1978). Latency of associative activation in memory. *Journal of Experimental Psychology: Human Perception and Performance, 4,* 455-470.

Fiske, S. T., & Taylor, S. E. (1984). *Social cognition.* Reading: MA: Addison-Wesley.

Fogelin, R. J. (1978). *Understanding arguments.* New York: Harcourt, Brace Jovanovich.

Forster, K. I., & Chambers, S. M. (1973). Lexical access and naming time. *Journal of Verbal Learning and Verbal Behavior, 12,* 627-635.

Foss, D. J. (1982). A discourse on semantic priming. *Cognitive Psychology, 14,* 590-607.

Galambos, J. A. (1981). *The mental representation of common events.* Doctoral Dissertation, University of Chicago.

Galambos, J. A. (1983). Normative studies of six characteristics of our knowledge of common activities. *Behavioral Research Methods and Instrumentation, 15,* 327-340.

Galambos, J. A., & Black, J. B. (1982). Getting and using context: Functional constraints on the organization of knowledge. *Proceedings of the Fourth Conference of the Cognitive Science Society.* Ann Arbor, MI.

Galambos, J. A., & Black, J. B. (1985). Using knowledge of activities to understand and answer questions. In A. C. Graesser & J. B. Black (Eds.), *The psychology of questions.* Hillsdale, NJ: Lawrence Erlbaum Associates.

Galambos, J. A., & Rips, L. J. (1982). Memory for routines. *Journal of Verbal Learning and Verbal Behavior, 21,* 260–281.

Gentner, D., & Stevens, A. L. (Eds.). (1983). *Mental models.* Hillsdale, NJ: Lawrence Erlbaum Associates.

Gentner, D., & Tenney, Y. J. (1984). *What makes analogies accessible: The water flow analogy for electricity.* Paper presented at the Twenty-fifth Annual Meeting of the Psychonomic Society, San Antonio, TX.

Gick, M., & Holyoak, K. (1980). Analogical problem solving. *Cognitive Psychology, 12,* 306–355.

Gick, M., & Holyoak, K. (1983). Schema induction and analogical transfer. *Cognitive Psychology, 15,* 1–38.

Glenn, C. G. (1978). The role of episodic structure and story length in children's recall of simple stories. *Journal of Verbal Learning and Verbal Behavior, 17,* 229–247.

Goffman, E. (1959). *The presentation of self in everyday life.* Garden City, NY: Anchor Books.

Goffman, E. (1974). *Frame analysis.* Cambridge, MA: Harvard University Press.

Goldiamond, I., & Hawkins, W. F. (1958). Vexierversuch: The logarithmic relationship between word-frequency and recognition obtained in the absence of stimulus words. *Journal of Experimental Psychology, 56,* 457–463.

Goldman, S. R. (1985). Inferential reasoning in and about narrative texts. In A. C. Graesser & J. B. Black (Eds.), *The psychology of questions.* Hillsdale, NJ: Lawrence Erlbaum Associates.

Goodman, G. S. (1980). Picture memory: How the action schema affects retention. *Cognitive Psychology, 12,* 473–495.

Gordon, B. (1983). Lexical access and lexical decision: Mechanisms of frequency sensitivity. *Journal of Verbal Learning and Verbal Behavior, 22,* 24–44.

Gough, P. B., Alford, J. A., Jr., & Holley-Wilcox, P. (1981). Words and contexts. In O. J. L. Tzeng & H. Singer (Eds.), *Perception of print: Reading research in experimental psychology.* Hillsdale, NJ: Lawrence Erlbaum Associates.

Graesser, A. C. (1978). How to catch a fish: The memory and representation of common procedures. *Discourse Processes, 1,* 72–89.

Graesser, A. C. (1981). *Prose comprehension beyond the word.* New York: Springer-Verlag.

Graesser, A. C., & Clark, L. F. (1985). *Structures and procedures of implicit knowledge.* Norwood, NJ: Ablex.

Graesser, A. C., Gordon, S. E., & Sawyer, J. D. (1979). Recognition memory for typical and atypical actions in scripted activities: Tests of a script pointer + tag hypothesis. *Journal of Verbal Learning and Verbal Behavior, 18,* 319–332.

Graesser, A. C., & Murachver, T. (1985). Symbolic procedures in question answering. In A. C. Graesser & J. B. Black (Eds.), *The psychology of questions.* Hillsdale, NJ: Lawrence Erlbaum Associates.

Graesser, A. C., Robertson, S. P., and Anderson, P. A. (1981). Incorporating inferences in narrative representations: A study of how and why. *Cognitive Psychology, 13,* 1–26.

Graesser, A. C., Robertson, S. P., & Clark, L. F. (in press). Question answering: A method for exploring the on-line construction of prose representations. In J. Fine & R. O. Freedle (Eds.), *New directions in discourse processing.* Norwood, NJ: Ablex.

Graesser, A. C., Robertson, S. P., Lovelace, E., & Swinehart, D. (1980). Answers to why-questions expose the organization of story plot and predict recall of actions. *Journal of Verbal Learning and Verbal Behavior, 19,* 110-119.

Graesser, A. C., Woll, S. B., Kowalski, D. J., & Smith, D. A. (1980). Memory for typical and atypical actions in scripted activities. *Journal of Experimental Psychology: Human Learning and Memory, 6,* 503-515.

Green, E., Flynn, M. S., & Loftus, E. F. (1982). Inducing resistance to misleading information. *Journal of Verbal Learning and Verbal Behavior, 21,* 207-219.

Greenwald, A. G. (1968). On defining attitude and attitude theory. In A. G. Greenwald, T. C. Brock, & T. M. Ostrom (Eds.), *Psychological foundations of attitudes.* New York: Academic Press.

Grice, H. P. (1975). Meaning. *Philosophical Review, 66,* 377-388.

Grosz, B. J. (1977). The representation and use of focus in a system for understanding dialogs. *IJCAI, 5.*

Guindon, R., & Kintsch, W. (1984). Priming macropropositions: Evidence for the primacy of macropropositions in the memory for text. *Journal of Verbal Learning and Verbal Behavior, 23,* 508-518.

Haberlandt, K. (in press). Reader expectations in text comprehension. French translation in *Bulletin de Psychologie.*

Haberlandt, K., Berian, C., & Sanderson, J. (1980). The episode schema in story processing. *Journal of Verbal Learning and Verbal Behavior, 19,* 635-650.

Haberlandt, K., & Bingham, G. (1978). Verbs contribute to the coherence of brief narratives: Reading related and unrelated sentence triples. *Journal of Verbal Learning and Verbal Behavior, 17,* 419-426.

Haberlandt, K., & Bingham, G. (1982). The role of scripts in the comprehension and retention of texts. *Text, 2,* 29-46.

Halliday, M. A. K., & Hassan, R. (1976). *Cohesion in English.* London: Longman.

Hamilton, D. L. (1979). A cognitive-attributional analysis of stereotyping. In L. Berkowitz (Ed.), *Advances in experimental social psychology, 12.* New York: Academic Press.

Hammond, K. J. (1983). Planning and goal interaction: The use of past solutions in present situations. *Proceedings of the National Conference on Artificial Intelligence, AAAI.* Washington, D.C.

Hastie, R., & Kumar, P. A. (1979). Person memory: Personality traits as organizing principles in memory for behavior. *Journal of Personality and Social Psychology, 37,* 25-38.

Haviland, S. E., & Clark, H. H. (1974). What's new? Acquiring new information as a process in comprehension. *Journal of Verbal Learning and Verbal Behavior, 13,* 515-521.

Hayes-Roth, B., & Hayes-Roth, F. (1977). Concept learning and the recognition and classification of exemplars. *Journal of Verbal Learning and Verbal Behavior, 16,* 321-338.

Hovland, C. I., Janis, I. L., Kelley, H. H. (1953). *Communication and Persuasion.* New Haven, CT: Yale University Press.

James, C. T. (1975). The role of semantic information in lexical decisions. *Journal of Experimental Psychology: Human Perception and Performance, 1,* 130-136.

Jaspars, J., Hewstone, M., & Fincham, F. (1983). Attribution theory and research: The state of the art. In J. Jaspars, M. Hewstone, & F. Fincham (Eds.), *Attribution theory: Essays and experiments.* New York: Academic Press.

Johnson, H. H., & Watkins, T. A. (1971). The effects of message repetition on immediate and delayed attitude change. *Psychonomic Science, 22,* 101-103.

Johnson, S. C. (1967). Hierarchical clustering schemes. *Psychometrika, 32,* 241-254.

Johnson, W., & Kieras, D. (1983). Representation-saving effects of prior knowledge in memory for simple technical prose. *Memory and Cognition, 11,* 456-466.

Johnson-Laird, P. N. (1980). Mental models in cognitive science. *Cognitive Science, 4,* 71-115.

Johnson-Laird, P. N. (1983). *Mental models.* Cambridge, MA: Harvard University Press.

Johnson-Laird, P. N., Legrenzi, P., & Legrenzi, M. S. (1972). Reasoning and a sense of reality. *British Journal of Psychology, 63,* 305–400.

Jones, E. E., & Davis, K. E. (1965). From acts to dispositions: The attribution process in person perception. In L. Berkowitz (Ed.), *Advances in experimental social psychology* (Vol. 2). New York: Academic Press.

Jones, E. E., & Kohler, R. (1958). The effects of plausibility on the learning of controversial statements. *Journal of Abnormal and Social Psychology, 57,* 315–320.

Jones, E. E., & Nisbett, R. E. (1971). The actor and the observer: Divergent perceptions of the causes of behavior. In E. E. Jones, D. E. Kanouse, H. H. Kelley, R. E. Nisbett, S. Valins, & B. Weiner (Eds.), *Attribution: Perceiving the causes of behavior.* New York: General Learning Press.

Just, M. A., & Carpenter, P. A. (1980). A theory of reading: From eye fixations to comprehension. *Psychological Review, 87,* 320–354.

Kanouse, D. E., & Abelson, R. P. (1967). Language variables affecting the persuasiveness of simple communications. *Journal of Personality and Social Psychology, 7,* 156–163.

Katz, J., & Fodor, J. (1964). The structure of a semantic theory. In J. Fodor & J. Katz (Eds.), *The structure of language.* Englewood Cliffs, NJ: Prentice-Hall.

Kay, D. S., & Black, J. B. (1984a). Summarizing and recalling narratives with self-contained episodes. Paper presented at the 1984 Conference of the American Educational Research Association.

Kay, D. S., & Black, J. B. (1984b). Summarizing the Wall Street Journal. *Proceedings of the Sixth Annual Conference of the Cognitive Science Society,* Boulder, CO.

Keil, F. (1979). *Semantic and conceptual development: An ontological perspective.* Cambridge, MA: Harvard University Press.

Keil, F. (1981). Constraints on knowledge and cognitive development. *Psychological Review, 88,* 197–227.

Kelley, H. H. (1967). Attribution theory in social psychology. In D. Levine (Ed.), *Nebraska Symposium on Motivation.* Lincoln, NE: University of Nebraska Press.

Kelley, H. H. (1972). Causal schemata and the attribution process. In E. E. Jones, et al. (Eds.), *Attribution: Perceiving the causes of behavior.* Morristown, NJ: General Learning Press.

Kemper, S., Estill, R., Otalvaro, N., & Schadler, M. (1985). Questions of facts and questions of inferences. In A. C. Graesser & J. B. Black (Eds.), *The psychology of questions.* Hillsdale, NJ: Lawrence Erlbaum Associates.

Kintsch, W. (1974). *The representation of meaning in memory.* Hillsdale, NJ: Lawrence Erlbaum Associates.

Kintsch, W., & Greene, E. (1978). The role of culture-specific schemata in the comprehension and recall of stories. *Discourse Processes, 1,* 1–13.

Kintsch, W., & Keenan, J. (1973). Reading rate and retention as a function of the number of propositions in the base structure of sentences. *Cognitive Psychology, 5,* 257–274.

Kintsch, W., Kozminsky, E., Streby, W., McKoon, G., & Keenan, J. (1975). Comprehension and recall of text as a function of content variables. *Journal of Verbal Learning and Verbal Behavior, 14,* 196–214.

Kintsch, W., & van Dijk, T. A. (1978). Toward a model of text comprehension and production. *Psychological Review, 85,* 383–394.

Kleiman, G. M. (1980). Sentence frame contexts and lexical decisions: Sentence-acceptability and word-relatedness effects. *Memory and Cognition, 8,* 336–344.

Kneale, W., & Kneale, M. (1962). *The development of logic.* Oxford: Clarendon.

Kolodner, J. L. (1983). Reconstructive memory: A computer model. *Cognitive Science, 7,* 281–328.

Kolodner, J. L. (1984). *Retrieval and organizational strategies in conceptual memory: A computer model.* Hillsdale, NJ: Lawrence Erlbaum Associates.

Kolodner, J. L., & Simpson, R. L. (1984). Experience and problem solving: A framework. *Proceedings of the Sixth Annual Conference of the Cognitive Science Society,* Boulder, CO.

Kucera, H., & Francis, W. N. (1967). *Computational analysis of present-day American English.* Providence, RI: Brown University Press.

Lakoff, G. (1972). Linguistics and natural logic. In J. Davidson and G. Harman (Eds.), *Semantics of natural language.* New York: Humanities Press.

Lakoff, G., & Johnson, M. (1980). *Metaphors we live by.* Chicago: University of Chicago Press.

Lalljee, M., & Abelson, R. P. (1983). The organization of explanations. In M. Hewstone (Ed.), *Attribution theory: Social and functional extensions.* Oxford: Blackwell.

Lalljee, M., Watson, M., & White, P. (1982). Explanations, attributions, and the social context of unexpected behavior. *European Journal of Social Psychology, 12,* 17–29.

Landauer, T. K., & Meyer, D. E. (1972). Category size and semantic-memory retrieval. *Journal of Verbal Learning and Verbal Behavior, 11,* 539–549.

Lebowitz, M. (1980). Generalization and memory in an integrated understanding system. *Technical Report No. 186,* Computer Science Program, Yale University.

Leddo, J., Abelson, R. P., & Gross, P. (1984). Conjunctive explanations: When two reasons are better than one. *Journal of Personality and Social Psychology, 47,* 933–943.

Lehnert, W. G. (1978). *The process of question answering.* Hillsdale, NJ: Lawrence Erlbaum Associates.

Lehnert, W. G. (1981). Plot units and narrative summarization. *Cognitive Science, 5,* 293–331.

Lehnert, W. G., Black, J. B., & Reiser, B. J. (1981). Summarizing narratives. *Proceedings of the Seventh International Joint Conference on Artificial Intelligence,* Vancouver, B.C.

Lehnert, W. G., Robertson, S. P., & Black, J. B. (1984). Memory interactions during question answering. In H. Mandl, N. L. Stein, & T. Trabasso (Eds.), *Learning and comprehension of text.* Hillsdale, NJ: Lawrence Erlbaum Associates.

Levine, J. M., & Murphy, G. (1943). The learning and forgetting of controversial material. *Journal of Abnormal and Social Psychology, 38,* 507–517.

Lichtenstein, E. H., & Brewer, W. F. (1980). Memory for goal directed events. *Cognitive Psychology, 12,* 412–445.

Loftus, E. F. (1973). Activation of semantic memory. *American Journal of Psychology, 86,* 331–337.

Loftus, E. F. (1975). Leading questions and the eyewitness report. *Cognitive Psychology, 7,* 560–572.

Loftus, E. F. (1979). *Eyewitness testimony.* Cambridge, MA: Harvard University Press.

Loftus, E. F. (1981). Mentalmorphosis: Alterations in memory produced by the mental bonding of new information to old. In J. Long & A. Baddeley (Eds.), *Attention and performance IX.* pp. 417–434. Hillsdale, NJ: Lawrence Erlbaum Associates.

Loftus, E. F., & Green, E. (1980). Warning: Even memory for faces may be contagious. *Law and Human Behavior, 4,* 323–334.

Loftus, E. F., Miller, D. G., & Burns, H. J. (1978). Semantic integration of verbal information into a visual memory. *Journal of Experimental Psychology: Human Learning and Memory, 4,* 19–31.

Loftus, E. F., & Palmer, J. C. (1974). Reconstruction of automobile destruction: An example of the interaction between language and memory. *Journal of Learning and Verbal Behavior, 13,* 585–589.

Mandler, J. M. (1978). A code in the node: The use of story schemas in retrieval. *Discourse Processes, 1,* 14–35.

Mandler, J. M., & Johnson, N. S. (1977). Remembrance of things pavsed: Story structure and recall. *Cognitive Psychology, 9,* 111–151.

Marcus, M. (1980). *A theory of syntactic recognition for natural language.* Cambridge, MA: MIT Press.

Markus, H. (1977). Self-schemata and processing information about the self. *Journal of Personality and Social Psychology, 35,* 63–78.

McArthur, L. A. (1972). The how and what of why: Some determinants and consequences of causal attribution. *Journal of Personality and Social Psychology, 22,* 171–193.

McClelland, J. L., & Rumelhart, D. E. (1981). An interactive model of context effects in letter perception: Part I. An account of basic findings. *Psychological Review, 88,* 375–407.

McCloskey, M., & Zaragoza, M. (1985). Misleading postevent information and memory for events: Arguments and evidence against memory impairment hypotheses. *Journal of Experimental Psychology, 114,* 1–16.

McKoon, G. (1977). Organization of information in text memory. *Journal of Verbal Learning and Verbal Behavior, 15,* 247–260.

McKoon, G., & Ratcliff, R. (1980a). Priming in item recognition: The organization of propositions in memory for text. *Journal of Verbal Learning and Verbal Behavior, 19,* 369–386.

McKoon, G., & Ratcliff, R. (1980b). The comprehension processes and memory structures involved in anaphoric reference. *Journal of Verbal Learning and Verbal Behavior, 19,* 668–682.

McKoon, G., & Ratcliff, R. (1982). *Contextually-determined aspects of meaning.* Paper presented at the Twenty-third Annual Meeting of the Psychonomic Society. Minneapolis, MN.

Meyer, B. J. F. (1975). *The organization of prose and its effect upon memory.* Amsterdam: North-Holland.

Meyer, D. E., & Schvaneveldt, R. W. (1971). Facilitation in recognizing pairs of words: Evidence of a dependence between retrieval operations. *Journal of Experimental Psychology, 10,* 227–234.

Meyer, D. E., & Schvaneveldt, R. W., & Ruddy, M. G. (1972). *Activation of lexical memory.* Paper presented at the meeting of the Psychonomic Society, St. Louis, MO.

Meyer, D. E., Schvaneveldt, R. W., & Ruddy, M. G. (1975). Loci of contextual effects on word recognition: In R. M. A. Rabbitt & S. Dornic (Eds.), *Attention and performance V,* New York: Academic Press.

Miller, J. R., & Kintsch, W. (1981). Knowledge-based aspects of prose comprehension and readability. *Text, 1,* 215–232.

Minsky, M. (1975). A framework for representing knowledge. In P. H. Winston (Ed.), *The psychology of computer vision.* New York: McGraw-Hill.

Mitchell, D. C. (1982). *The process of reading: A cognitive analysis of fluent reading and learning to read.* Chichester, England: John Wiley & Sons.

Mitchell, D. C., & Green, D. W. (1978). The effects of context and content on immediate processing in reading. *Quarterly Journal of Experimental Psychology, 30,* 609–636.

Mitchell, D. C., Sharkey, N. E., & Fox, J. (1983). *Search and evidence-collection models of lexical access: Problems for both approaches.* Paper presented to the Tenth Experimental Psychology Conference. Tasmania, Australia.

Morton, J. (1969). The interaction of information in word recognition. *Psychological Review, 76,* 165–178.

Moyer, R. S., & Dumais, S. T. (1978). Mental comparison. In G. H. Bower (Ed.), *The psychology of learning and motivation, 12.* New York: Academic Press.

Murachver, T., Murray, K. E., & Graesser, A. C. (1985). Answering some questions about a model of question answering. In A. C. Graesser & J. B. Black (Eds.), *The psychology of questions.* Hillsdale, NJ: Lawrence Erlbaum Associates.

Neely, J. H. (1976). Semantic priming and retrieval from lexical memory: Evidence for facilitatory and inhibitory processes. *Memory and Cognition, 4,* 648–654.

Neely, J. H. (1977). Semantic priming and retrieval from lexical memory: Roles of inhibitionless spreading activation and limited-capacity attention. *Journal of Experimental Psychology: General, 106,* 226-254.

Nelson, K., & Gruendel, J. M. (1981). Generalized event representations: Basic building blocks of cognitive development. In A. Brown & M. Lamb (Eds.), *Advances in developmental psychology.* Hillsdale, NJ: Lawrence Erlbaum Associates.

Newell, A. M. (1982). The knowledge level. *Artificial Intelligence, 18,* 87-127.

Nisbett, R. E., & Ross, L. (1980). *Human inference: Strategies and shortcomings of social judgment.* Englewood Cliffs, NJ: Prentice-Hall.

Norman, D. A., & Bobrow, D. G. (1979). Descriptions: An intermediate stage in memory retrieval. *Cognitive Psychology, 11,* 107-123.

Norman, D. A., & Rumelhart, D. E. (1975). *Explorations in cognition.* San Francisco, CA: W. H. Freeman.

Nottenberg, G., & Shoben, E. J. (1980). Scripts as linear orders. *Journal of Experimental Social Psychology, 16,* 329-347.

Owens, J., Bower, G. H., & Black, J. B. (1979). The "soap opera" effect in story memory. *Memory and Cognition, 7,* 185-191.

Papageorgis, D. (1963). Bartlett effect and the persistence of induced attitude change. *Journal of Abnormal and Social Psychology, 67,* 61-67.

Piaget, J. (1926). *The language and thought of the child.* New York: Harcourt Brace.

Piaget, J. (1960). Equilibration and the development of logical structures. In J. M. Tanner & B. Inhelder (Eds.), *Discussions on child development.* London: Tavistock.

Pichert, J. W., & Anderson, R. C. (1977). Taking different perspectives on a story. *Journal of Educational Psychology, 69,* 309-315.

Reder, L. M. (1982). Plausibility judgments versus fact retrieval: Alternative strategies for sentence verification. *Psychological Review, 89,* 250-280.

Reder, L. M., & Anderson, J. R. (1980). A partial resolution of the paradox of interference: The role of integrating knowledge. *Cognitive Psychology, 12,* 447-472.

Reed, S. K., & Johnson, J. A. (1977). Memory for problem solutions. In G. H. Bower (Ed.), *The psychology of learning and motivation* (*Vol. 2*). New York: Academic Press.

Reiser, B. J. (1983). Contexts and indices in autobiographical memory. *Technical Report No. 24,* Cognitive Science Program, Yale University.

Reiser, B. J. (in press). Knowledge-directed retrieval of autobiographical memories. In J. L. Kolodner & C. K. Riesbeck (Eds.), *Experience and reasoning.* Hillsdale, NJ: Lawrence Erlbaum Associates.

Reiser, B. J., & Black, J. B. (1982). Processing and structural models of comprehension. *Text, 2,* 225-252.

Reiser, B. J., & Black, J. B. (1983). The roles of interference and inference in the retrieval of autobiographical memories. *Proceedings of the Fifth Annual Conference of the Cognitive Science Society.* Rochester, NY.

Reiser, B. J., Black, J. B., & Abelson, R. P. (1985). Knowledge structures in the organization and retrieval of autobiographical memories. *Cognitive Psychology, 17,* 89-137.

Reiser, B. J., Black, J. B., & Kalamarides, P. (in press). Strategic memory search processes. In D. Rubin (Ed.), *Autobiographical memory.* New York: Cambridge University Press.

Reiser, B. J., Black, J. B., & Lehnert, W. G. (1982). Thematic knowledge structures in the understanding and generation of narratives. *Technical Report No. 16.* Cognitive Science Program, Yale University.

Reiser, B. J., Galambos, J. A., & Black, J. B. (1982). Retrieval from semantic and autobiographical memory. Paper presented at the Twenty-third Annual Meeting of the Psychonomic Society, Minneapolis, MN.

Revlin, R., & Leirer, V. (1968). The effect of personal bias on syllogistic reasoning. In R. Revlin & R. E. Mayer (Eds.), *Human reasoning,* Washington: D.C.: Winston-Wiley.

Richey, M. J., McClelland, L., & Shimkunas, A. M. (1967). Relative influence of positive and negative information in impression formation and persistence. *Journal of Personality and Social Psychology, 6,* 322–327.

Rieger, C. (1975). Conceptual memory: In R. C. Schank (Ed.), *Conceptual information processing.* Amsterdam: North-Holland.

Riesbeck, C. K. (1978). An expectation-driven production system for natural language understanding. In D. A. Waterman, & F. Hayes-Roth (Eds.), *Pattern-directed inference systems.* New York: Academic Press.

Riesbeck, C. K. (1983). Knowledge reorganization and reasoning style. *Technical Report No. 270.* Computer Science Program, Yale University.

Riesbeck, C. K., & Schank, R. C. (1979). Comprehension by computer: Expectation-based analysis of sentences in context. In W. J. M. Levelt & G. B. Flores d'Arcais (Eds.), *Studies in the perception of language.* Chichester, England: John Wiley.

Rips, L. J., Shoben, E. J., & Smith, E. E. (1973). Semantic distance and the verification of semantic relations. *Journal of Verbal Learning and Verbal Behavior, 12,* 1–20.

Robertson, S. P., Black, J. B., & Lehnert, W. G. (1985). Misleading question effects as evidence for integrated question understanding and memory search. In A. C. Graesser & J. B. Black (Eds.). *The psychology of questions.* Hillsdale, N.J.: Lawrence Erlbaum Associates.

Robinson, J. (1976). Sampling autobiographical memory. *Cognitive Psychology, 8,* 578–595.

Rosch, E. H. (1973). On the internal structure of perceptual and semantic categories. In T. E. Moore (Ed.), *Cognitive development and the acquisition of language.* New York: Academic Press.

Rosch, E. H. (1978). Principles of categorization. In E. H. Rosch & B. B. Lloyd (Eds.), *Cognition and categorization.* Hillsdale, NJ: Lawrence Erlbaum Associates.

Rosch, E. H., & Lloyd, B. B. (1978). *Cognition and categorization.* Hillsdale, NJ: Lawrence Erlbaum Associates.

Rosch, E. H., Mervis, C. B., Gray, W. D., Johnson, D. M., & Boyes-Braem, P. (1976). Basic objects as natural categories. *Cognitive Psychology, 8,* 382–439.

Roseman, I. J. (1984). Cognitive determinants of emotions: a structural theory. In P. Shaver (Ed.) *Review of personality and social psychology* (Vol. 5). Beverly Hills, CA: Sage.

Rosnow, R. L. (1966). Conditioning and direction of opinion change in persuasive communication. *Journal of Social Psychology, 69,* 291–303.

Rubenstein, H., Garfield, L., & Millikan, J. A. (1970). Homographic entries in the internal lexicon. *Journal of Verbal Learning and Verbal Behavior, 9,* 487–494.

Rumelhart, D. E. (1975a). Notes on a schema for stories. In D. G. Bobrow & A. Collins (Eds.), *Representation and understanding.* New York: Academic Press.

Rumelhart, D. E. (1975b). Understanding and summarizing brief stories. In D. Laberge & S. Samuels (Eds.), *Basic processing in reading, perception and understanding.* Hillsdale, NJ: Lawrence Erlbaum Associates.

Rumelhart, D. E. (1980). Schemata: The building blocks of cognition. In R. J. Spiro, B. C. Bruce, & W. F. Brewer (Eds.), *Theoretical issues in reading comprehension.* Hillsdale, NJ: Lawrence Erlbaum Associates.

Rumelhart, D. E., & Ortony, A. (1977). The representation of knowledge in memory. In R. C. Anderson, R. J. Spiro, & W. E. Montague (Eds.), *Schooling and the acquisition of knowledge.* Hillsdale, NJ: Lawrence Erlbaum Associates.

Sanford, A. J., & Garrod, S. C. (1981). *Understanding written language.* Chichester, England: John Wiley.

Schallert, D. L. (1976). Improving memory for prose: The relationship between depth of processing and context. *Journal of Verbal Learning and Verbal Behavior, 15,* 612–632.

Schank, R. C. (1972). Conceptual dependency: A theory of natural language understanding. *Cognitive Psychology, 3,* 552–631.

Schank, R. C. (1973). Identification of conceptualizations underlying natural language. In R. C. Schank & K. M. Colby (Eds.), *Computer models of thought and language.* Hillsdale, NJ: Lawrence Erlbaum Associates.

Schank, R. C. (1975a). A story understander. *Yale A.I. Project Research Report, No. 3.* Yale University.

Schank, R. C. (1975b). The structure of episodes in memory. In D. G. Bobrow & A. M. Collins (Eds.), *Representation and understanding: Studies in cognitive science.* New York: Academic Press.

Schank, R. C. (1975c). *Conceptual information processing.* Amsterdam: North Holland.

Schank, R. C. (1978). Predictive understanding. In R. N. Campbell & P. T. Smith (Eds.), *Recent advances in the psychology of language—formal and experimental approaches.* New York: Plenum Press.

Schank, R. C. (1980). Language and memory. *Cognitive Science, 4,* 243–284.

Schank, R. C. (1982). *Dynamic memory: A theory of reminding and learning in computers and people.* New York: Cambridge University Press.

Schank, R. C. (1984). The explanation game. *Technical Report No. 307.* Computer Science Program, Yale University.

Schank, R. C., & Abelson, R. P. (1975). Scripts, plans and knowledge. *Proceedings of the Fourth International Conference on Artificial Intelligence,* Tbilisi, USSR.

Schank, R. C., & Abelson, R. P. (1977). *Scripts, plans, goals, and understanding.* Hillsdale, NJ: Lawrence Erlbaum Associates.

Schank, R. C., Lebowitz, M., & Birnbaum, L. (1980). An integrated understander. *American Journal of Computational Linguistics, 6,* 13–30.

Schank, R. C., & Riesbeck, C. K. (1981). *Inside computer understanding.* Hillsdale, NJ: Lawrence Erlbaum Associates.

Schank, R. C., & Seifert, C. M. (1985). Modelling memory and learning. In M. G. Shafto (Ed.), *How we know: The inner frontiers of cognitive science.* Harper & Row.

Schmidt, D. F., & Sherman, R. C. (1984). Memory for persuasive messages: A test of the schema-pointer-plus-tag model. *Journal of Experimental and Social Psychology, 13,* 112–135.

Schneider, W., & Shiffrin, R. M. (1977). Controlled and automatic human information processing: I. Detection, search, and attention. *Psychological Review, 84,* 1–66.

Schuberth, R. E., & Eimas, P. D. (1977). Effects of context on the classification of words and nonwords. *Journal of Experimental Psychology: Human Perception and Performance, 2,* 243–256.

Schuberth, R. E., Spoehr, K. T., & Lane, P. M. (1981). Effects of stimulus and contextual information on the lexical decision process. *Memory and Cognition, 9,* 68–77.

Schustack, M., & Anderson, J. R.(1979). Effects of analogy to prior knowledge on memory for new information. *Journal of Verbal Learning and Verbal Behavior, 18,* 565–584.

Schvaneveldt, R. W., & McDonald, J. E. (1981). Semantic context and the encoding of words: Evidence for two modes of stimulus analysis. *Journal of Experimental Psychology: Human Perception and Performance, 7,* 673–687.

Seidenberg, M. D., Tanenhaus, M. K., Leiman, J. M., & Bienkowski, M. (1983). Automatic access of the meanings of ambiguous words in context: Some limitations of knowledge-based processing. *Cognitive Psychology, 14,* 489–537.

Seifert, C. M., & Black, J. B. (1983). Thematic connections between episodes. *Proceedings of the Fifth Annual Conference of the Cognitive Science Society,* Rochester, NY.

Seifert, C. M., & Black, J. B. (in press). On-line processing of pragmatic inferences. *Journal of Memory and Language.*

Seifert, C. M., McKoon, G., Abelson, R. P., & Ratcliff, R. (1986). Memory connections between thematically similar episodes. *Journal of Experimental Psychology: Learning, Memory and Cognition, 12,* 220–231.

Seifert, C. M., Robertson, S. P., & Black, J. B. (1982). On-line processing of pragmatic inferences. *Technical Report No. 15*. Cognitive Science Program, Yale University.

Seifert, C. M., Robertson, S. P., & Black, J. B. (1985). Types of inferences generated during comprehension. *Journal of Memory and Language, 24*, 405-422.

Sharkey, N. E. (1982). *The locus and control of script priming effects*. Unpublished Ph.D. Thesis, Exeter, England.

Sharkey, N. E. (1983). The control of mundane knowledge in memory. *Technical Report No. 20*. Cognitive Science Program, Yale University.

Sharkey, N. E., & Bower, G. H. (1984). The integration of goals and actions in text understanding. *Proceedings of Cognitive Science, 6*.

Sharkey, N. E., & Mitchell, D. C. (1981a). *Match or fire: Contextual mechanisms in the recognition of words*. Paper presented to the Experimental Psychology Society, Oxford.

Sharkey, N. E., & Mitchell, D. C. (1981b). *New primes for old: Passive decay versus active suppression of scripts in working memory*. Paper presented to the British Psychological Society. Cognitive Psychology Section, Plymouth, England.

Sharkey, N. E., & Mitchell, D. C. (1985). Word recognition in a functional context: The use of scripts in reading. *Journal of Verbal Learning and Verbal Behavior, 24*, 253-270.

Sharkey, N. E., & Sharkey, A. J. C. (1983). Levels of expectation in sentence understanding. *Technical Report No. 21*. Cognitive Science Program, Yale University.

Sharkey, N. E., & Sharkey, A. J. C. (in preparation). The influence of scripts on sentence processing.

Sidner, C. L. (1978). The use of focus as a tool for disambiguation of definite noun phrases. *Proceedings TINLAP, 2*.

Singer, M. (1985). Mental processes of question answering. In A. C. Graesser & J. B. Black (Eds.), *The psychology of questions*. Hillsdale, NJ: Lawrence Erlbaum Associates.

Smith, E. E., Adams, N., & Schorr, D. (1978). Fact retrieval and the paradox of interference. *Cognitive Psychology, 10*, 438-464.

Smith, E. E., & Collins, A. M. (1981). Use of goal-plan knowledge in understanding stories. *Proceedings of the Third Conference of the Cognitive Science Society*. Berkeley, CA.

Smith, E. E., & Medin, D. L. (1981). *Categories and concepts*. Cambridge, MA: Harvard University Press.

Solomon, R. L., & Howes, D. H. (1951). Word-probability, personal values, and visual duration thresholds. *Psychological Review, 58*, 256-270.

Stanners, R. F., Jastrzembski, J. E., & Westbrook, A. (1975). Frequency and visual quality in a word-nonword classification task. *Journal of Verbal Learning and Verbal Behavior, 14*, 259-264.

Stein, N. L. (1979). How children understand stories: A developmental analysis. In L. G. Katz (Ed.), *Current topics in early childhood education, 11*. Norwood, NJ: Ablex.

Stein, N. L., & Glenn, C. G. (1979). An analysis of story comprehension in elementary school children. In R. Freedle (Ed.), *Multidisciplinary perspectives in discourse comprehension*. Hillsdale, NJ: Lawrence Erlbaum Associates.

Swinney, D. A. (1979). Lexical access during sentence comprehension: (Re)consideration of context effects. *Journal of Verbal Learning and Verbal Behavior, 18*, 645-659.

Taylor, S. E., & Crocker, J. C. (1981). Schematic bases of social information processing. In E. T. Higgins, P. Herman, & M. P. Zanna (Eds.), *The Ontario symposium on personality and social psychology, 1*. Hillsdale, NJ: Lawrence Erlbaum Associates.

Thorndyke, P. W. (1977). Cognitive structures in comprehension and memory of narrative discourse. *Cognitive Psychology, 9*, 77-110.

Thorndyke, P. W., & Hayes-Roth, B. (1979). The use of schemas in the acquisition and transfer of knowledge. *Cognitive Psychology, 11*, 82-106.

Thorndyke, P. W., & Yekovich, F. R. (1980). A critique of schema-based theories of human story memory. *Poetics, 9,* 23–49.

Trabasso, T., Secco, T., & van den Broek, P. (1984). Causal cohesion and story coherence. In H. Mandl, N. L. Stein, & T. Trabasso (Eds.), *Learning and comprehension of text.* Hillsdale, NJ: Lawrence Erlbaum Associates.

Tulving, E. (1983). *Elements of episodic memory.* New York: Oxford University Press.

Tulving, E., & Thomson, D. M. (1973). Encoding specificity and retrieval processes in episodic memory. *Psychological Review, 80,* 352–373.

Tversky, A. (1977). Features of similarity. *Psychological Review, 84,* 327–352.

van Dijk, T. A. (1980). *Macrostructures: An interdisciplinary study of global structures in discourse, interaction, and cognition.* Hillsdale, NJ: Lawrence Erlbaum Associates.

van Dijk, T. A., & Kintsch, W. (1977). Cognitive psychology and discourse: Recalling and summarizing stories. In W. U. Dressler (Ed.), *Trends in text-linguistics.* New York: DeGruyter.

Waly, P., & Cook, S. W. (1966). Attitude as a determinant of learning and memory: A failure to confirm. *Journal of Personality and Social Psychology, 4,* 280–288.

Warren, R. E. (1972). Stimulus encoding and memory. *Journal of Experimental Psychology, 94,* 90–100.

Wason, P. C., & Johnson-Laird, P. N. (1972). *Psychology of reasoning: Structure and content.* Hillsdale, NJ: Lawrence Erlbaum Associates.

Watts, W. A., & McGuire, W. J. (1964). Persistence of induced opinion change and retention of inducing message content. *Journal of Abnormal and Social Psychology, 68,* 233–241.

Whaley, C. P. (1978). Word-nonword classification time. *Journal of Verbal Learning and Verbal Behavior, 17,* 143–154.

Whitten, W. B., & Leonard, J. M. (1981). Directed search through autobiographical memory. *Memory and Cognition, 9,* 566–579.

Wilensky, R. (1978a). Understanding goal-based stories. *Technical Report No. 140,* Computer Science Program, Yale University.

Wilensky, R. (1978b). Why John married Mary: Understanding stories involving recurring goals. *Cognitive Science, 2,* 235–266.

Wilensky, R. (1983). *Planning and understanding: A computational approach to human reasoning.* Reading, MA: Addison-Wesley.

Williams, M. D., & Hollan, J. D. (1981). The process of retrieval from very-long term memory. *Cognitive Science, 5,* 87–119.

Wilson, B. A. (1980). *The anatomy of argument.* New York: University Press of America.

Wilson, W., & Miller, H. (1968). Repetition, order of presentation, and timing of arguments and measures as determinants of attitude change. *Journal of Personality and Social Psychology, 9,* 184–188.

Author Index

Subject Index